Once Upon Abundance

Fred Van Dyke

Relive fond memories of childhood adventures, never ending fun, first kiss, a dream girl you're missing, but have never met. Reminisce a captivating time when life was simple; freedom was felt in the uncrowded natural environment of mountain streams, Redwood forests, isolated California and Hawaii beaches, unspoiled fishing, surfing, and hiking. Share the pleasure of anticipation, the challenge of life threatening experiences. Enjoy an appealing story, love of animals, people, nature that provides a sane and sacred way of life. Enter the Golden Gate; wander a romantic California that no longer exists. Travel west to an alluring Hawaii, a golden abundance that is timelessly held in your heart and soul.

Fred Van Dyke has written four other books :

Thirty Years of Riding the World's Biggest Waves

Riding Huge Waves With Ease

Once Upon A Wilderness

Two Surf Stories For Children (Ages 6–10)

Once Upon Abundance:

Coming of Age In California and Hawaii

Fred Van Dyke

Chuck ~ Pedro is
my origina. I love
the place and
come from Hawaii
every year to be
here.
aloha
Fred Van Dyke

Once Upon Abundance
by Fred Van Dyke

First Edition, 2001

Second printing 2002

Printed in Thailand

Published by Anoai Press 2001

ISBN 0-9702618-1-0

Distributed by
Anoai Press
3349-A Anoai Place
Honolulu, Hawaii 96822, USA
Phone (808) 988-6109
Fax (808) 988-1119
Web page: www.anoaipress.com
E-mail: kukui@lava.net

Contents

Contents

Acknowledgements

This book, Once Upon Abundance, was solely my own creation, until I invited my wife, Joan Marie, a retired English teacher, to read and edit the finished manuscript. She jumped into the project like a dive into Boulder Creek.

Spell check is good, but lacks knowledge, understanding, and sensitivity. The manuscript was only partly finished before she helped me to feel more deeply the importance of word choice. The book has been embellished beyond my fondest dreams. It now has esoteric completion, touched by her energy, creativity, spirit, and depth. I learned about myself through Joan's advice. She feels things that only a woman who knows herself can.

Joan Marie is the heroine of the book, my female mentor, and I have trouble separating the events we shared in the book and this other world. She is my companion, the love of my life, and our magic never grows old. Thanks, for helping me when I most needed it, after the manuscript was finished, or so I thought.

Ted Gugelyk, first a true friend, whose belief in my writing encouraged me to reprint two of my earlier books and now publish a story from my heart. Ted is publisher of Anoai Press.

Steve Curry PhD, University of Hawaii English Professor, a talented poet and editor can put me back in the 8th grade with severe, but true criticism as he moved my book forward to publication.

Both Ted and Steve are surfers and when the first copy is in hand, we will all go surfing to celebrate!

"The earth does not belong to us; we belong to the Earth . . .
We did not weave the web of life; we are merely a strand in it.
Whatever we do to the web, we do to ourselves."
Chief Seattle

When we try to pick out anything by itself,
we find it hitched to everything else in the universe.
John Muir

And only when we are no longer afraid
do we begin to live in every experience, painful or joyous;
to live in gratitude for every moment,
to live abundantly.
Dorothy Thompson

Love of God's creation, the whole and every grain of sand in it.
Love every leaf, every ray of God's light.
Love the animals, love the plants, love everything.
If you love everything, you will perceive the divine mystery in it.
Once you perceive it,
you will begin to comprehend it better every day.
And you will come at last to love
the whole world with an all-embracing love.
Feodor Dostoyevsky

These are the things I prize and hold dearest worth:
Light of sapphire skies, peace of the silent hills,
shelter of the forest, comfort of the grass,
music of little rills, shadows of clouds quickly passing,
And after showers, the smell of flowers
and of the good brown earth—
And best of all, along the way, friendship and mirth.
Henry Van Dyke

Introduction

Looking into memories may blemish reality and some of the truth, but if taken as mostly accurate, the minor exaggerations are pulled into a vacuum of fact and after many years sometimes become accepted as that. A familiar reference to "Those were the good old days" rings constant. Were they that great or did I simply sift out only the good experiences?

I am not sure about that and very little concerned. I have something to share, a depth of me, a picture, a saga of America as many have never seen and never will again. A triangle has less depth as it reaches its apex. I have lost many friends along the climb to the peak. Many are gone from my San Francisco 1946, Abraham Lincoln High School graduation picture.

These experiences I share are almost daily vivid flashes to the past, especially when situations feel like they are closing in on me.

Driving in heavy commuter traffic, enclosed in a four engine jet, fishing elbow to elbow on a favorite stream, struggling to catch a wave on the North Shore of Oahu, Hawaii when two hundred surfers are out are some of the situations that bring forth these wonderful memories.

These escapes to a slower less crowded time of abundance save me from the effects of the five billion plus people competing for space on the planet Earth.

This book, in part, was created by many of my students at Punahou School in Honolulu. Before retiring I spent some time each day in class "Talking story," a popular way that kids get you off the subject being taught.

One day the students and I were talking about surfing and how it has changed so much, gotten so crowded. Some of the kids in the class were mentioning a favorite Honolulu spot and how it had gone beyond capacity. I asked them. "When had it not been crowded?"

They answered. "Two years ago."

I laughed and retorted. "I quit the Honolulu side for surfing twenty years ago because it got too crowded." That's when it dawned on me that time, crowds, places as they were existed in the eye of the beholder. It was all relative and so are my experiences that I am going to relate.

Chapter 1

Days of Old

In 1932 I was three years old and lived across the street from Golden Gate Park in San Francisco, California. I remember Christmas time and looking out the window to the snow covered ground outside. I had never seen snow, heard of it, and I wanted to go out and touch it. My mother let me go.

I looked at the flowers all white. They were beautiful and I wanted to pick a bouquet for my mother. I brought them into the house and handed over the lovely white flowers. My mother told me to take the flowers back outside because they would melt. I did not understand and proceeded to put the flowers into a vase as the snow melted from them. Bursting into tears, I ran to my mother and buried my sorrow deeply in her apron. She comforted me, but I had experienced my first consciousness with the facts of change, that nothing remained the same no matter how much you wanted it that way.

On warm spring days my mother would take my brother, Gene, and me to the Golden Gate Park. My mother would make us look both ways and then cross Lincoln Way with not a car in sight. There were few parked cars by the curbs. Once in the park it was as if I had entered a wilderness, trees filling in the sky, and swans swimming upon the little lake on 41st Avenue. I loved the warmth of the sun and my mother always brought little pieces of bread to feed the ducks and swans.

The policeman who patrolled the park on horseback would stop and chat. I wanted to ride upon his horse, which seemed to me to stand fifteen feet high. As suddenly he was gone up the trail and we ate our picnic lunch, played while my mother read a magazine.

My father came home one evening and announced that he was going to buy a car. The garage mechanic, who was selling the car, arrived and took us for a ride. It was a 1926 Buick. Such a car, the insides with little flower vases against the woolen upholstery, shining mahogany dashboard and silver gear shift. My brother and I sat in the back seat, and we were off as my father yelled, "In a cloud of manure."

In those days my father bartered for a lot of what we got. No one had cash. Not many had jobs. It was the Depression years. I had been born on the year of the stock market crash, 1929, I think my father extracted a couple of teeth and gave the man thirty dollars for the car. I remember that his dentistry was mostly paid for in carpentry, eggs, sometimes a chicken or two, whatever was available.

Money was tight then, and when our landlord cut the heater thermostat down, we had to go over to Marin County and gather logs from Stinson Beach.

The trip was an adventure, getting in line to move the car onto the ferryboat, the forty-five minutes to cross the Bay, and then disembarking. My dad proudly drove the car up to us at the pier in Sausalito.

We piled in and headed up toward the summit. Somewhere below Mount Tamalpais, long below the crest line, steam shot out from under the hood. My father left us and walked back to Sausalito. The gas station attendant closed his station and drove my father back to our car. He opened the hood and they both looked inside. My father yelled at me to stay clear of the car, as the water was still hot.

The station attendant poured some oatmeal mixed in water into the radiator, then filled the remaining with water from a can. "The oatmeal will clog up the holes. When you come back check with me and we'll see if you need more water."

"How much do I owe you?" my father asked.

"It's on me, Sunday, you know. You've got a mighty nice looking family there." No one had money during the Depression beginning in 1929. There was a spirit of community and concern for your neighbor. Even a complete stranger, like the station man who helped clog our leaking radiator, and did not charge us, that was the way people dealt with one another. The attendant lit his pipe and was gone. The Buick held together and we wandered Stinson Beach looking for logs. We filled the trunk and my mother set out a tablecloth and we sat down to eat. After lunch we lolled in the sand waiting for the hour to pass before my dad would allow us to play in the water. We all got sunburned, and on the trip back across the bay my brother threw up all over us.

That next week we basked in the warmth of the fireplace, huddling after dinner to burn that wood we had all collected.

Chapter 2

Let's Go Camping

Sunday's were special living near the beach in San Francisco. The fog was thick in the morning and my father would take us, only two children then, to the beach off of Judah Street. Going with him gave my mother a much-needed break. Two blocks walking to Judah Street and one to the tunnel that went under the Great Highway. There were others on the beach, but you rarely saw them for the sand dune shelters everyone built to keep out the west wind. We ran the dunes, always staying within calling distance of my father. We didn't quite understand why he just liked to sit in the windbreak when there was so much to explore. As the fog lifted in the early afternoon, if it did, my mother would show up with a picnic lunch. Again wait an hour and my father would take us down to the shorebreak. We ran through the foam, dove over the already breaking waves rushing up the beach, and occasionally watched a fisherman land a huge striped bass.

Walking back through the tunnel my brother and I shivered in the semi-darkness. My mother always stopped us near the bathroom and we hosed off feet, shook out bathing suits, towels wrapped around, and changed so no sand would make it into our house. Once home, we all had to take baths and the tub had an inch of sand on the bottom when we finished. Even though the fog usually persisted most of the day, we all had sunburned backs and arms. The baths cooled our bodies and we climbed into pajamas to ready for dinner and bed.

The next morning right after my dad had left on the streetcar for downtown and work, my brother and I got to play out front. On Monday it was special for the garbage men came. My brother and I would follow them with our makeshift bags upon our shoulders, helping them to throw garbage into the truck until our mother yelled to get back in front of our house. She'd come out with a mid morning snack and we would all sit down and wait for the produce man to come. When we heard the "Rags, bottles, and sacks" being uttered, we knew that the produce man would be there soon. The rags, bottles, and sack man coached an old horse with his cut down whip, but the horse barely moved beyond a snail's pace. Most everything in those times moved slowly. We'd run up to the horse, fight over who got to pet him, and my mother would grab us up and put us back on the stairway to wait. She told us that the man was a bum who made his living collecting junk. "Stay away from him. He might kidnap you," as his wailing disappeared in the distance.

The produce man looked the same to us, but my mother met him with a friendly smile and a warm, "What have you got today?" My mother had given us each a carrot to feed his horse while she bargained.

Whenever he mentioned prices we thought that our mother was suddenly angry with the man, but she explained after he left that you don't accept the first price and getting or acting angry always saved a few pennies. In those days my mother was given a dollar a day to spend on groceries.

Friday afternoon my father came home early. He announced that the friends next door and across the street were taking a camping trip down to La Honda and we were invited. My brother and I jumped for joy. We had never been camping. My mother did not take to the idea. "Those people across the street are hangers on and the ones next door are on welfare."

My father retorted to my mother. "It'll be fun, Billie, and all we have to bring is our own food and camp equipment. Jack is taking his old pickup truck. We'll all fit in it. We leave Saturday noon."

My brother and I got yelled at as everything was piled on the truck. We just wanted to help and could not understand why they did not find us useful. The men were drinking beer while they tied down the tent poles to the side of the truck. My brother and I got to sit in the back of the truck bed with my mother who was complaining

5

about the moist fog. We could care less. We were going camping! I rarely saw my mother in a joyous mood.

In 1935 there were no freeways. They hadn't even been in the minds of the current architects. The Golden Gate Bridge was in its embryonic form and would not be finished until about 1938. The road we headed south on was called Skyline Boulevard. We had gotten on the highway just below Lake Merced. We meandered through fields of vegetables. They were called truck farms. It was before insecticide sprays. Everything was grown organically. The soil was a soft black loam. It was so healthy that vegetables and fruits thrived in it. What insects there were did not attack in mass. The plants were so resistant because of healthy unpolluted soil. Fertilizers were unheard of except for different manures, horse, chicken, cow, and the like. Aside from the clear cutting lumber companies, a great deal of California was semi-virgin, covered deeply by untouched portions of redwood trees. Just forests and vegetable farms. The men in the cab up front were speaking loudly and lone beer bottles bounced out behind us on the highway.

Suddenly we careened off to the soft shoulder and Jack, my father, and Jim the next-door neighbor ran down the pavement. They returned with the poles to hold the tents up. They were laughing and swearing. My mother was saying, "No more beer until we get to La Honda." The men grumbled, but got into the car and for the next miles I heard none bounce on the pavement behind.

We rolled around a curve and headed to a dividing section in the lakes. The two-lane road went right down the middle. Across the section we saw a herd of deer scamper ahead of us, veer off into the trees. My brother and I had never seen deer. Moving into the curved climb my mother talked about deer, bears, and mountain lions when she had lived in Idaho and told us how coyotes would follow her to school. I noticed that the car was slowing down, coughing and sputtering. Looking back down I could see the lake far below. Ahead lay thick soupy fog. The truck lost more power and Jack shifted down to the next lower gear. We moved upward for a time and then I heard him shift again, but to no avail.

Jack pulled the truck off the highway and stopped. He said, "This calls for another beer." We all got off the truck and my mother told us not to wander and to watch out for rattlesnakes. The men opened beers and did a lot of laughing and swearing. Sometime later my mother sought us out and said that we were ready and that the truck could not pull the load up to the summit. The men were going to push and Jack's wife would drive. My mother was to help, too. We wanted to run behind and help, but were yelled at again. "You're too young, you want to get run over?" my mother added.

They pushed. The car belched, blew black smoke out the exhaust, but we made it to the top. Jack said, "We'll need to rest her, let the radiator cool. Time for a beer." This did not bother my brother and me, but my mother and the other two wives were ready to blow.

Dusk we arrived at the La Honda camping park. The camp, nearly deserted, was nothing like today when you have to call ahead or wait long lines of cars to get a campsite, and, they are close together making for inter dissension. It was wonderful, huge redwood trees, wonderful lush undergrowth, and a ground cover deep enough to sink deeply into with each step. My mother was fit to be tied. We had come approximately thirty miles and it was nearing darkness. Now commuters from this area drive to San Francisco in about a half an hour, excepting rush hours. My brother and I ran down to the stream that lay below the camp chosen. We explored in the nearing darkness until I heard my mother calling for us.

Rushing up the embankment toward camp we were greeted by a sight never before witnessed by my brother and me. A campfire reached upwards ten feet. Tents were up and we saw a lean-to crudely constructed. My mother told us that was where my brother and I were to sleep. She said that after dinner we could sit by the fire for a while and then go to the lean-to. There was nothing to fear for the open end of the lean-to faced the campfire.

Tucked under our blankets, and lying upon evergreen branches, we settled in for the night, that is until one of the men took out a banjo and started playing some music. I sat up and watched my mother climb a tree and swing back and forth like a wild monkey. I didn't like this and climbed out of bed.

"Mother, it is not lady like for you to swing in a tree, and I am afraid that you will hurt yourself." Everyone roared in laughter except my mother.

"Listen here young man. I won't swing anymore, but you get back into bed and not a word from you again."

I was happy when dawn broke and I could see all was well. My mother took us down to the creek and we washed up, brushed our teeth and drank from the stream. My mother told us that the fish surfacing were rainbow trout and that after breakfast we would try and catch some. The stream temperature was in 40s. We balanced upon rocks. Gene slid into the water first, followed soon after by me. My mother yelled for us to go up and get warmed by the fire.

The men were drinking beer before breakfast was served. It was a cool morning until the coastal fog lifted, sunshine streaming between redwood branches, creating steam to rise from verdant undergrowth.

I walked toward where the men were hunched over, tying lines to hooks. My father handed me a switch from a smaller tree branch, and said that was my fishing pole. We walked down to a place where the creek had been dammed.

Looking into the crystal clear water, I saw dozens of trout moving back and forth, most of them sitting head forward into the current. They dashed back and forth, flipped their tail to the surface and returned to where they finned, holding position.

Jack handed me a worm. "Put it on your hook like this. Then swing the baited hook in front of one of the trout." He demonstrated, and a silver side turned upwards, moved onto the worm, felt the hook, and took to the sky. Jack landed the fish immediately and looked to me. "See, that's how it's done."

I tried, once, twice, a lot of times, but not a touch. It was the same for my brother, mother, and father. Jack's wife was able to land a few trout, but he kept on flipping them up on the bank. About every fourth fish my father would ask him if he needed another drink. By noon the fish stopped hitting and Jack took the catch below the dam to clean them. None were large fish, but they shone rainbows in the sunlight.

"This'll make a wonderful lunch soon as you ladies cook them up. As for me, I'm going to take a swim. How about it Doc?"

My father told him as soon as he got the kids into their bathing suits. He carried us down to the dam again and dove into the icy water, standing up about a yard out from shore. "Son, dive in and I will catch you."

I panicked. The water looked like it was a hundred feet deep. My father beckoned again. "Come on, don't be a sissy."

He grabbed me and pulled me into the deep water. "Relax, put your face down. I'll hold you."

I screamed, scratched at him. My mother showed up and told him to let go and let me play in the shallow rock pools further away from the dam. I, half in a trance, concentrated on bouncing in the shallow water. It was fun, but I didn't want to get near that deep water. My father was apologizing to his friends about my outburst. No one really cared except for him.

My brother didn't like the small trout fried in butter, but I took an immediate liking for those crispy morsels, eating four of them myself. It redeemed me in the eyes of my father who listened to Jack as he said. "That's some kid you got there. I'd like to take him fishing sometime."

"Yes, as soon as he learns to swim," my father retorted.

My brother and I sneaked up on deer, chased squirrels, threw rocks at water snakes, and then we were packed into the car for the return journey. West winds blew and it was cold sitting in the back of the open jalopy.

Coming over the peak of King's Mountain, we headed down to the Spring Valley Lakes. Even at such a young age I still remember the wonderful blue ocean to the left, furrows of mixed light through the redwoods, a deer jumping in front of the jalopy, screeching of what brakes there were, a stop for the men to have a drink and a smoke.

The Spring Valley Lakes were a series of creeks that originally cascaded down the steep valleys, emptying into the San Francisco Bay. The dam gathered all of the small streams into two huge lakes. Besides the small streams which helped to fill behind the dam, water was piped from the Sierra Nevada range to the Spring Valley Lakes, pristinely pure water to supply the people of San Francisco County with an abundance of quality drinking water. To this day it remains the same and the City hires riders who patrol the shores of the lake on horseback to insure that trespassers are chased out after being given tickets.

Continuing down the winding two-lane road we crossed between the two Spring Valley Lakes, waves cresting out in the middle of each lake. The air temperature warmed as we turned off Skyline Boulevard into the Lake Merced plateau.

Twenty minutes and we were home, jumping off the tailgate and rushing up our front stairs. The next day my brother and I played in the backyard, fishing with imaginary poles, and drinking imaginary beers.

Chapter 3

Fishing Is So Much Fun?

Living on 47th Avenue was remote. In the thirties there were few routes to the beach with vast amounts of sand dunes in all directions. The Sunset District avenues were mostly disconnected from 20th Avenue to about 45th Avenue, from Golden Gate Park to Taraval Street. There were some homes on each side of these boundaries, except for the park. Directly across from the park was Lincoln Way and homes lined it for most of its distance to the beach.

Playland lay between Golden Gate Park on its north boundary and the Cliff House, which still hangs over the ocean. Droves of people, mostly San Franciscans, flocked to the amusement park on weekends, but other than that it was mostly deserted.

Although my brother Gene and I were forbidden to go to the beach a block away, my father took us on most weekends to play in the sand and cavort in the surf. We could not swim, but that mattered little. From as far back as I can remember we had been taught about the dangers in San Francisco surf.

The beach had a gentle slope to it in most places, resulting in strong whitewater pushing to the beach at all times. We were warned about the deeper holes that had side and deep ocean directed currents. It was not a time of surfing and many who did get caught in these riptides drowned.

We always waded in water that was not over shoulder height. My father taught us how to dive under the oncoming soup and grab the sand to hold position. The next wave we would throw ourselves in front of it and bounce in the foamy soup to the sand. It was great fun and we never tired or got cold. At least we didn't realize it until my father or mother would usher us up the beach wrapped in towels, lips blue, and shivers taking precedence.

The Sunset District was aptly named as you most often only saw the sun in the late afternoon after the fog had cleared. The winter surf on quiet nights would awaken you, and, if it was really starry, you could hear the lions at the zoo at Fleishacker screaming. Otherwise, a soft silence predominated. No cars were parked on the streets at night and only a few during the day. The police patrolled the beach on horseback. The only litter on the beaches, besides parts of ships that had gone aground, was horse manure, and it broke down into soil. There was no plastic and bags were at a premium, used over and over again.

There were no supermarkets until the late thirties and Safeway was the first out on 43rd Avenue and Judah Street. Prior to the super markets you shopped at a meat market, vegetable market, and dairy market.

Everything moved slowly. There was time for focusing on hiking, fishing, and swimming in the surf. We played in the street until dark, basketball, football, hop scotch, chase the tin can, and no parents felt anxious or fearful that we would be hurt or harassed by some pervert. Children were safe and we knew it. Any crime was considered unusual.

We camped as scouts, but also on our own. We trusted adults to act like dependable grown ups. We knew that they kept a watchful eye on us. Sometimes it was spooky to go into foreign neighborhoods, and occasionally we would have confrontations with bullies, but mostly we got along and felt safe.

Refrigeration was at a premium, ice cream and candy something special, and for my father to buy me a hotdog at Playland was a super duper treat. We made coolers from old boxes hung out the shady side of the house with a porous sack kept wet on the down side of the wind. It worked pretty well, except for dairy products and meat. I got food poisoning often, but recovered, accepted it as part of growing. The pay off, which I did not realize at the time, was open space, uncrowded places, unobstructed views, wildlife in your backyard, clean air, and you could drink from streams.

There were deer in the sand dunes, raccoons, hawks, and some snakes, most non-poisonous, but even an occasional rattlesnake. It was not unusual to see the raccoons in your backyard at night. Less than ten miles down Skyline Boulevard, Highway 5, and mountain lions roamed some nights. Much of the land, which is premium now, was just about worthless. People laughed when anyone talked of building homes on the sand dunes.

The boundary line between 48th Avenue and the beach was The Great Highway, a three-mile stretch of road suspended on top of the berm separating the ocean from the streets on the other side. However, in 1936 a huge North Pacific storm, which reached all the way to Hawaii, swept the sea across The Great Highway and into our garage on 47th Avenue. Tropical fishes were washed ashore along with fishing boats and huge redwood logs. The storm lasted for many days, and, when finally abating, my parents took me and we stood atop The Great Highway watching giant waves wash thirty feet high foam across the beach. The foam remained after the waves subsided and we ran down into it during low tide, completely lost in mountains of air filled foam.

The last memory of 47th Avenue was one Sunday when our family went down to Rockaway Beach. It was a clear, glassy, and quiet day, no waves breaking on the beach. Rockaway Beach lay north of Pedro Point, now called the Pacifica region.

We walked to the southern portion of the cove and set our blanket down. The sun warmed us quickly and my father suggested a dip. Walking down to the sea I noticed that the sand was different here, more coarse with millions of sparkling like diamonds embedded. The sand, unlike San Francisco, was shiny white. It felt like it could cut your feet.

I watched my father dive into the sea, surface, turn over on his back and let out a whoop. The sea, also unlike San Francisco, was crystal clear, deep, and reminded me of La Honda Park.

There was some shimmering kelp and shellfish on top the submerged rocks. I could see fish swimming beneath the surface. Overwhelmed by the wonder, the beauty, the perfection of this little protected cove, I wanted to dive in and swim to my father, but I did not know how to swim. He held my hand and I walked in up to my shoulders.

Ducking my head under the icy water I felt extreme exhilaration. My father told me to hold my breath and float face forward toward shore on the next swell. My first separation from the bottom, my eyes open wide, being able to see the sandy bottom, and I ran out of air too quickly.

"Again, Dad, I want to do it again." He stayed with me for a long time. I still remember the crispness and clear water, the kelp and abalone. A wonderful day, great abundance.

That year we moved to 13th Avenue off Judah Street. Feeling a great loss upon moving from the beach, I concentrated on playing in our backyard, looking forward to the Saturday matinee on 14th Avenue and Irvine Street. Becoming totally engrossed in a serial movie, *Hawk Of The Wilderness*, a chapter each week, I found deep identification with Hawk.

My mother bought me a length of rope twenty-five feet long, sewed for me a duplicate of Hawk's clothes, and I was gone into Golden Gate Park every day after school. I swung from tree to tree, ran through the jungle in my mind, chased monkeys, lions, and jumped from branches onto deer.

One night after I had stowed my rope and clothes in my cave in the attic, I heard my father telling my mother that on Sunday Roy and he were going fishing down at Pedro Point. "I want to take Fred with me."

As excited as could be, I slept little Saturday night. Morning came before it was light and we ate a piece of toast and I had some hot chocolate. My mother handed me a brown bag lunch and my father and I got into Roy's car, headed down the coast to Pedro Point.

The boat ramp smelled of old sardines and it was foggy. I watched two fishermen launch into the surf. They slid down the ramp, one of them guiding the boat into the sea, while the other pulled on the outboard motor starter line. They sped away into the fog.

We were next. Roy and my father piled the fishing equipment into the boat and then Roy lifted me. "You get the free ride. We'll jump in when you hit the water." They pushed me off. I screamed, saw the sea coming up to me. I was terrified when the skiff hit the ocean, saltwater splashing over the bow and drenching me. Tears poured from my eyes and my father fell into the boat, followed by Roy. Roy was yelling at my father. "Grab the damned oars and paddle to sea. I'll start the motor." More waves over the bow, and the motor jumped into action. We chugged into the fog barely making it over what appeared to me to be mountainous ground swells.

The fog slowly cleared and Roy pointed to some rocky outcroppings offshore. "We'll anchor there." They put their rods out, leaned them against the oarlocks, and Roy pulled a bottle of whisky from his hip pocket. "This'll warm you up, Doc."

He handed me a drop line and baited the hooks for me. The swells were feathering all around us when Roy decided that we were too close to the rocks.

I had just thrown up and was begging to be taken back to the beach, sobbing in-between puking.

Roy kept pulling on the starter and it wouldn't take. "It's too damned wet, Doc. We got to row away from those rocks."

I lay in the bottom of the boat wishing that I had gone to confession. It was all over as far as I was concerned. "I'll give you a dime if you take me back to shore."

"God damn it, Doc, shut that kid of yours up. I told you we shouldn't have taken him." Doc rolled to the bow and threw up over the side. Roy was stuck with rowing, fighting the swell away from the rocks.

What seemed like an eternity passed; the fog tightened its grip and with it the sea glassed off. There was chop, but the white caps that came over the bow had ceased. Roy dropped the anchor and told us, "This place is in deep water and we don't have to worry about one of those waves filling the boat."

I felt a little more assured of survival, but continued throwing up next to my father. Roy yelled again. "I got him." He pulled his line over the side, two huge black fish hooked. He had his line in the water again in seconds. Again he pulled in two fish.

"We're in a school of fish. Get your lines in the water." I didn't know what he meant. I tried to picture fish in school.

"I didn't know that fish went to school."

"Don't get wise kid. Get your line into the water."

My line was not long enough to get down to the school of rockfish, but I caught a few smelt and felt a hair better. Roy was not ready to give up. He was filling the boat with fish and I was afraid that we would sink. I started to cry again and Roy said. "That's it Doc, we're going in." I saw a deep smile part my father's lips.

Not on shore more than a minute and I felt wonderful. It was stable land that I had needed. No one said anything to me all the way back to San Francisco. When Roy emptied the gunnysacks full of fish I was excited. I had never seen so many fish, different colors, sizes, shapes. Roy bent over and neatly cleaned all of them, leaving us with more fillets than we could eat in a week. It had been a day of abundance in fishing.

Chapter 4

Buck Shot
In Dark Places

In what seemed no time, my family moved again, this time to Lawton Street and 11th Avenue, a move that came as pleasant relief to me. Many of my friends who attended Saint Anne's Grammar School with me lived up there. From our new home we could see across the Golden Gate and watch the last preparations in finishing the bridge.

15th Avenue, which lay to our west four blocks, was an area of hills, shrubbery, and some Monterey Pines. If was mostly uninhabited, a few houses on the side of the hill facing the Golden Gate. There was a natural pond sitting in an indentation on 15th Avenue. Whenever it rained for more than a few days the pond would fill to near the rim of the circular crater. None of us knew how to swim, but we overcame that obstacle by carrying lumber up from a building project to the west on 16th Avenue. Henry Doelger was just beginning to develop the west side of this slope.

After the carpenters left we would sneak into the unfinished buildings and take scrap lumber, nails, and tin strips left from opened lumber. With these we constructed our raft. There were other kids hanging around, but they didn't know of our private lumberyard. We were the lords of the pond until one of the other kids, who also could not swim, pushed off on the raft one afternoon before we arrived. He drowned and that ended our adventure in rafting. The City and County Department constructed a fence around the water.

17

Of course, we still would sneak in whenever the occasion presented itself, but interest waned after the kid had drowned.

It was kite season and my friends confided in me that the best kite flying, because of wind and no overhead electric wires, were the "Hills." The west wind blew in from the ocean and it was perfect kite country. Each of us vied for the choice position, which was above the now enclosed pond. My friend, Dave Devine, told me that it was not safe to fly your kite alone as their were gangs of "Big Kids" who ran the "Hills" and found much glee in cutting the line to your kite and if you resisted they'd tie you to a tree and torture you. I thought that he was putting me on until one late afternoon I had my kite out about five hundred feet further than all the rest. My friends, one by one, rolled their kites in and left the area. I was alone and it was descending to dusk, but the wind was still strong and I basked in the thrill of my kite being so far up in the sky, that is until I saw a bunch of kids running up the hill toward me.

My first thought was to wind the kite in on the run down the opposite side of the hill, but when I looked back I could see that they were gaining on me. My next thought was my own survival. I had put a lot of care and work into getting that kite just light enough so that I could feed it out so far. This kite was the envy of my kite flying friends. Those things you built yourself.

Now there was about fifty yards between my pursuers and me. The kite slowed me down. I looked back again and saw the biggest of them waving a large wooden sword constructed from slats that were used to hold plaster in place. I saw the point swinging above his head, heard his curses.

Dropping the ball of twine I had been feverishly rolling, I sprinted forward with renewed strength and speed. The last of daylight descended as I ran the stairs to my front door, looked back into darkness, and heard the gang continue on past my house, shouting obscenities.

In school the next day I told Dave about the attack and he said that it had happened before and the best thing to do was to not go up into the "Hills" until things died down. Dave passed out notes to all of our gang. The essence of the note was that we were all to meet on 7th Avenue after school below the trail into Sutro Forest.

Changing into my play clothes I hurried down to our meeting place. Ray Helms, John Mc Bride, Dave, and I were the complete roster. Dave led us up the trail to the forest. I had never been into it before. As we ascended, Dave told of the different places to watch. One, in particular, was a fenced area that we approached. He said that there was an old guard who attended the vegetable garden and kept people from stealing vegetables. Dave further mentioned that one of our missions today was to climb the fence, steal carrots and tomatoes, and get back out without the guard seeing us.

The trail, as Dave knew it, ended at the gate to the garden. Forest, pines and ferns, grew right up to the fence, which stood way above our heads.

Dave laid out his plan, whispering to the small group, which resembled a football huddle. "We crawl to the other side of the fence where you can see that little opening where the sun is strongest. There are some animal trails there. We climb over the fence, spread out, and grab as much as we can. Be quiet."

Edging around the fence, Dave was first over and I climbed last. Inside I went toward the tomatoes. They were fat and red. I reached over, picked a ripe one and ate it. Delicious! I wanted more and stuffed the inside of my shirt until there was no more room.

Balloom! I heard the shotgun blast. Jumping up I ran for the fence, scratched feverishly to make the other side, but as I peaked the fence I felt a hot flash of pain sear my buttocks. It didn't stop me. The screaming man only added to my speed.

I emerged from the depths of the forest scratched from head to toe and my backside was burning pain. Staggering down the trail toward 7th. Avenue and safety, I came across Dave and Ray. They were laughing so hard when they saw my hands grasping my butt that tears ran their faces.

"He got you, he got you, the salt and pepper load. We've all been hit. It was just your turn to find out that that old geezer means business and you've got to run in, grab and right out, no sitting around savoring tomatoes."

The next two days in school were miserable. I couldn't sit. I didn't know what was happening during math, but volunteered to work at the board just so I could stand.

Aside from the old geezer Sutro Forest was an exciting place to explore. It was bounded by University Of California on the north and La Honda's old peoples home on the south. It covered hundreds of acres, had its population of deer, snakes, raccoons, coyotes, and other undiscovered animals that lived in its depths. Besides pine trees there were abundances of eucalyptus trees, and a little brook ran into a reservoir on the 7th. Avenue side. We drank from it when the sweat exuded our pores. There were also older gangs that ran the forest. We avoided them at all risks for some of them carried B-B guns. We avoided them until a frontal confrontation occurred on the trail up to the garden. I saw them first and warned my friends. They scattered into the bushes and I ran down the trail, but was headed off by the rest of the gang coming up from 7th. Avenue. I sidetracked and ended up looking down a precipice that dropped one hundred feet nearly perpendicular.

Sizing up the situation I felt the gang descending. There was no out and they knew it. I looked down the cliff. There was a little protrusion about fifty feet down. The gang, moving full speed, was twenty-five feet distant. I slid off the cliff, gained momentum, pushing large amounts of gravel ahead of me, and landed on the small protrusion, only slowing down long enough to look up and see the gang picking up rocks.

I slid all the way down that wall of shale and loose particles. It seemed like an eternity, but I reached the bottom running full speed. I didn't look back until I was coming into 11th Avenue.

Sneaking into the basement of my house so that my mother would not see me, I checked out my wounds. I was bloody and picked gravel from cuts, but all in all I was alive, would survive, and I had gotten away from them.

Soon afterwards the people living on 7th Avenue heard screams late at night, eerie screams, like a cat in heat. One resident described the screams to the local newspaper reporter. "It sounds like a cat fight, but I never heard one that loud."

A state trapper was called in and the hunt began. The animal was seen once or twice. It was a huge cougar. No one knew for sure how it had gotten there. After a week of pursuit, the forest being closed, the lion showed up in one of the basements on 7th Avenue.

It was trapped and moved to a less populated area in the coastal range above San Mateo.

San Francisco, although filling in with homes, was still a place of wildness. It was so much more fun to never know what we might find on an exploration. There was a siege in Golden Gate Park, and the phenomenon never explained, of huge increases in the garter snakes that we saw once in a while. Ray and I were wandering one day in the park and Ray yelled, "Come quick." I ran to him and wriggling on the ground were snakes everywhere. We turned to run and snakes had filled in our path of escape. They squirmed around our feet moving up our pant legs. We gingerly walked like on eggs to the road. We did not come back to the park for a month, and cautiously so on our first re-entry. There were no snakes, like it had never happened. We asked a gardener. He laughed and said that we were making up the story. I can still see in my mind those thousands of snakes. It never occurred again, but neither of us forgot the incident.

Chapter 5

Dynamite
Steelhead Fishing

The house on Lawton Street was going to be refurbished. My father and mother found a good rental on 19th Avenue near Ortega Street. The family had enlarged to four children, a sister Gretchen and brother Peter the youngest.

Aside from the fact that Doelger and a new competitor, Galli, were expanding into the sand dunes, there were in 1939 very few homes beyond 19th Avenue. Doelger and Galli were expanding only where pre-existing roads were. It was virtually sand dunes from about 19th or 20th Avenue to 48th Avenue.

Mostly, I spent my free time wandering either the sand dunes or the "Hills." During a Saturday matinee my friends and I had seen some skiing in a newscast. Ray got the idea to ski in the depths of the sand dunes. There were huge mounds of sand and deep gullies in-between. We got old barrel staves, waxed the bottom with my mother's canning parowax, and tied the skis to our feet. It worked, not as fast as we had seen in the movie, but it was as good as roller-skating.

Doelger did the ridiculous. He bought up all of the land in the sand dunes for a few cents an acre. The experts who had built San Francisco told him that he was crazy and that you could not stabilize a house in that shifting sand. Doelger didn't listen and offered a three-bedroom home with view of Marin County and the San Francisco ocean for $6,000. At the same time we received notice from the City and County that they were going to widen 19th

Avenue. We could move out for the months it would take and come back if we chose. My father, tired and disgusted with so many moves in the years past, decided to buy one of Doelger's lots.

We drove in from Judah Street on the road that had only gone as far as Lawton Street. New pavement lay ahead as we moved past Moraga Street to our lot. It just looked like a lot of sand that I had wandered. Yes, you could see the ocean and, yes, Marin County and part of the Golden Gate Bridge.

The house would not be finished until late August and it was only May. What to do? My father mentioned the problem to his dental patients as they filed in for help. One of them was a lumberman who owned a vast amount of acreage up near Boonville, California. He volunteered a place.

Jake Pesula looked up at my father from the dental chair. "Doc, I'll build you a platform, put two tents up on it and you can stay until the house is finished. It'll be rugged, but the kids get out of school soon. Make it a summer vacation."

My father discussed the offer with my mother at the dinner table. She replied. "Over my dead body." We all chimed in on my father's side.

"Come on, mom. It'll be fun. We can learn to swim. We can camp like at La Honda." I was the spokesman for the others.

My father added, "Jake wants me to come up this weekend and look at the place. I'll take Gene and Fred with me."

We drove the hundred plus miles in our '34 Chevy. It was a two lane winding road—country I had never seen unfolded and then it got dark as we entered Boonville. My father said that we were supposed to meet Jake in the local bar. There was only one in Boonville then. Jake and my father hoisted drink after drink. My brother and I got hungrier and hungrier.

Walking across the street to a small motel, my father looked for the owner. The place hadn't opened yet. It was only May. Jake said, "Give the kids something to eat. We'll have another drink and then you can stay up at the lumber mill at my place."

My father pulled two sandwiches from a bag my mother had packed and put us into the car to eat. "I'll be back soon and then we'll go to the camp." Gene and I were scared, left in this strange

23

town, alone, while my father disappeared into the bar. We waited, waited and then they both came from the bar arm in arm, giving each the support needed.

Turning off the main highway a mile out of town, we bounced up and down over a rickety dirt road. The dust climbed skyward and we moved into the darkness.

Jake, driving ahead of us in a pick up truck, suddenly came to a stop. Gene was asleep and I climbed out of the car with my father. Jake turned the spotlight in a hundred and eighty degree angle. Back and forth and then he stopped. "Shh, Doc, see the deer? I blinded it with this light; hand me my gun. It's in the case on the front seat."

My father returned. Jake took aim carefully. I saw the deer turn sideways. It was a beautiful animal, much like the ones my brother and I had chased and sneaked up on at La Honda. Just as Jake was pulling the trigger I deflected the gun with my hand, the bullet glancing off the top of an oak tree, Jake screaming, "What the hell you doing kid? That was dinner."

Jake mumbled under his breath all the way back to the truck. We followed, my father lecturing me about hunting and how I had better apologize. Arriving we walked up the front stairs to Jake's cabin. "Listen Doc, I haven't any room here for the kids. I got an Indian crew man and they can sleep in his cabin."

Terror struck my heart when I met this man, disheveled, drunk, scratching his head continually. "Don't worry, he's got a few coodies in his hair. He won't bother you."

The next morning I heard my father and Jake talking. Looking out the one window in the Indian's cabin, I saw them loading things into the truck.

I heard Jake, "Since that kid of yours ruined my shot last night, we can go down to the stream and get some steelhead trout for food."

At a place where we had to drive through the stream to get to the other side, I saw fish moving upstream, big fish. I jumped out of the car and Jake yelled at me, "You get down stream and hide behind that tree. Soon as you hear the dynamite blow run down stream and watch for stunned fish." He passed a bottle of whisky to my father and said, "Better drink some of this cause you're the one who's going to swim the dynamite out to that hole where the steelhead are hiding."

I watched my father string the line connected to the dynamite and then cross back over the stream. He had dove under the low cliff overhang and planted the dynamite right above the fish. He emerged from the water blue and shivering.

Jake yelled, "Take cover. I'm gonna blow er."

Water flew fifty feet into the sky. The water settled and Jake was yelling, "Watch for the floating fish. Grab them." I didn't see anything until my father emerged downstream holding a huge pink-sided fish. Jake grabbed another, threw it up on shore, and plunged forward to grab a third fish. He laid them on the bank. They still quivered and the slash rainbow down their sides shimmered in the morning sun.

Arriving back at camp, Jake handed the fish to the Indian man and told him to clean and prepare one for lunch. He told him to put the rest in the icehouse.

Some drinks later my father told us that lunch was ready and that we should come sit at the table. We had ice water from the stream and the three men drank straight shots out of the bottle. The steelhead was delicious, tasting somewhat like the salmon my mother cooked for Friday night dinners. Both my brother and I filled up on the fish and fried potatoes.

Jake looked over to my father, "Well, these kids will do all right up here. There's plenty of fish."

Arriving home Sunday afternoon, after my mother listened to the tales of the weekend, she put us into a hot bath and washed our hair with Lysol. Sleep came easy.

Chapter 6

Sharing Camp
With Rattlesnakes

May sifted into June. School closed for the summer and we packed what we would need in our camp outside of Boonville. Excitement reigned. My mother was not sharing our enthusiasm as she held three-year-old Peter on her lap. Passing through Cloverdale, a small town of about 1500 people, we read the sign, "Boonville 35 miles."

The countryside changed. There were rolling hills, meadows, interspersed with redwood trees, and the narrow highway wound up and down hairpin turns, sometimes in hot sun, other times covered with deep undergrowth overhead. It was early morning and we saw deer feeding in the meadows. A coyote ran across the road some distance ahead.

Dropping down a long stretch of straight road, we saw Boonville in the distance. It was a one street town, a gas station, ice cream parlor, grocery store, and some small businesses. The total population of the town was 750 people and most of them lived on the outskirts. There were two farm trucks parked in front of the grocery store and one lumber truck loaded with redwood spars in the gas station.

My father had filled the gas tank on the outskirts of Cloverdale and proceeded toward the dirt road outside Boonville. Turning up the redwood picket fenced road, we waved at a lady watering her roses, passed a one-room schoolhouse atop the knoll, and followed the lumber road to Indian Creek Lumber Mill. It was nine miles on this dirt road, which at one place we had to ford a small stream. My father got a good head of power going before dropping onto the gravel bottom. We made it with splashes of water coming over the hood.

Passing two farmhouses in long intervals between, our Chevy chugged to the summit and we looked down into a lush valley covered with redwood trees, virgin growth. We could see the road far below in only a few places as the heavy growth mostly hid it.

Dropping into the redwood canopy suddenly the temperature dropped to a coolness that my father rolled up his window. On the floor of the valley we saw a beautiful stream accompanying the road, the same stream where earlier in May we had blasted the Steelhead trout. Aside from the road, a lush carpet of redwood cones, leaf needles, and fallen branches filled the area under the trees. Very little sunlight filtered beneath these giant trees. The silence was somewhat deafening, and the crisp air stimulated your lungs to inhale.

Crossing a redwood bridge held up by giant logs laid across the stream, we entered the camp. Quiet reigned, except for some angry blue jays pecking at a squirrel climbing an oak tree.

We stopped in front of Jake's cabin and climbed out, ascending his porch, knocked and knocked, but Jake was no where to be seen.

My mother saw a woman down by the stream washing her clothes. She walked down and asked where Jake might be. "This time a day he's at the mill. Follow the road through camp. You friends of his'n"?

My mother introduced herself and told the lady that she was going to be staying in a tent for the summer. "I hear all about you, the four kids. I wouldn't think of doing that, the snakes, mountain lions, and bears. You have a gun?" She spoke with a strong Swedish accent. "What if the kids get sick? Nearest doctor Boonville. Only the lumber trucks going out, sometimes not every day."

My mother replied, "Jake has the pickup truck. He can take us to town if we need to go."

"Hah, Jake drunk most the time. He stays in town sometime a week. What you do then?"

Deep silence pervaded the Chevy as we continued through the camp, four or five log houses, roofs covered with branches and needles from the redwoods hanging overhead. Another stream to ford in our car, but this part not as deep. Easy!

Jake met us, climbed down from the caterpillar, and shook my father's hand. "Hello, Mrs. Van Dyke. Let's take a look at your campsite. I hope those guys built the platform. I told them last week." He climbed into our car and we turned to head back through the camp and over the redwood bridge. "Stop, turn left here and stop next to the creek," Jake instructed.

We looked at the small clearing, logs and branches scattered helter and skelter, the platform adjacent to the stream, a high cliff with oak trees hanging above us. My father, Jake, and my mother erected the two tents next to each other, leaving a small walk space around the decking. Jake showed my mother where he had hung a wooden box with open front covered with gunnysack material. "This is your cooler and I had that pot bellied stove brought over so you can cook. I have to get back to work."

As Jake walked away my mother asked him, "Where do we go to the bathroom?"

"You can use my outhouse. It's close enough to the bridge, just a short walk, and the kids can go in the bushes. Sunday I'll come over and Doc and I can dig an outhouse for all of you."

The outhouse, finished, consisted of two boards suspended between branches over a hole of five feet deep. After a couple of days as you sat balancing on the two boards, hundreds of bees buzzed beneath your bottom. At best it was hazardous. Sunday night my father waved goodbye to us and yelled, "See you next week. I will get the supplies. Don't worry."

A routine established itself. We gathered wood. My mother showed us how to pile kindling and large pieces. She started the fire.

We huddled near for warmth, morning and night. My mother made breakfast, packed a lunch of sandwiches, and we hiked down the dirt road to a trail, which led to a redwood dam that the lumberjacks had constructed. It was a swimming hole for them to swim in after work.

The sun faded into the afternoon, disappeared, and we headed back to camp. My mother told us that the water was too deep and that we would go back only after Gene and I had learned to swim.

That was fine with Gene and me for the creek in front of the camp was only hip deep and the sun shone on it until about one o'clock. Gretchen and Peter were too young to wander freely, but Gene and I, after playing in the creek, would sneak over the ridge and watch the lumberjacks at work. One day one of the men spotted us and beckoned us to come. We were scared, but reluctantly moved forward. "You want to be a lumber jack? You help us. I show you how to stack the lumber." It was just more play for us and we were now lumberjacks.

Days passed and the explorations continued after breakfast. My mother would settle in with Peter and Gretchen and Gene and I would explore. Our first discovery was up by the Swedish lady's cabin. The stream there had a log jam and the water backed up, forming a six-foot deep hole. We climbed out on one of the logs and peered down into the depths. Trout swam back and forth, small trout, middle sized, and some almost as large as the steelhead we had dynamited. There were hundreds of trout stacked in this logjam.

I raced Gene back to camp, asking our mother if she would give us two pins from the diapers, some string. We constructed crude poles out of skinny redwood branches, attached bent pin and line. All we needed was bait. "Where can we get worms?" I remembered fishing at La Honda.

My mother told us to look for moss and wet soil, dig quickly, and we would find worms. It worked and we had a discarded empty can of chicken gumbo soup filled with worms in a few minutes. We rushed back to the deep hole, sneaked out on the log and softly lowered our lines into the depths. I watched the worm slowly settle to the bottom, wriggling, but it never made it. A trout snatched the worm, impaling its lips on the pin. It dove straight for the bottom and made a lunge upward, clearing the surface. I lifted the pole and swung the fish over my head onto the moss on the beach. It was nearly ten inches long, a deep slice of red piercing its gill plate and underside. I admired the fish and practically got hit in the face by my brother's trout. It was somewhat bigger than mine, about fourteen inches. We hung the fish by a twig in the shade and went back to fishing. We caught ten more fish and ran out of worms. The Swedish lady came out her door and inspected our catch. "Not bad; my son, he's a lumber jack. After work one day he fish here and land one hundred and eight trout before it come dark. He feed the whole camp."

29

Screaming as we entered camp, my brother held up the fish. "You have dinner for us. Let me show you how to clean them." I said that I would help because I had learned from Roy when he had cleaned the other fish in our backyard. We went below the camp a goodly distance for my mother said that she did not want to attract animals. She made us bury the entrails.

My mother fried the fish in a big pan with Crisco, salt, and pepper. We feasted and after dinner my mother said that we should go and catch a whole bunch, for my father was coming up from San Francisco to visit Friday. The next day we caught more trout. My brother hooked one the size of a steelhead but it was gone, hook, line, and my brother cried, tears streaming down his cheeks. We had the trout for our father, though.

My dad arrived late Friday night, smelling heavily of alcohol. We ran up to the car, the fish in our hands, the headlights illuminating them. My father said that he'd have them for breakfast, that he had stopped in Boonville for a beer and Jake was there. He reached into the backseat and pulled a half crushed brown bag of groceries out, handed them to my mother, and went to sleep in the tent. My father had moved out of the house on 19th Avenue and was staying at his mother's. She had dogs and so he had brought our tomcat, Rasputen, with him. We took Rasputen to bed with us who seemed confused, but interested more in exploring the night. He bounded out the tent flap. Toward dawn we were awakened by loud screaming noises. Rasputen came running into the tent with us kids. My mother yelled to me from the other tent. "I have Rasputen, don't worry."

I answered back. "You can't. I have him." Whatever I was holding dug deeply into my hands and was gone through the tent flap. This was the beginning of a long string of adventures at night with Rasputen and his new friends, enemies? We never did see the other creatures that he brought back to camp.

Breakfast was relished, trout for my father who wasn't feeling very well and bacon and eggs, toast and jam for us. We had run out of food by Thursday and this was tantamount to a feast. My mother finished washing the dishes in the stream and we were off to the dam. My dad wanted to swim off his hangover.

I loved the dam and sat in the shade looking into the pool. It dropped off into deep water abruptly. Climbing out on a submerged log that hung over the water, I imagined myself diving into this pool and swimming to the other side, settled for jumping near shore into the hip deep water. It was a wonderful place, framed in redwoods, moss covered rocks beneath the dam, and the water so pure that I would bend over and vacuum in this freezing water many times during the day. We were all brown like bears. Our feet toughened from running the forest floor, our lungs healthy from fresh air; we were like part of the animals in the forest. I liked seeing the deer, raccoons, squirrels, chipmunks, eagles, and hawks.

I felt that time had stopped in this wonderful forest. It was so different from the city. The sun shone all day and the nights were crisp with billions of stars flooding the sky above. I fell asleep to the night sounds, the woodpecker who lived in an oak tree, the coyotes at dusk, dawn serenading the forest, and the occasional unidentified growl from the depths of darkness.

My mother had complained to my father that the supplies were not lasting. My father assured her before he drove off, "I left money with Jake and he said that he was going into town so don't worry."

Wednesday morning we had no more food. We didn't even have grease to fry trout. The Swedish lady had eight kids plus a hungry lumberjack husband to feed. She had no surplus. We boiled some trout, but that was it. Peter and Gretchen needed milk. My mother asked the Swedish lady if anyone was going to town? She said, "No," and then told my mother that there was a farmer three miles up the road where she could get raw milk. She said that it was important to leave early in the morning for by eleven a.m. it would be too hot to walk the road.

Leaving at the earliest light, we trudged up the grade toward the summit. It was cool, but most difficult for my mother, as she had to carry Peter most of the time and Gretchen was petering out by time we reached the farmer's house. Gene and I had carried two empty quart bottles to be filled. The farmer's wife was very nice and invited us in for some toast and fresh milk. It was the best food I had ever tasted. We stayed too long and the sun was high in the sky when we departed, my mother carrying Peter and Gene, Gretchen, and me stumbling in the hot sun carrying the milk.

Suddenly we heard a crashing through the bushes and a large buck deer emerged taking long leaps and bounds. The crashing continued and a huge mountain lion bounding after it stopped its chase and looked at us. My mother put Peter down, told us not to move, opened her purse and pulled out the thirty-eight revolver my father had left with her. She again reached deeply into her purse groveling for the bullets. She had left them in camp.

The lion looked at us more closely, lifted its paw into the air, and let out a scream. It moved to within ten feet and repeated the scream, ending with a foofing sound like an angry domestic cat. We stood frozen in our paths. My mother pointed the gun at the animal. It took one last look and bounded off after the deer. We nearly half ran the rest of the distance to camp. However, we still had the two quarts of milk. I tasted it and spit. All of the jumbling on the return trip plus the heat had soured the two quarts. My mother sat down and cried.

My mother tried calming us by playing a game. We had magazines that had food ads in them. She told us to make believe that we could have any food that we wanted from the ads.

Then when we had chosen she cut the pictures out and said that we were to play make believe again and enjoy the meal in front of us. It worked for a short time. We needed food!

We pounded on Jake's cabin door to no avail. My mother boosted me up at the back entrance, a screened window at top. I peered through to his cooler and could see a piece of meat hanging and some potatoes. "That's it," my mother told me. "We're breaking in, now!"

We tore the screen off and I climbed through to the cooler, grabbed the piece of meat, stuck potatoes in my pockets, and we ran to camp. It took little time for my mother to get a fire burning in the stove.

She diced the potatoes and cut the slab salt pork into bacon-sized pieces. Cooking the entire ingredients together its fragrance filled our camp. We stood in line and she doled out food. The pork was really salty, but the potatoes absorbed a good deal of the fat and salt. It was a substantial meal, a filler. We would survive another day. Jake never did show, but my dad arrived early in the afternoon. He had taken off for the long Fourth of July weekend.

The next day was my birthday and we had doughnuts and hot chocolate. My mother put ten candles in the doughnut in front of me and I blew them all out, wishing a secret that was to come true, and soon.

While we waited that hour before going in the water in front of camp, the sun climbed directly above. It was a perfect day, my birthday. My brother and I played in the water and my father watched. I remembered the game he had shown me down at Rockaway Beach and tried it in the waist deep water. I took a deep breath, fell forward toward shore, and floated. It worked. I showed my brother, Gene, and he tried it, too. We competed to see who could float the longest distance and soon were moving fifteen feet.

My father said, "Why don't you move your arms like this." He motioned a crawl stroke and we tried it. We were swimming. It was shallow water, but we were both swimming. "Let's go to the dam. It's my birthday."

It was hot afternoon sun when we arrived at the dam. My father dove in and swam to the mossy bank shaded by redwoods. He climbed out of the water, didn't pause, turned and dove head first into the path he'd just swum. He leaped out of the water and came running across the narrow beach, yelling, "There are snakes all over that moss." We laughed, but my father did not think it was funny.

My mother explained. "When we come down here once in a while we have to clear the snakes away before we can get into the water. Watch." She picked up a hand full of rocks and threw them in the direction of the mossy bank. Snakes glided into the water and dispersed in all directions. "See, that's all you have to do. There are snakes everywhere." My father stayed on the sandy beach most of the afternoon. I sat upon that log and visualized the dive into the water, surfacing, holding my breath, and taking the necessary strokes to the mossy bank.

I looked beneath the surface for a long time, seeing trout dart back and forth, some slapping their tails on the surface. "It's time," I thought out loud. "Dad, watch me while I dive off and swim to the other side."

He stood beneath the log and I aimed for a dive as close to the other side as possible. I knew that I had to come to the surface, get air, and negotiate a few strokes to the moss. I calculated again. It looked good. Leaning forward, I lost balance and jumped. Hitting the water I felt myself shooting down into the depths, my first time in water over my head.

I held my breath, bounced off the bottom, pushed hard, and shot to the surface, took the needed breath, put my head down and stroked. I bounced against the moss two strokes under my estimate. My mother and father stood and cheered. Including the long jump, I had covered about fifteen feet in deep water. I was ecstatic, waited until chills emanated from my torso, and dove, this time forward. It was a belly flop, and almost before I landed on the water I was stroking. My father told me that the next step was to make me water safe.

"What do you mean?" I asked.

"Being able to change direction, tread water."

My father showed me these things and even though I was freezing, I tried each, the changing direction the easiest, treading water a little more frightening, but I got the idea. I had something to practice when he was in the city. My mother would have to take us to the dam now for I could swim. I might even be able to act as a lifeguard helper for my mother.

Next week we spent most of the sunny part of the day at the dam. It was wonderful practicing. I would edge my way into the deeper water and tread for two or three minutes. I loved going up beyond the log where no one could see me and I would tread water, experiencing the full wonder of the exhilarating water, looking at the azure blue sky.

Next weekend my father brought twenty pounds of potatoes, carrots, canned beef, flour, syrup, butter, and Crisco, some canned juices. We felt like we were in heaven. Everything was perfect.

My father decided to take us for an explore down the stream. He said that it finally ended at the dam and we could not get lost. One hundred yards below camp the stream widened and became swifter. There were huge boulders protruding the surface, the beaches, sandbars filled with excrement from many different kinds of animals.

My father had been an Eagle Scout and he thought that he could identify some of the feces that lay there. With each discovery he gave it an identity, bear, elk, deer, raccoon, some kind of cat, maybe Rasputen or a mountain lion, coyote. The coyotes were the easiest for they all had hairballs in the offal. We wandered deeper, climbed under deadfall, under moss covered trees, and walked knolls to see what lay ahead. It was a beautiful, rugged wilderness. I could feel the presence of animals.

I asked my dad if he thought anyone had ever walked where we were. His answer. "This is so remote that I do not believe that anyone has ever been here." A half an hour later we rounded a turn in the stream and there before us was the dam, clothed in shade, quiet, some trout feeding on the surface near the darkly shaded banks.

Cool as it was we bathed in the icy water. It was great, the contrast from heavy perspiring in the hot sun to this hideaway. Walking back through the woods on the trail we were silent, basking in our good fortune.

Back at camp, Gretchen complained of an itching in her ear. My father examined it and found a tick attached to her eardrum. He reached with tweezers, but they were too thick. Kerosene didn't seem to move the insect. The decision was made to drive to Boonville, visit the doctor.

The doctor said that it had been a wise decision as these ticks can cause severe infection. He removed it carefully making sure that he extracted the head, poured some disinfectant into the ear, and filled it with gauze.

"If she does not complain don't bother to come in again. I'll give you these pills. They will make her sleep better." My father took us to the ice-cream parlor, our first treat in a long long time. We savored each lick.

In those days your resistance either cured you or you perished. There was no penicillin. She was fine the next day. My father left for San Francisco late Sunday night.

Less and less sun shone upon our camp. It was moving toward fall and things were dryer than when we first arrived. An old oak tree hanging above our camp creaked in the hot sun. My brother and I played on a huge fallen redwood log. It was at least ten feet in diameter. It was great fun to climb the semi-perpendicular side and slide down the rounded edges, flying off into space where the angle turned under. We had been at it for an hour or more when suddenly I saw a huge snake slither from beneath the log to under our platform. I yelled for my mother. She came and I pointed toward where the snake had disappeared.

We ran to Jake's cabin and he wasn't home. Crossing the dirt road, we knocked on the Swedish lady's house. Her youngest son appeared and asked what the matter was.

"There's a huge snake under our platform. Can you help us?" He followed, a pitchfork in hand. Arriving at the camp, my mother showed him where the snake had gone. He pulled out a flashlight and looked into a series of beady eyes. There was a nest of rattlesnakes under our platform. We had lived there most of the summer and that was the buzzing we had heard in the evenings, thinking it was crickets. He jammed the pitchfork into the area over and over, pulled back and had three snakes on the fork's points. They were rattlesnakes, big ones, and he thought there might be more of them. He looked with the flashlight for a long time, but saw no movement or eyes reflected.

"I think you'll be all right now. Rattlesnakes don't like to be close to people. If there are anymore they'll probably clear out."

It was hot that week, unusually dry and hot. With the rising sun we heard the oak tree creaking throughout the day. My mother was nervous. We found Jake at home and asked him to come by and check the tree. He looked at it and said, "Hell, that tree's been hanging on that cliff for at least a hundred years and it'll probably hang another hundred. In hot weather the sap expands and contracts. Don't worry."

The tree continued to creak and crack. My brother and I had listened to the lumberjacks cut trees down. Just before the tree was beyond the point of no return it began to creak and crack. It usually was a matter of a few minutes before it toppled. We played in the creek and half listened. The creaks and cracks became more pronounced and my mother quickly summoned us out of the water and placed all of us next to the huge redwood trunk that Gene and I played upon.

The oak tree continued to crack and creak. It swayed slightly, forward, and then the cracking grew into a continuous cacophony of splitting lumber. It seemed like two or three minutes passed, a continuous splintering, and then it happened. This huge oak, suspended a hundred feet above our camp in slow motion fell sideways up the stream throwing water in all directions when it hit. It fell the length from the bridge to our camp, missing us by about ten or fifteen feet.

My mother burst into tears, cursed at the top of her lungs, screamed. "That's it. We're leaving, as soon as your father arrives. I don't care if our house is finished or not. We're leaving." She received no dissension.

We left this place of beauty, quietness, the pristine redwoods, the pure mountain air, the drinking from the stream, fishing in virgin environs, the freedom of an eagle, the danger ever present of wilderness isolation.

We left this place, but each of us took a part of it with us forever.

Chapter 7

Dead Man's Rock

Another move, this time to our new house on 34th Avenue between Moraga and Noriega Streets. Noriega Street came down from 19th Avenue to the beach. There were no connections to Taraval Street on the other side of the sand dunes except for 36th Avenue, which was a boulevard that went from Golden Gate Park to Lake Merced on the south. Some city planners had seen the potential many years ago and it was a link to the Highway 5 called Skyline Boulevard. There were five houses on our block, nothing between the beach and us aside from vastness of dunes.

The view was incredible, no houses to block it, Marin County, part of the Golden Gate Bridge, and Ocean Beach. When the wind blew hard, as it does in San Francisco, we would get sanded in instead of snowed in. The dunes would reclaim our exit and until bulldozers could clear a path, we were stuck, our car sitting in the garage, useless. It was three and a half blocks to the N streetcar on Judah Street.

Discovering the fun of fishing more and more, enjoying supplementing the family food supply, I explored the fishing in San Francisco. Ray Helms, John Mc Bride, and I started at Muni pier, newly constructed especially for fishing. It made a half moon toward Alcatraz Island, close to a mile out into the bay. The fish that came in or out on the tides were funneled past the pier. It was perfect.

Most of the fishermen were of Chinese, Japanese, Italian, and Filipino descent. One day when my mother drove down and picked us up she was aghast. "You should not associate with those people. They cannot be trusted. I do not want you to fish there again." I didn't understand. These people were my new friends. We never remembered to bring lunches. These people shared lunches with us whenever we looked like we were about on the edge of starvation, watching them savor big fat French bread sandwiches.

Regardless of the tide coming in or out, from about 1 p.m. until about 2:30 p.m. daily, the fish, as it was referred to, were "Running." Suddenly, after long periods of no bites, the bay would explode with life, sea gulls diving, pelicans vying for their share, carrying shiners, perch, smelt, an occasional striped bass in their beaks. It reached fever pitch. We were catching smelt every time our line touched the water. We rigged up half a dozen hooks. Same thing, full hooks, fish flopping everywhere on the pier.

Our faces flushed, pink with excitement, we filled gunnysacks with mixed species. I wanted big horse smelt, the fish that fought so hard, but hardly any one ate because they had worms. I found out that all fish have some parasites and if cooked it made no difference, much like pork.

It was the abundance of sardines, herring, anchovies that packed the bay, created that frenzy in birds and fish, people. Everything fed on the baitfish. We bought sardines at the bait shop. Some fish would bite on worms or shrimp, but all fish relished sardines. Some days the bay channel got so choked with bait fish that they were being pushed onto shore, flopping in the sand, gulls feasting like the Romans in days of old.

Smelling of a day of baiting and cleaning fish, our gunnysack of fish slung over our backs, we boarded the streetcar most often at the beginning of rush hour home from work traffic. No one stood near us and sometimes the conductor kicked us off. The double transfer to reach Muni Pier kept our visits down to a minimum.

This lack of transportation did not hinder our hours fishing. The only real impediments were my mother refusing to allow me to go or Sunday Mass. We beat the latter by meeting at St. Anne's church for the 5 o'clock a.m. service. Sometimes Ray even talked us into skipping the church ceremony, promising that he'd confess for all of us.

We ran the Golden Gate Park after school and one late afternoon we saw movement on a lake adjacent to 21st Avenue. There were swishes and swirls near the tules. Sneaking up on the phenomenon, suddenly a huge fish slapped its tail on the surface and disappeared into the depths. I looked at Ray and Mc Bride. Our minds synched: a carp.

In our excitement, notes were passed back and forth during school. Mc Bride got sent to the Mother Superior, came back with welts on his knuckles. He cared less, was an artist, and continued to draw the huge carp that we had seen, the drawing hidden from the sight of Sister Felicitas.

We ran the distance from school to the lake, hid in the tules, and stripped long sinews of cuttyhunk line from our pockets, attached one hook, baited with left over sandwich bread, swung the line overhead and let go. Three soggy pieces of bread fell off each hook and sank beneath the muddy surface. We baited again, tried more sensitive precision, and the baits lay motionless on the surface. I saw the swirl, the carp sucking in my bread bait, and then it dove. I set the hook and the lake exploded, the carp flying two feet into the air, landing on its side. I felt that it was heard all the way to Lincoln Way.

Allowing the fish to run, I only turned it when I was running out of line, retrieved some footage, and then the fish was off again. It tried that three times, and then I pulled hand over hand until the fish lay flopping on its side in the tules. It was the biggest fish I had ever caught. I grabbed it through the gills and held it up to admire.

Ray was first to see the gardener sprinting toward us, waving a machete over his head. The gardener yelled something half Filipino and English. "Let's get out of here," whispered Ray. We split in three different directions, the gardener choosing me to chase.

I was carrying the huge fish. I cut into a dark channel of brush, jumped over a culvert, and made it to the edge of Lincoln Way. I didn't look back until I opened the side door into the garage. I hung the fish in the basement and weighed it on a pull scale, seven pounds.

Mc Bride showed up and we snacked up in the kitchen. "What are you going to do with it?" he asked.

"Eat it, what do you think?"

My mother did bake it, after pictures taken out on the lawn, but it was not a feast. It tasted lake muddy, and bones were throughout the meat. Rasputen chewed on it for a couple of days.

Coming into winter we fished less and less until one day Mc Bride, who wandered over the city by himself, came to school, his hands filled with drawings. We sat down and looked at them during recess. They were pictures of a rugged set of rocks looking into the Golden Gate, ferocious waves pounding up against the rocks, and fishermen clinging precariously to little perches on the cliffs. Mc Bride told us that these fishermen were catching huge horse smelt, giant redtail perch, and once in a while a bass. He swore us to secrecy if he told us where it was and how to get there. We were on our knees.

Plans unfolded. Excitement dominated. We didn't have poles or reels, but we all were expert at casting our drop lines into the Ocean Beach where we caught some perch. We would go Saturday, early, leaving our homes at 4 a.m. It was necessary, Mc Bride told us, for the choice spots on the cliffs were taken early.

The 5 a.m. trolley came, slowed down, and I jumped aboard, seeing my two friends sitting up front. The trolley took us to the end of the line, which was still far below the Cliff House and our destination on the edge of the bay.

Climbing the ledge that led to our destination, Mc Bride pointed to where the first cliff protruded. "That's Camel's Back. It's kind of dangerous so we'll go on to Dead Man's Rock where the old Frank Buck boat grounded in heavy seas."

The trail in the semi-dawn was slippery and most of it precipitously arranged over piles of boulders and crashing sea. Mc Bride pointed. Dead Man's lay ahead and below our trail. Mc Bride led us to a branching pile of rock and shale. There were occasional iron bars dug into the trail and toward the flattened deck of rock a rope hung. We worked our way down the last ten feet hanging to the rope with one hand.

As we landed safely on the flat granite, faces peered at us from beneath hats, woolen scarves. There was one man wearing the uniform of a milkman delivery person. Looking over the flat ledge to the sea below, we saw some fishermen hunched, poles between their legs, smoking. The rank odor of cigar smoke rose from one older man. He looked up.

"God damma Kindagarten coming on us."

We were not a welcome sight and when we settled into fishing it got worse. Mc Bride, who was blind in one eye, swung his drop line around his head. One of the Italian fishermen stood up from bending and baiting his hooks. The drop line wrapped around his neck, the lead weight smacking his head. "God damma kids. Where's your mommy?"

Mc Bride apologized profusely and the man turned a shoulder to him, cast out toward the Frank Buck boat, and backlashed his reel. He cursed the line, the reel, the god damma kids, and just about everything.

The sun climbed over the mountain behind us and changed that black sea below us into a semi-clear surf, sand and rock, kelp moving to and fro with the surge. We caught huge horse smelt, twenty inches plus, and tied them with rope, stuck them in shade and cast again. We saw striped bass tied to the rocks. Some of the men had two or three bass, ten to twenty pounds.

Mc Bride made a long cast that almost landed on the Frank Buck boat. He fought a fish away from a snag. We helped him hoist it up over the rocks. It was a four or five pound cabezone, an ugly green spotted fish in the cod family. The milkman fisherman told us that it was a delicacy and the meat turned white when baked. I caught horse smelt, one after another. This fishing was a dream come true.

Suddenly gulls and pelicans appeared, then sea lions. The froth created from millions of anchovies, sardines, herring, erupted the entire area for as far as you could see. From atop the ledge you could see huge bass lunge into the schools of fish, tear away, and blood covered the surface, the smell of the oily fish filling our noses. It smelled like sweet and pungent fresh air.

The fishermen went into a frenzy. Everyone had bass on. Lines tangled. Gaffs were brought down to a ledge where they landed the huge bass, a two-man endeavor. One pulls the fish in on top of a swell, the gaffer bends, holding onto a rock protrusion with one hand, and tries to gaff the fish before the next swell.

Ray waits for use of the gaff and Mc Bride volunteers, climbs down, leans to gaff the bass, and a swell washes him off the ledge into the sea. He disappears and the next swell breaks. We see his feet sticking up as the whitewater dashes him onto the rocks. Mc Bride grasps the moss-covered rocks and clings. One of the fishermen runs to a position above Mc Bride and lowers a rope to him. Mc Bride is saved and by this time one of the other fishermen has gaffed Ray's fish. It is at least ten pounds and we all sit in envy, wishing for our own striper. Before we are forced to leave as starvation threatens, I catch a fish about seven pounds. That plus the horse smelt and fishing equipment is a burden I shoulder happily, admiring that huge bass as we climb to safety.

Rounding the point, we settle into a Monterey Pine canopy. The wind does not get into this place and it is the first time since early morning that we have not been near hypo-thermia.

We arrived home from the strenuous walk and after carrying the load, I am exhausted, but my mother and father take picture after picture. What little neighborhood there is, comes, admires my catch. My parents want to see Dead Man's Rock. I'm not sure that is a good idea, but after church the next morning we drive to the parking lot near Sutro Baths. It is a warm day, the wind non-existent.

I lead them through the pines and out onto the open trail. My mother pauses at Camel's Back rock and peers toward the Frank Buck. "You are not going to fish here anymore. That's it. Let's go home." All the way back to 34th Avenue she harangues me about falling from the rocks, drowning, washing out to sea.

I knew I should have kept my mouth shut about this secret place. My father never said a word. We had the bass for Sunday dinner. It was delicious, fed the entire family, and there were leftovers for sandwiches for school lunches.

Chapter 8

The San Lorenzo Valley

My father had patients just about everywhere or so it seemed to me. One Sunday he piled us into the car and headed south, past the La Honda Park cut off, beyond the summit above Saratoga, and descended into the San Lorenzo Valley. None of us had ever heard of this place except that my father told us that it was in the Santa Cruz Mountains.

My father took the cut toward the coast, fog hanging on the edge of the ridge across the valley. It was sunny on Highway 9, a winding road, two lanes, and not lined all the way. We drove by a sign that read, "Right Turn Big Basin," then wound down deeply into a huge redwood forest. Most of the sunlight was shadowed by these monsters towering above us. They stood stately, almost in appearance like the pre-historic growths of the dinosaur age.

Our eyes focused on the narrow road unwinding, a good-sized stream ran parallel to it and moved slowly through the undergrowth. Where were we headed? My father broke the silence. "One of my patients has a summer cabin down in Boulder Creek. That's a few miles further and he told me of a real estate office in the town, a guy named Carl Connolly runs it. Everyone goes up to the Russian River. It's too crowded, too commercial. This is supposed to be the same kind of area, but without the congestion."

The town ran four blocks in its entirety; bright sun shone, and the bluest sky I had seen since Boonville. We stopped at the real

44

estate office and us kids were left in the car. Opening windows barely cooled us. It was hot and we wanted to go swimming. I climbed out of the back seat and walked into the real estate office. "Dad, how long are you going to be? We want to go swimming."

It was Connelly who answered, telling my Dad, "Follow me with your car. I've got time before I show you around." My father followed back through the town to where we turned off on a side road that led into dirt and deep bumps. Suddenly and before us lay this river, a deep pool across a white sandy beach. No one was in the water. "Sure beats the Russian River, right?" Connelly interjected.

We changed in the car and ran to the streamside. I stuck my foot in and recoiled. It was like ice water. The sun beat down on my back. Leaning forward, I sprayed water on my forehead, underarms, slowly moved inch by inch into deeper water, and dove forward. I felt my entire body contract. Surfacing, I let out a whoop! It felt great. Treading water I looked to the opposite side, a steep granite slab, a tree or two hanging precariously fifty feet upwards.

My father swam by me, followed by Gene. Gretchen and Peter played in a little side stream called Boulder Creek that emptied into the San Lorenzo River at the Junction swimming hole.

I swam after Gene and my father, caught up just as my father was hoisting himself up on a ledge a foot above the water. I climbed onto the ledge and sat down in the sun, experiencing the wonder of a tight icy body, but the sun shining so brightly that I felt the warmth melting all cold away. In a short time my body was warm, and my brother and I explored the ledge. It climbed upwards toward the trees above. We went about ten feet up and looked down into the depths, crystal clear, but so deep we could not see the bottom in places. My dad climbed up next to us and dove off the ledge, clearing the granite with room to spare. I hesitated, scared of the depth, and that I had never jumped that far.

Gene jumped first and I followed, felt my self shoot down deeper and deeper. The water temperature dropping degrees brought on the need for air and I struggled upward, burst through the surface. "Again," I thought. Both Gene and I repeated the jump until we were blue from head to toe. My mother yelled, "We have to go with Mr. Connolly up the Big Basin road to look at a house."

The house, tucked under redwoods and huge first growth Douglas fir caught the warmest sunshine of the day. It was mid-noon and Connolly said, "It cools off here by 2 o'clock everyday. You sit out on that porch after the shade comes and be perfectly comfortable. Come around to the back of the porch and you look down on Boulder Creek. That's the creek that emptied into the San Lorenzo River where you swam."

My father, mother, and Connolly sat on the back porch and talked business, something I had no interest IN. The rest of the kids shared my boredom.

"Take the kids down and check the creek while we do business. I'll yell when I want you to come up."

Gretchen and Peter threw stones into the creek and Gene watched them. I boulder hopped up stream a hundred yards and came upon a deep pool. It was partially shaded. I sneaked up and saw trout finning on the edge of the shade. They were six to eight inches maximum, but there were many.

Sneaking closer, I wadded up a piece of paper into spitball size, flipped one above where the trout finned. Two fought for the morsel, ripping at it and then discarding. I moved to the head of the pool, repeated the move, and a little bigger trout grabbed the spit ball half way to the bottom. Hearing my mother's voice, I ran the boulders only slipping and getting one shoe wet.

"Well, how do you like it? This is ours now. We closed the deal and we now have a place to spend our summers." My father beamed.

I was excited, the other kids shared my enthusiasm, and my mother chided, "It's a lot better than Boonville." We returned to San Francisco to await the closing of school and our first summer in Boulder Creek.

I called Ray and told him about the stream, the trout. He told me that the bass were beginning to run at the Ocean Beach and Dead Man's.

After school Monday we took our drop lines to Ocean Beach, baited up, and cast as far as possible. There were many fishermen with fancy poles who cast out much farther than we could. We caught a few smelt, and a big redtail perch, but we wanted bass. Everyone but us caught bass that afternoon.

By the weekend the bass run was dominating the sports section of the Chronicle and Examiner papers. Pictures of huge bass, some as big as thirty-five pounds were displayed. Soon the fishing column published the daily catches, where and total poundage. The bass would be at the beach until the end of June and then head up into the bay and finally the delta to branch into their own spawning beds.

Back in the City, meanwhile, Doelger was going full blast in building. Houses sprouted everywhere around us. The sand dunes to Noriega Street were filling with houses. No longer did we have to worry about being sanded in. Houses covered the dunes, more and more scheduled. We didn't lose our view, but 35th Avenue filled quickly. I wanted a fishing pole badly and one good thing about all this growth brought people who needed lawns cut, cars washed, babies taken care of so parents could go out. I worked at every job I could get.

Visiting Roos Brothers sport shop I saw the pole, the reel, the equipment I wanted. It would cost me about $12 for the entire outfit. I rode the streetcar daily and looked at my pole and reel. One day I put a down payment on it so that it could be held until I had the total. In a few weeks, it was mine.

My first cast was in the backyard. I had watched the fishermen move forward, pull the weighted line and lead behind them, and then with a mighty heave, move the pole overhead, let go of the free running spool, and click the free wheeling off as soon as the weight settled on the water. The second cast backlashed, leaving a bundle of mixed cuttyhunk line tangled in tight coils. I learned, after some time, how to uncoil each little kink, and continued to practice. Saturday arrived.

My mother drove me to 48th Avenue and Noriega. She'd do anything to make sure that I wasn't fishing Dead Man's. I improved each time, again watching and mimicking the expert casters. Soon I was adept at getting the line out into deep water and not losing the sardine because of too abrupt an uphaul. I washed the cuttyhunk after each trip, spreading it down the length of 34th Avenue, drying it. I varnished my pole, oiled the Ocean City reel each time I went fishing. However, I was not catching bass. I did everything the same as the experts, but something was amiss.

An older man befriended me and told me to watch for birds and only fish the incoming tide. "No birds, don't bother to wet your line. Sit up on the dune and watch for the signs. Then fish. I watched and I watched.

One late afternoon my mother drove me to Noriega Street on the beach and said she'd be back around dinnertime. I walked across The Great Highway and set up my equipment, baiting with only choice tail pieces. The tide changed and moved in filling holes. I cast into one of these holes and stood waiting, watching the tip of my rod for any tell-tale sign of a strike.

It felt like a smelt jittering at the end of the line. I allowed it to play and then snagged backwards with great fervor. The pole bent double and I felt the thump, thump, thump of a solid fish. It ran, taking fifty yards of line and then sat on the bottom. I thought I was snagged, but at the Ocean Beach there were very few if any snags. The snag came alive, ran away with twenty-five more yards of line and I stopped it, turning the fish so I gained line. Walking back up the beach and making sure that I did not pull too fast or hard, I reeled.

I saw the swell approach, form into a wave, the bass swimming down the face. I reeled faster and pulled the fish right into the breaking wave. My line went limp and I thought that I had lost it.

Whitewater rushed up to the dry sand and the bass with it. I ran to the fish as water receded, kicked it up onto dry sand, and dove upon the fish. It was not going to get away. As I walked back across the beach to meet my mother, dusk descended. I looked back to the sea, the sun dropping into the Pacific, and held my fish in the gills. Its lines, the stripes, shone in the disappearing light. Its tail touched the sand as I held it above my waist. The gulls circled, dove into the darkening sea. The water was alive, in near darkness, with fish churning the surface, slapping tails. I was happy, fulfilled. This was the biggest bass I had ever seen. All was well in my world. It was the perfect moment. Nothing could get better.

December 7th, 1941, the bass run long gone, the Japanese bombed Pearl Harbor and The World War began. The lights went out on the coast with a total blackout enforced. Japanese submarines roamed the outskirts of San Francisco Bay. Depth charges were dropped by the Coast Guard every few minutes, and oil slicks, metal with foreign writing washed ashore. Soldiers armed with rifles patrolled the beaches. The entire coastline from Thornton Beach to the Golden Gate was strewn with barbed wire. No one could get near the beach without a special pass and we were too young to get one.

That didn't stop us. Mc Bride, Ray, and I sneaked by sentries who sometimes screamed. "Who goes there?" We were fired upon once, but lay still until the sentry moved to another post. No one was fishing Dead Man's Rock and we scored big. The fishing was fantastic, but the risk heavy. We had to keep hidden the entire day, and then sneak back out past the sentries.

Mc Bride told us that one afternoon he got caught by a sentry. "The guy was nervous as a cat. He told me that I was lucky it was light and he could see me. He said that they expected Japanese to swarm the cliffs and run across the beaches at night." He told Mc Bride that he had shot at some noise in the bushes a few mornings ago.

Mc Bride looked at Ray and me. "You know who he shot at?"

We gave up Dead Man's for the time being, concentrated on passing our Tenderfoot and Second class badges in the Boy Scouts. Then we pushed for the First class badge so that we could go on a weekend camp out at Lake Lagunitas located in Marin County.

When that day came, a Greyhound bus carried us to the little town of Mill Valley. It was a quaint place fashioned after alpine chalet villages. Redwood trees covered all the houses, lawns surrounding where trees didn't grow. Very little light filtered to the street. The bus drove to the edge of a mountain, stopped, and we clambered out, picked up packs, shouldered them, and began the hike up steep stairs to a trail that connected to Lake Lagunitas.

Sweat poured down my back. I needed water. A spring descended the mountain, covered in moss and watercress. Dropping my pack, I felt as if I might take off into the sky. Bending over and cupping my hands, I drank deeply of this sweet ice water. "Don't drink too much. We still have a climb ahead," yelled the scoutmaster.

Topping the mountain, we looked down into Lake Lagunitas a mile distant. We dropped into a shaded area of oak trees, a campground with circular pits for fire, and one pipe, a continuous stream of water exuding.

The scoutmaster supervised us in setting up camp, told us to collect wood, but we kept an ever-present eye upon the lake. "You're free for a couple of hours. I'll see you back here. Watch out for rattlesnakes, and don't go swimming in the lake. There's a place that is being set up for you so wait," exclaimed the scoutmaster.

We sprinted to the lake's edge, tested the water. It was not as cold as the springs. Exploring the north side, we worked our way along the shoreline to a dam. Looking over the dam, we watched the water cascade deeply down the canyon toward the bay. You could view the bay from here, a ship coming into the Golden Gate, the small fishing village of Sausalito, San Francisco a dot in the distance, nothing else but open space and bay.

Looking over the side into the dam we saw huge boulders, a mirrored surface, and trout cruising, big trout, twelve inches at least. Ray and Mc Bride looked at me. "Didn't bring any equipment. Did you?" It was a negative all the way around so we had to satisfy ourselves with watching those beautiful fish turn silver side upward, break the surface, and dive down with their captured prey, a small insect we could not discern. We did learn some things about surface feeding and it was fun.

Returning to camp along the shore, we walked into a canopy of trees. You couldn't see the camp. That meant that no one, not even a scoutmaster, could see us either. Stripping to birthday suits we swam back and forth, jumped from an overhanging branch into the lake, ducked each other many times, and floated looking up at the seemingly endless universe.

Silence, warmth, the solitude only broken by the flight of a deer fly, we sat on the edge of the mossy bank, dangling our feet. As we dried ourselves and bent to tie our shoelaces, the scoutmaster's voice shattered the calm, "I told you not to go swimming. Get back to camp!" Instead of swimming as the others did, we spent the afternoon collecting wood and piling it for the bonfire to happen that night. It had been worth it, though, to be able to swim freely, not hear the whistle of the lifeguard, be screened into certain boundaries like cattle in a corral.

The boy scouts, the rituals of flag raising, and the group singing didn't digest well with us and we dropped out of the scouts. It impeded our nature learnings, our growth. As Ray put it, "The scouts are all right for kids."

There was a certain amount of truth in his statement for we had associated with adults fishing the Ocean Beach, Muni Pier, and Dead Man's. The rules on Dead Man's were obvious, and we knew that if we broke them, nature would not be so kind as to give us a chore of collecting wood or cleaning up camp.

Chapter 9

A Strawberry Lake Kiss

As the war accelerated, things got rationed. Everything was sent to the service people overseas. Hardest hit was petroleum. We only got three gallons of gas per week. It was most difficult to make a trip to Boulder Creek that year so we just saved up gas coupons for another day. Money was still tight in 1942. If it were not for all those patients of my father we would have been in dire straights. It worked out so that we had plenty just in the gifts given in place of money for the dentistry my father performed.

One such instance that I remember vividly was my father's lab technician who owed him a sum of money, but was unable to collect from his debtors. He told my father that he had a cabin up at Pinecrest in the Sierra Nevada. If my father wanted to use the place he was welcome. For some reason, maybe because I was going on thirteen, I was chosen to spend the time with him up at Pinecrest.

Driving the long pace up into the Sierra the sun disappeared behind us. Darkness descended and my father started talking about my mother and their relationship. He told me that I should always please a woman before myself. He said that was the secret. I looked straight ahead. Ray had warned me that it was the time when fathers took you somewhere and told you about life. I already knew what I wanted to know, but listened as we pierced the darkness. He lifted a flask of whisky to his lips. He talked on and I wondered about the trout fishing in Strawberry Lake, our destination.

Arriving quite late, we worked our way to the front door. My father stopped and opened the electric box, pushing switches. A porch light lit. We walked into a rustic cabin, dank in odor, but we fixed that soon by lighting a fire. Sleep came quickly and I awakened early, hearing my father snoring. Looking out the front window I saw the lake in glassiness. Scanning the surface I noticed little dimples breaking the surface. It wasn't raining. These were feeding fish.

I ran down to the small pier, walked out to the end, and watched a man fly-casting. I stayed on his left side as he lifted the line from the water, deftly pitched it back behind his right shoulder. The line straightened and at that moment he pushed the rod forward. The line hovered above the lake, and the man gave a tiny flick of his wrist, the line dropping softly to the surface. The fly sat for a moment, and then the man retrieved it in short jerks, repeated the cast, let the fly settle, and lit his pipe. The swirl engulfed the fly. The tail flipped and his reel whined. I saw the fish take to the air forty yards out on the lake, flop on the leader and disappear.

The man looked to me. "Can almost predict a strike if I light that pipe." I assuaged his pain in loss and told him what a wonderful cast he made.

"I wish that I could do it like you do it." I asked him if he caught any fish.

"Yes, these two." He held up a string with two sixteen inch rainbows attached. "Time for my breakfast. Nice talking to you."

Picking up his gear, he headed up the trail. I watched the lake for a while. Fish, periodically rose in different parts of the lake. I heard my father's voice, turned, and he was motioning me to come. We walked to the little village at Pinecrest. There was a general store where I bought some salmon eggs and then we ate breakfast at the one restaurant. Hurrying home, I told my father that I was going down on the pier and catch some trout. He said, "Go ahead, I'm going to set up my kayak and then we can go across the lake."

The sun rose high in the sky, the heat with it, and the dimples on the lake stopped. My father needed some help launching the kayak so I reeled in my line and assisted him. "Can I bring my fishing stuff with me?"

"Sure, let's shove off." We passed a couple of boats anchored in the lake with fishermen humped over their rods. I trolled a spinner crossing the lake, got a strike, grabbed the pole, and watched a rainbow jump. It took time to bring the fish to the boat, but we finally netted it, a twelve to fourteen inch rainbow. "We've got dinner," my father smiled.

A rushing stream poured into the lake on the northwest side. Sticking my hand into the water, I realized that it was much colder here. My father told me that stream mouths like this always add colder water to a lake.

I steadied the kayak as my father climbed onto shore. It was all granite and the stream was a cascading mass of water through huge boulders. My father wanted to walk up the stream to explore. I voted to stay in the kayak and fish. Drifting a few yards off the mouth of this stream, I grabbed an overhanging branch, tied the bow rope to it, and set up my rod, baiting it with double salmon eggs. Casting toward the mouth of the stream I let the salmon eggs and line settle. I saw the abrupt stop in line, knew that the sinker had touched bottom, and settled back. For a while I watched the tip of my line, but got diverted with an eagle's flight. It swooped, scratched the surface, and flew away with a trout clutched in its talons. "What a sight! Wait until I tell Ray about that."

The middle of the lake was all whitecaps, but in this cove not a breath of wind. It was quiet, except for the water rushing from the stream, the sun soothingly warm. I slipped into a half sleep. The late night, the paddling, the excitement of discovery caught up with me and I melted into the kayak.

My father's voice interrupted my dream. He yelled, "Look, your line is moving, your pole bending." I lunged forward, immediately awake, like the morning alarm clock. I lifted the rod and felt the fish. It had mostly fought itself out and I netted another rainbow, a twin to the first one. My father climbed in and we paddled toward the far shore.

What had appeared from the cove as small whitecaps turned into swells frothing on top and spitting over the bow. I was scared, my father fighting the oars to make headway. We took turns as fatigue overwhelmed our arms, back, and then we passed from the whitecaps to calm water. The beach had a few bathers on it and a lifeguard sat in his tower. We landed, emptied the water from the kayak, and carried it to the front porch.

Making some peanut butter and jelly sandwiches, we ate lunch, and my father drank a beer. I cleaned the trout, put them in the cooler, and headed to the beach.

My father slept, and I saw people sunning themselves on a raft about twenty-five yards out on the lake. There was rope from the raft to shore. It defined an area for swimming. I figured the swim to be easy, but kept close to the rope just as added insurance. Climbing up onto the raft, I stretched out, face downward to sun myself. I must have dozed again for when I looked up there was only one other occupant on the raft, a young girl about my age. She looked away from me and I looked away from her. She turned and spoke. "Was that you I saw paddling across the lake?"

"Yes," I coughed out. "My father and I like the rougher parts of the lake." I wondered to myself why I had lied. I had been terrified.

"I could never do that," she retorted.

"It's easy and fun. I'll take you, if you want, for a ride." Names exchanged, where each lived, what grade in school, favorite foods, and we swam to shore together.

My father sat on the beach smoking a cigarette, drinking a beer. "Can I take Barbara for a kayak ride?"

He looked at me; a smile crossed his lips. "Yes, I guess so, but be careful. Don't scrape the boat on any rocks, and stay away from the whitecaps."

We paddled most of the afternoon. I saw my father waving me in, but made believe that I didn't see him. The lifeguard stood in his tower; the whistle in his mouth screeched across the lake. He summoned me. Walking up the beach he told me that my father had told him to get me out of the water when he was going off duty. Barbara walked away, turned, and asked. "Are you going to the bonfire tonight? It's on the edge of the lake and they tell stories and we sing."

"Sure, of course, wouldn't miss it. Are you going to be there?"

"I'll see you there," and she headed to a cabin down the lake.

She found me although I searched the fire reflected faces for hers. We sat together, sang, listened to the stories. My father told me that he'd see me at the cabin and left. Two scary stories later, and I felt her hand touching mine. I clinched and walked to her cabin tied together until I said goodnight, walking away with new sensations emanating my body. It was something akin to the strike and first run of a fish, but I knew it was more.

Sunday I was first on the beach, scanning toward the cabin where Barbara stayed. Two hours passed. I swam, walked the beach, talked to the lifeguard, threw skipping stones until my arm ached, and then I saw her walking down the beach. "I thought you were going fishing this morning. You said that you always got up early to fish"

Fishing was the last thing on my mind that day. We swam to the raft, paddled the kayak. I taught her how to use the paddles, gripping her arms from behind to demonstrate the proper stroke. She smiled up at me and I felt my heart collapse.

The afternoon disappeared and her mother came to the beach. "Barbara, we have to pack and leave. Say goodbye to your friend." Her mother turned and left.

Barbara gave me her address, a little town in eastern California, called Niles. It might as well have been in Egypt.

She grabbed my hand, pulled me down to her height, and kissed me lightly on the cheek. That was the last time I ever saw her although we wrote each other once a week for a year.

Ray, Mc Bride, and I fished the rest of that summer, but it was not the same. Something had happened. I still loved fishing, but longed for something else. There was more out there than STRIPED BASS.

Chapter 10

Exploring
Santa Cruz Mountains

What had been regarded as a minor skirmish that we would clean up in a couple of weeks turned into a major war. The Germans, Italians, French, Japanese, Russians, Americans were involved in World War II. The allies and our country were not doing very well, especially in the South Pacific.

Fortunately I was too young to be drafted, but the ranks of men were so depleted that it appeared, at times, that there were no men left in America, except for the very old and the under eighteen. My dad, being a doctor, was considered essential and did not get drafted. It was like everything shut down except the creation of a gigantic war effort. Food rationing, gas coupons, tires, all of these basics were transformed into an industry which produced only to boost allied attacks on Germany and Japan. Civilians were lost between the cracks. We got nothing, not even cigarettes or liquor. I had tried both. I can remember walking the streets looking for discarded cigarette packages that might contain one or two, rolling tobacco with Bull Durham, an extremely strong and throat burning substance.

However, when we finally went down to Boulder Creek for the summer it became a time of abundance for me. I was going on fourteen, had grown five inches in the past year, and lifted weights as a pre-football training schedule. Appearing older than my years, I was sought after by the many women who had few choices. Being the swimming instructor at Forest Pool a mile outside of Boulder

Creek put me into focus for whoever came to the pool. I listened to one of the hit parade songs of the week, "They're either too young or too old. What's good is in the army; what's left will never harm me." I rode that false wave of importance until one day my sister saw me with a lady who was obviously five or six years my senior. I was showing off for this lady and was about ready to approach her for a date. Gretchen stood on the diving board and announced to all, "He's going to be fourteen July second."

That ended all of my abundance with the exception of a couple who had less scruples than most of the ladies searching for a man. I turned my energies to exploring the mountains and fishing Boulder Creek. Awakening at pre-dawn, I forced myself to climb out of my snug bed on the porch overlooking the creek. Dressing, no breakfast, I was gone down to the creek.

Baiting my hook became tedious soon as I got my hands wet. The creek was icy cold and the air temperature stifled from warmth until late morning when sunrays pierced the redwoods. I moved quickly, becoming expert in rock hopping, but of course, slipping enough to have wet shoes and pant legs to the knees.

Each trout I slipped into my creel pushed the feeling of coldness from my reality. Approaching the steelhead hole, I dropped to all fours, and crawled to a vantage point. There he lay, finning in the current suspended beneath the rocky overhang. He turned sideways, displaying an orangish pink stripe. The fish appeared out of place in such a binding environment. I pictured this grand trophy sized trout swimming the ocean, slashing through schools of anchovies and sardines. At that time I did not know that some of the spawning steelhead got trapped when low water came and they had to wait until the next fall for rain. Some, finding the creek cuisine to their liking, became permanent residents.

Reaching for the bottle of salmon eggs, I picked two out and quietly flipped them above the trout. He moved, but allowed the eggs to pass. I flipped more. He showed half interest. Next, I baited my hook with two new salmon eggs and deftly pitched the line upstream. The eggs drifted naturally past his nose. I tried it again and he dove deeply into the depths beneath the overhang. It was no use so I moved upstream, searching for more of these trapped monsters.

Catching three more small rainbows, I moved up towards a hole with tree branches hanging above. Great clusters of leaves covered the pool in sections. I carefully cast my line in-between these leaves and into the depths where clear water lay. Watching the salmon eggs sink, almost out of sight, my concentration interrupted, like a huge airplane flying overhead, except this movement swift and lithe shot past my salmon eggs still sinking toward the bottom. For a second the eggs were blotted out by this huge form. I only got a glimpse, but saw that it was at least ten pounds, a steelhead. It disappeared beneath those leaves, leaving me with a hummingbird heartbeat.

Sun filled the surface of most pools now, and I decided that I had better head down stream. Besides, I had some swimming lessons coming at 10 a.m. and the dark and mysterious pools passed earlier were flooded with sunlight. I looked into the depths as I hopped from boulder to boulder and saw many eight-inch trout scamper before me, the two-legged intruder.

Looking at the sun, which was still on a relatively severe angle, I realized that it was not as late as I thought. Coming upon the pool where the steelhead hid, I changed to a small Colorado spinner, I sneaked through the bushes and emerged across from that ledge, cast the spinner into the fast water at the head of the pool. It fluttered into the depths and moved toward the overhang, disappearing in the shadows. My line stopped. I figured that it was snagged and gave a slight tug to try and free it. This was my only spinner.

The snag turned into a huge trout which leapt clear of the stream, landed on its side, and sprinted into the current upstream, ran the shallow rapids, sulked on the bottom in the pool above.

I could see it, rubbing its jaw against a boulder. I forced the fish off the bottom, turned it toward the end of the pool. It accommodated by rushing down the rapids to hide under the overhang where it had first consumed my spinner. Applying pressure I felt the fish move toward me slowly, then rush into the rapids, only gaining a few yards before drifting back into the depths of slow moving water. The fish was tiring. I applied all the pressure I could upon fly rod, leader, and fish. I gained foot after foot, and the fish rolled onto its side. I pulled it ashore, the hooks on the spinner falling out of its mouth.

Pouncing upon the steelhead, I grabbed it firmly through the gill slot, held it up to the sun, and let out a whoop. Running all the way home, I sprinted the hill to the house, flopped the fish into the kitchen sink. It barely fit. My mother hadn't believed me when I had told her of this huge fish I saw most mornings, but never caught. It had become a family joke, Fred's fish tale fantasy. Here was the proof staring my mother in the face, all twenty-five Inches.

Swimming lessons were much sought after and I filled Band-Aid can after Band-Aid can with cash. Charging a dollar and a half for a thirty-minute lesson I always got at least a fifty-cent tip. Feeling eight feet high, and completely fulfilled, I walked home along the highway to our house a half-mile away. It felt wonderful to walk, bare footed all summer, let the dust sift through my toes, feel the warmth from sunshine penetrate my back. The only time I put clothes on beyond my bathing suit was for the nightly dance up at the Forest Pool.

Today was going to be different. The sky was overcast and a slight drizzle fell upon the redwoods. The owner of the pool closed down for no one wanted to swim. I walked back home, looked mountainward. The redwoods climbed the long slope two thousand feet. I wondered what lay up in those woods.

Lacing boots, I pulled a shirt over my head, and affixed a canteen filled with water on my belt. I told my mother I was going to take a hike up behind the house, left and began the climb into the redwood forest. It was steep and brush grasped me, manzanita bush unbending, gnarled in all directions. I made slow progress for about four hundred yards and emerged on a deer trail. It led angularly upwards. Ascending a half-mile or so I saw a redwood chute hanging above. I climbed up and watched water cascade downward to where I did not know. Filling my canteen, I moved upward, came upon an old abandoned cabin. I explored its depths. The cabin was falling apart and I cautiously stepped upon rotted wood, turned at the sound of buzzing, and looked squarely at a coiled rattlesnake. It was big and angry, but retreated into timbers beneath a crack in the floor, and continued buzzing. I got out of there, shaken to the bones, climbed higher, and was more aware that every step could be another rattlesnake that might strike me.

Reaching the summit, I emerged from timber into high clouds. I could see the ocean, to the left a few miles, and Santa Cruz. The view was expansive, the breeze cool and refreshing. I sat up there for an hour basking in front porch view of sea and ascending forest below.

A deer and its fawn came from the woods, looked at me and turned bushy tails in flight back to the security of the forest. I watched hawks ride the convection currents, swoop, and grab an occasional mouse.

Descending, I found the sluice carrying water, and decided to follow it down to where it ended. Besides, the trail next to it made walking much easier than beating the brush. The trail got wider, and I looked down onto a huge redwood storage tank, a small dam. This was the Boulder Creek water supply. "No Trespassing" signs discouraged further exploration, so I slid down a mossy bank to a dirt road that led into Boulder Creek. It was a mile walk up Highway 9 to my house.

Summer ended and I went back to school. Late January, I read the paper and it said that the steelhead were running up on the Russian River. I wondered if there was a goodly run of steelhead on the San Lorenzo River and Boulder Creek.

Talking my parents into spending Christmas at our cabin was not an easy task, but with promises that I would cut a couple cords of wood per day convinced my father that it might be fun.

We arrived a couple of days before Christmas Eve and cleaned up the cabin. It was dank and the fire we built in the fireplace forced warmth to permeate the cabin. The sleeping porch that surrounded our cabin, lay outside, freezing in winter, but screened in from insects. I began cutting wood and created a sizeable load under the house. It was great exercise and I felt my biceps, chest muscles bulge. Sweating profusely, I wondered if a swim might cool me off.

I didn't tell my mother, but all of us kids climbed down to the creek, walked up to the hole where I had caught my big trout last summer. The water ran clear, the stream a foot higher than summer. We dared each other to test the water and swim.

Stripping down to our underclothes, we edged into the pool. It was twice as cold as summer. My body contracted, turned blue immediately. Diving toward the overhanging ledge I reached for a protruding rock and hoisted myself up the precipice. The cliff climbed a hundred feet above the pool. Fifteen feet up I looked down into eight feet of water, a gravel sandy bottom. The kids yelled. "Jump." I sized it up again, jumped and bounced off the bottom feet first. They all followed suit and we jumped and swam until the pool was completely muddied, the fun ending when my mother screamed for us to get home immediately. She was furious. "Do you want to get pneumonia? What's wrong with you kids?" We sat, shivering, but each of us knew that we had broken through one of those major barriers that keeps adults from having fun.

I cut wood for the rest of the afternoon, carried a load up as it darkened outside, and built up the smoldering fire. My father commented, "Great fire, warms the whole place. Yes, this was a good buy."

The next morning, before cutting wood, I walked down to the bridge at the entrance to our road. Peering down into the pool that lay below I let out a war whoop!

Fish, huge fish, bigger than the one I caught last summer, lay stacked in unison, finning forward. I climbed down for a closer look. They only changed position for a moment and returned quickly to formation. Some were salmon, some steelhead. They filled the pool. Every so often one or two would run the pool, swish their tails up the rapids, over rocks, and disappear into the pool above. It was a show, the most exciting thing I had experienced, so many fish in such a small stream.

Walking up the stream past my house, I reached a place called Brackenbrae. The people who owned cabins on this part of the creek had dammed up the water creating a wonderful private swimming hole. I had fished it last summer and swam after filling my creel, but now the redwood dam staves were piled up on the side. The stream ran free with some fast moving water interspersed with holes no deeper than three feet. Finning on the gravel bottom, steelhead and salmon, smaller trout fought for position.

I watched what I gauged to be a twenty-pound salmon, move quickly into position in fast moving water. Another salmon, I guessed a male, moved in behind her, and dug holes in the gravel with his tail. The female in front exuded salmon eggs. They drifted toward the male who shot forward and secreted a white filmy ooze onto the eggs. Swimming above the eggs the salmon's tails dug some of the eggs into the gravel. Those eggs that continued to drift attracted the smaller trout that moved in to feed.

The male slapped his tail into the trout and two landed up on the bank. They flopped while I grabbed up as many as the salmon would flip onto the bank. They were bigger fish than summer average.

I found out that they were called spawn eaters, younger steelhead that followed the runs and returned to the sea to grow bigger and mature. All the way back down to the cabin, I watched huge fish run the rapids, jump three feet into the air. The abundance of fish overwhelmed me. Christmas Day dinner was enhanced by these fifteen inch pink meated fish that lay beside the small roast my mother had saved ration points for months.

When we shopped in Boulder Creek, the meat man told me, "Those big salmon down below your house all die after they spawn." He took me out in the back shed and handed me a pitchfork. "Ain't legal, but how about getting me some fish?"

I agreed. My mother thought it was a stupid idea until I laid five fifteen to twenty pound salmon on the front deck. Returning the pitchfork, I gave the butcher three of the salmon, kept two, and we headed for San Francisco.

It snowed heavily on the summit above Saratoga and we had to wait an hour for the snowplow, which was a bulldozer. It rarely snowed there, but for us it was all fun. We ran, rolled in the drifts, and built a snowman before the bulldozer plowed us a path to a lower elevation and San Francisco.

I thought, "There was a war, somewhere?"

Chapter 11

In The Mood

Abundance comes in rationed quantities and sometimes in flooded proportions. For some it rarely or never arrives.

Entering my fifteenth birthday in a matter of three days, I arrived back in Boulder Creek for the summer. Swimming lessons were slow so our family went down to the place on the San Lorenzo River called The Junction. There was no admission fee here. The County took care of damming the river each summer. There was no lifeguard and you were able to do pretty much what you wanted unless some of the locals decided that it was against their code. These kids, mostly, were the sons and daughters of the lumberjacks who worked the Santa Cruz Mill, and they were tough. I broke into their group, slowly, with many hindrances, the top of the list my having come from San Francisco, and having a father who was a professional. They were suspect of both.

Otherwise only one young lady and her three-month-old baby occupied the sandy beach. I saw some of the locals, dressed in Levis only, move to the top of the beach, form a line, and sprint across the sand, dive as far as they could, landing flat as a pancake, and chop stroke to the granite hanging above the water. The dust took minutes to settle, and by the time it did, they had reformed and were again sprinting across the beach. I could see that my father was annoyed and that the lady off by herself was picking up her belongings. She moved toward our blanket and settled down. "Damned brats," she echoed, and grabbed a cigarette. She introduced herself as Carol and asked my father if he had a match. Grabbing my Levis I reached deeply and bent toward her to light the cigarette.

She said, "Hells bells, that's no way to light a match. Let me show you." Cupping her hands around the match she struck it on the flint box. "See, you keep the wind out and get a light every time. Can't waste anything these days. My husband's in the South Pacific. He's got nothing but cigarettes; I'm lucky if I can get a pack a week."

Looking straight at me, she asked, "Anyone for a swim?"

"Sure," I answered. She dove into the water, cleanly leaving a fine line, while Gene and I lumbered in best that we could. We did not know how to dive.

Climbing up onto the granite overhang we sunned ourselves and watched Carol climb ten feet up the side. She poised for a moment and then dove, a perfect swan dive, again no splash. Hoisting herself upon the ledge my brother and I sunned ourselves, she said, "Only thing lacking is a cigarette."

Sucking in the cue like that big steelhead swallowing my spinner I volunteered. She told me to go over and look in her purse and swim back with the matches and cigarettes above my head. "Can you do that?"

I jumped into the water, swam across, and climbed out. My mother interrupted. "What are you doing in Carol's purse?"

She wants a cigarette and I said I'd get it. "Don't drown yourself getting it back to her." I felt the sarcasm, but grabbed the cigarettes, matches, wrapped them in a towel, and lowered myself into the iciness, holding my left arm high above my head.

"Chivalry hasn't died. Some lucky girl some day." She reached for the towel.

"I'd sure like to have a cigarette with you, but my mom keeps a close eye out."

"How come you and your brother jump instead of dive? Would you like me to teach you how?"

She held my brother first, around the waist, told him to lean forward, lose his balance, and then push off. "Keep your head down," she yelled as Gene belly flopped, the splat resounding to the beach. He was game to try again, but it was my turn. She repeated the process to me and I kept my head down, splitting the water like an anchor, descending ever into the depths.

Faint shimmers of light met my upward gaze. I struggled to the surface and climbed upon the ledge. Gene and I both dove a number of times from the foot high ledge, and then Carol looked at us. "You guys ready or are you scared? Let's go higher."

She ascended to the ledge where she had dove. I followed and looked down. It looked like a hundred feet to me. "Who's first?" She tauntingly prodded.

Both Gene and I peered downward, a ledge protruding slightly just before you entered the water. I wondered if we could make it, not bounce off the granite. She sensed our fear. "Don't worry, you have longer legs than I so you can push farther out."

I judged it once more and jumped, clearing the ledge easily. Climbing back up, I readied myself. "Count three, dive. One, two, two and a half", and I sprung as hard as I could. Smashing the water, I felt it rush up my nose, push against my ears as I bounced off the bottom.

Now an expert, I climbed back up and gave my brother instruction, told him how easy it was. Carol spoke to me, "Not bad for the first, gonna have to learn to keep those feet together."

Shadows crept across the beach and my father told us to pack up, time to go home. Driving up the road to our house my father commented, "Nice girl, too bad her husband is overseas. Probably misses him a lot, guts, lots of guts."

"Yeah, lots of guts," replied my mother.

Saturday night after dinner we heard the music playing up at Forest Pool. My father suggested that we take a walk up and see what was happening. Arriving there we were stamped with a florescent type symbol so that we could go in and out. Gene and I ran up to the dance floor.

My father, mother, Peter, and Gretchen sat by the huge bonfire beneath the dance floor. Glenn Miller's "Tuxedo Junction" serenaded us from the jukebox and we watched the dancers. I knew a faint two-step from eighth grade parties and asked a local girl, Dorothy, to dance. My stumbling and bungling feet made her laugh. She danced with me for a few dances until a jitterbug session began. I stood next to Dorothy watching those who performed steps I couldn't even fantasize.

Asking Dorothy if she wanted to walk outside, she reached and grabbed my hand. I saw the Big Dipper, a shooting star, the moon poking its head up over the redwood-lined ridge, but I couldn't think of anything to say. We walked. She asked me questions, but I didn't know how to answer.

We walked past the guard at the gate and mellow music, "Moonlight Serenade," transformed the dance floor into a tranquil scene of undulating bodies, cheeks to cheek, and deep embraces. A gangly local boy approached us, looked at me like he was getting ready to fell a tree, and asked Dorothy to dance. I stood there more on my head than my feet, walked over to the juke box, and stared at the selections, dropped a dime in, and played two Glenn Miller songs.

Turning, I saw Gene attempting to dance, the lady's back to me, a slender blonde. She was teaching my brother to dance and all the town's people sat on the benches nodding approval. The music stopped and she turned. It was Carol. I didn't really recognize her at first. She sat Gene down with some old ladies and glided toward me. I blushed, smiled, looked down at the floor.

The music began. "Would you dance with a married woman?" I told her that I wasn't too good and that I would definitely step on her feet, but she insisted. "Can't show favoritism, just try it."

She followed my awkwardness with extreme dexterity and I felt a pang, but dismissed it. The music ended and I told her that there was another song coming for I had chosen it. Miller again, "In the Mood," and we moved across the floor. She whispered. "I saw you dancing with that cute little girl. I bet you have lots of girls chasing you."

"Dorothy's one of the girls who swims down at The Junction. She has that boyfriend who cut in on me. He's too big to argue with. He can have her."

"Well, if I were your age, I know who I would choose." The dance ended and my mother walked across the floor, told me that we were heading home, said goodnight to Carol.

After lunch the next day my father told us all that he was giving us a treat. "We're going to Forest Pool today."

"I've got a date at The Junction with Dorothy. You go. I'll walk down to The Junction."

"Wait at least an hour before you go swimming," my mother grafted upon me.

A hot day, a gentle breeze, dust oozing between my toes, I walked the mile and a half. Sweating, I arrived, looked at the placid, clear Junction water, and stripped to my bathing suit. I lay back, peered at the cliff across the water, saw an older man up under the first line of trees. He was half squatted, his arms and legs strained. From my vantage it looked like at least fifty feet to the water.

Springing from his perch, the man cascaded toward the water, missing the ledge by not more than two feet. A pause and he appeared in knee-deep water, popping up, blowing air diffused with river water. He sauntered up the beach, picked up a towel, and dried himself.

"Beautiful, dive. How high is that? You only cleared that ledge by a couple of feet." I walked toward him, sat down. "How do you clear that ledge? Aren't you afraid of hitting it?"

"Miss is good as a mile;" he answered. "Got a smoke?"

"No, I ran out."

"Don't matter anyway, trying to quit. I work the Mill six days a week, grewed up here, and I swim every Sunday till it hits early fall. You want to dive off that there cliff. You work your way up. There's about three steps, the ten foot."

"I did that already."

"The twenty-two foot, and then the fifty foot, no in-between. Last one took me half of my childhood, but now no one beats me. I even climbed up that tree hanging over and jumped, won a fifty-dollar bet. Massy's the name."

We shook hands; I laid down my towel, and dove into the water. The freedom I felt convinced me that this was better than Forest Pool where a lifeguard was always blowing his whistle, telling you something was wrong. He never would have allowed people to dive off these cliffs.

I saw the blue 1936 convertible Ford pull into the parking area. Carol climbed out, carried a baby crib to the beach, and returned to get a blanket, and her purse. Climbing to the twenty-two foot ledge I sat and waited. It looked too far, and that ledge was sticking out. Carol sat down in the neatly spread blanket, and waved to me. I stood up, leaned, strained and pushed out into space, remembered, "You've got to keep those feet together," pressed my toes into place and sliced the water.

Holding my breath to shore I popped to the surface, smiling from ear to ear, walked up the beach, grabbed my towel, and moved to sit down next to Carol.

"Hey, you're a fast learner, and your feet perfectly together. I don't even dive from up that high."

"By the end of the summer I'm going to be diving from under that tree. That old guy over there just did it before you arrived."

"Where are your parents?"

"They went to Forest Pool. I like it better down here. There's more to do and it's really pretty. I like that icy water and no chlorine to burn your eyes."

Carol grabbed her purse, took out a pack of Lucky Strike's and offered me two and a book of matches. I stuck the cigarettes into my mouth, cupped my hands, and lit the match. The flame burned my semi-closed hand, but I covered and lit both cigarettes, handing her one of them, deeply inhaling on the one remaining in my mouth. Feeling dizzy, I lay face down and coughlingly exhaled.

"Just start to smoke?"

"Naw. I've been doing it for a long time."

Finishing our cigarettes, we swam to the cliffs, climbed up and lay back against the warmth of granite. I could see the sun piercing her legs, turning them dark tan. Contrasted with the sky, the clear water reflecting her image, I felt strong, controlled, and excited. I didn't know why, but it was fun and made me feel good all over.

We laughed about my dancing, and the baby cried, softly at first, but quickly created a giant crescendo of noise, Carol changing in attitude, appearing tight, bothered. She excused herself, dove into the water, and swam to the baby. I felt alone, but made believe that I was just getting cool, dove and followed her. She stood with the baby in arms and said. "I have to leave. He needs to be fed and bathed. If you want to you can come over to my cabin later tonight and I'll teach you to dance better."

Dinner passed and I sat in front of the fireplace. A long silence and I looked at my father. "I'd like to go up to Forest Pool for a while. Ok?"

"Ask your Mother," he replied.

"Yes, you can go, but take Gene with you."

"I'm meeting Dorothy."

Walking down the highway the pitch darkness closed in on all sides. My only path was the open spaces where the road followed, stars my compass. Falling off the roadside, my eyes finally adjusted and I could barely make out the white line, enough to keep me on the road. Two miles, the turn out, I lit a match, looked for the mail box with Carol's name on it, saw a light in a window many trees and darkness ahead.

I walked toward it, stumbled a few times, and finally knocked on the front door, looking into the living room where Carol sat in front of a slowly dying fire.

The evening passed too quickly for me and we only danced a few times. I knew that the walk home would take an hour and I also knew that my mother would wait up for me in front of her own fire.

I opened the front door to leave and Carol took my hand. "I get scared out here at night. Someone hits on my pipes a couple times a night. It would be nice if you could come by once in a while."

The next evening we sat in front of the fireplace. We sat there listening to the radio, talking, once in a while dancing, but the pipes never were banged.

To get an early start so that I only walked one way in the dark, I left home right after dinner, early dusk. Rushing, I could be at her place before the last rays of light disappeared, but on the walk out there I had to pass many little cabins with people sitting out on their porches. Quickly they figured where I was going.

One early afternoon after swimming, Carol asked me if I could help her by carrying the baby while she shopped. I told my mother that I would meet her at the grocery store and left in Carol's convertible, holding the baby in my arms. Arriving at the store we shopped and I carried a screaming child, Carol thanking me profusely for helping.

My mother sauntered in, began to shop. I followed her and the owner walked up and said in front of all. "Mrs. Van Dyke, I didn't know that you had a grandchild."

Walking the long mile to our cabin, I little thought about the three bags of groceries suspended in my arms. "Are those groceries heavier than that kid you carry all over town? What are you doing? I'm so embarrassed. Johnny wasn't the first one. From now on you go with us everywhere."

Slamming the groceries down on the kitchen table, I grabbed my rod and took to the solace of the creek below. Some time later my mother yelled, "Dinner."

"I'm not hungry."

"If you don't eat you're not going out tonight."

"I thought you grounded me."

"Well, I've been thinking. Just stay away from that woman. Find Dorothy. She's your age. You want to be tied down before you get out of high school?"

"Nothing's going on. We just enjoy each others company. She gets scared living out there alone. Don't worry."

I left, sneaked down by the San Lorenzo River, attempting to bypass those gawkers, but the river's edge got steep, and I was forced to climb to the road. They gawked. I walked as fast as possible.

Arriving at Carol's we took a walk, carrying the baby in arms, taking turns. It was a quiet evening, cool, and a finger moon sat next to the first star. We both stopped, looked at the moon, the descending light, and made a quiet wish upon the star.

"A penny for your wish." Carol handed me the baby.

"If I tell you then it won't come true." I kept it to myself and we walked back to the cabin. I sat on the porch and smoked a cigarette while Carol put the baby to bed. I heard the shower door close and water stream. Darkness descended and a cool breeze forced me indoors. Carol walked from the bathroom, her hair up in a bun, and sat down by the fireplace. I moved in next to her and she looked up at me. "I'll give you a cup of sugar and a penny for your thoughts."

"Where can you get a cup of sugar in these times?" We sat in silence, watching and stirring the last embers. It was past time for me to be heading for the walk in darkness. I got up and opened the door. Carol got up and walked to the door, opened it and a deep chill emanated from the room. I only was clothed in a T-shirt.

"Look, the baby's asleep. It only takes a few minutes to drive to your cabin. Let me take you home. I'll feel better and it's late anyway."

Arriving at the entrance to the steep road up to my cabin, Carol parked under a tree, turned off the lights, and looked at me. "Two cups of sugar, and a penny for your thoughts."

We lit a cigarette and shared it between us. I smudged it out in the ashtray and looked up at the sky. I said. "Three cups of sugar for your thoughts." I knew what my thoughts were and slightly suspected hers. It seemed out of place, unreal to me. My underarms flowed perspiration, my hands clammy, heart pounding. She looked at me and moved closer.

"I think that you are beyond your age. I know you're six years younger than I am, but I like being with you. You don't try things with me like all the other men. My wish is that you kiss me."

Pulling her close to me, I bent and kissed her, broke away, and she grabbed me and lay across my lap. I kissed her again. She moved her tongue deeply into my mouth. My lips quivered in deep pleasure, nerves tingled in harmony. I pulled away. "I don't know if this is right."

She kissed me again, slowly moved my hand across her breasts so that I felt both nipples. Everything man in me turned fire hot. Pulling away, I looked up to the sky, the Milky Way miniscule in comparison

"I'm catholic. I can't do this until I'm married. I have no choice, marriage, celibacy, or eternity in hell."

"What's wrong? Did I do something wrong?"

She held me close, put her hand upon my thigh, kissed me deeply, and unbuttoned my Levis.

One more vague and weak thought, "Screw the catholic church." I made my decision for hell, moved my hand up between her legs, slipped panties below her knees, and moved my fingers deeply into pubic hairs. It was my first time and everything happened too fast.

We kissed goodnight and I staggered up the hill in darkness, head over heels in love.

Chapter 12

Bad Boys

Late the next morning, the first thing I heard was, "How come you didn't go fishing this morning?" My mother rambled on something about sleeping half the day away and missing breakfast. I looked at the clock, bolted out of bed. I had a lesson in ten minutes. Running the road to Forest Pool, I saw the mother sitting with her child, peering at her watch as I tried to casually walk past her.

"Be with you in a minute. Hi Janie, ready?" The girl, six years of age, moved toward me, adjusting her swim cap. I helped her into the pool and we both got wet, my mind wandering to a 1936 convertible and cups of sugar. The rest of the lessons went mostly the same, me not concentrating, thinking of Carol.

After stuffing the band-aid cans filled with money from lessons, I walked-ran to Boulder Creek. One car passed me on the way and it didn't pause for my extended thumb. Walking to The Junction my thoughts were interrupted by the beep of a horn. Turning, I saw Carol summoning me. Still embarrassed from last night's experience, I shyly looked away from her and said, "Hi."

"Fred, I have to go over to San Jose. My father is sick. I don't know when I will be back." She leaned forward and said that she'd like to kiss me, but that wouldn't look right. The '36 Ford disappeared on the first corner out of Boulder Creek. I turned, forlorn, wandered to the Post Office, collected the mail from our box, and saw a letter for me. It was from Ray and he said that he would accept an invitation

73

to come stay with me. Running into my mother at John's Cash Store, I told her the news. "He's coming in on the Greyhound Bus tomorrow at noon." We carried home more bags of potatoes, knowing that Ray was no lean eater.

Seeing the black fumes exude the bus, I stood while the driver pulled close to the sidewalk. The door opened and a few people paraded off, Ray being the next to last. He carried one small suitcase and his fishing rod in a case. We hadn't seen each other since school let out and I felt a little nervous, but eased up when I told him about my new adventure. He looked at me.

"Bullshit, Fred, tell me another story. When do I get to meet her?"

"She left for San Jose yesterday. She'll be back."

"Yeah, just like the bass run of '41. Show me where we swim. I'm hot."

We covered the brief distance to The Junction, suited up, and I dove flat, skimming the surface to the ledge, hearing Ray let out a Whoop! "This is ice," he screamed.

Ray swam slowly and cautiously, grabbed the granite, climbed out, lay out on the hot ledge, and said. "This is the life."

We swam till late in the afternoon, later than usual, and the wind died completely. Dimples appeared on the surface. Ray noticed them immediately. "Look at the trout. They're everywhere. Let's get our rods."

The sun set in the redwoods as we climbed the road to the cabin. Sweetly pungent fragrances floated in the early evening dusk, wild lilac, and redwood needles, drying in the brush. As we neared the cabin, the scent fried potatoes and onions dominated our senses. Rasputen sat on the deck under the sky reaching Douglas fir tree. Showing Ray his cot on the porch, I walked to the dinner table.

My mother carried platters of carrots, fried potatoes, melted with cheese, and cooked onions. Placing them on the middle of the table, she went to the kitchen and returned with two quarts of milk. "This'll have to do you. No milk deliveries here."

Having second thoughts about passing the platter of potatoes, onions, and carrots to Ray first, my mother interjected. "See if Ray wants to start the food around the table." This was it, potential starvation, but he surprised me, taking a generous portion, but far less than what I saw him do in the school lunchroom. After dinner he politely thanked my mother. I was wondering if this was the same Ray I knew.

Dinner finished, Ray and I walked down to the bridge. He took a pack of cigarettes from his pocket and handed me one. Lighting up we inhaled deeply, letting the smoke spew from nose and mouth as we planned the next day. "Let's spend the night somewhere up creek where there aren't any people. We can hitchhike up toward Big Basin and fish places rarely touched. I brought a sleeping bag and we can borrow some utensils from your mom."

Early the next morning we pooled our money and headed to Boulder Creek. Ray was a couple of years older than me. I had skipped a grade in elementary school. Nearing the only liquor store in town, Ray reached into his pocket, extracted a fake moustache, and put it below his upper lip. Next he looked into his wallet, pulled out a fake draft card. Entering the store, I stayed out of sight. He returned soon with one arm filled with beer, a cigarette hanging from his lips. We stashed the beer and cigarettes down under the bridge and went into the cabin to pack our necessities.

I kissed my mom goodbye and we walked to the bridge, picked up the stash, and headed up the highway. As we walked past the four-mile sign by the roadside, a car came upon us, stopped and we piled in. "Going to Big Basin. That any help?"

"Great, we're looking for the source of Boulder Creek and then we're going to fish down to where I live."

"The creek begins about a mile up, where the hairpin turn for Big Basin is. The creek jogs off into some deep brush and if you fight your way through that, it opens into redwood trees and a mossy bank. I fished there last May and there were some hold over steelhead, a few eggeaters up to twelve inches. They're wary, but if you sneak up and keep low, you can drop a worm right on top of some."

"They'll hit it if you get a natural drift."

I recognized him as the town pharmacist. He stopped at the turn and pointed. We thanked him and rushed off into the brush. It was like hitting a wall, not a break in it, except if you crawled along the creek bank, which we did. Ray led, on his knees, swatting at numerous gnats and mosquitoes. A quarter mile of that and it opened up into the forest that the pharmacist had described. I heard something, a sound like running water bouncing on metal, looked at Ray who had just stepped over a rattlesnake.

"Don't move," I yelled at Ray. He froze.

"What's wrong?"

"Turn slowly. Look where you just stepped."

Ray saw the four-foot rattlesnake, coiled and hissing as loud as our kitchen water faucet. He jumped about six feet to the side, and ran full blast to the creek. I picked up a rock, but the snake wound its way under some roots washed clear of the ground during high water.

"I never thought of rattlesnakes here. We've got to watch it." Ray was shaken.

"This is rugged country, not like the Russian River tourist trap. There are mountain lions, a lot of coyotes, and a couple of black bears still wandering where you don't find people."

We set up camp in as much open space as we could find. It was a great camp. Redwoods lined the mountains and the creek. Gravel bars interspersed with deep solid granite holes wet our appetites to fish. The water clean, but we could not see into the depths. There was too little light breaking through the huge trees. Ray cast into fast moving shallow water, white gravel lining its bottom. The salmon egg drifted through the rapids without a take.

"Try the deep darker holes. It's mid day and the fish are not working the fast water. Cast into that black pot hole covered with leaves."

Ray put the egg near the deepest part, watched the salmon egg disappear into the depths. He waited. A short jiggle on the end of his rod telegraphed a take. Lifting the rod it bent with solid resistance moving the line forward. Where the rapids began, the fish jumped. Ray dropped his tip forward and took the slam of the fourteen-inch rainbow on his leader. It held and seconds later, this beautiful, shining trout flopped on the granite slab.

We fished and caught five more trout, but none as large as the first. We cleaned them, tied a line through their gills, and suspended them in the fast water; then we tied the line to a branch and sank the beer into the granite pool. We gathered wood, piled it in front of our rock ringed campfire site, and explored upstream.

The creek got smaller and smaller, ending up a trickle coming from a steep incline. Walking down past camp we found three or four holes that held promise. Tomorrow, early!

Ray got the fire going and I put some oil in the frying pan, filled it with trout, and set the pan close to the coals, but not right in the heart of the fire, got up and walked down to the dark granite hole, lifted two beers out, and returned to camp. Ray lit a cigarette and we both sipped our beers, peering down at the creek, which was bathed in dusk.

Darkness descended; I pulled the fish from the coals, and built the fire up. Flames shot five feet into the air. The fish was fabulous, simmered to light brown on the skin. We ate them all, chewed chocolate bars, got four beers, and settled down to enjoy the fire.

We both jumped when we heard the splash in the creek at the deep granite hole. We knew what it was. We sneaked down to the edge of the hole, crawling on all fours, flipped the bait out over the water, and let it sink. I raised a beer to my mouth and sipped deeply. We waited and the moon rose slowly. It was the beginning of a new moon. I saw the splash this time and grabbed my rod, nothing. Ray let out a whoop and his pole was bent double. He let the fish run, jump. It went from pool to pool, Ray chasing behind, tripping, swearing, but the fish stayed hooked. Minutes later he yelled, "Help me. Get the net."

I swept the net under the tail of the steelhead and it dove again. "Not the damned tail, head first," swore Ray. "If you screw up on this fish you are dead meat."

I knew that he meant it. Carefully swooping the net underwater, I bent, and waited. Ray moved the barely moving fish right up over the net. I raised it, head first, and the fish disappeared into the net. We both ran to the campfire and admired this eight to ten pound steelhead. We tied a rope through its gills and hung it from a tree. It got mighty cold that night and dripping fog settled, wetting everything we slept upon or in, but it kept the fish in good shape. We broke camp at dawn, headed to the road, proudly displaying our huge trout. No cars passed and we ended up walking the five miles to the cabin, climbing the little hill, fighting starvation.

My mother was as excited as we were. "Wait until your father gets here Friday night. He'll be pleased. We can have the fish for dinner Friday." Days passed and I thought of Carol. We fished, swam, used Ray's phony draft card to buy beer and cigarettes. The cigarettes we could get were foreign and tasted terrible. Drinking three or four beers before attending the dance at Forest Pool eased my loneliness. We got pretty sloppy a couple of nights and none of the girls would dance with us. I had my excuse that I missed Carol, but I didn't understand Ray's because he never told me.

We planned a hitchhiking trip to Santa Cruz. We figured that we could get better cigarettes there and no one knew us.

It was Saturday night and we got three rides, ending up on Front Street. Ray walked into a liquor store, returned with beer and a pint of whiskey, some Lucky Strike's. We walked to the San Lorenzo's river mouth into the ocean, sat, watched the breakers, drank, and smoked. Ray passed the last swig of liquor to me and I tossed the bottle into the waves, stood up, and fell on my face. Ray threw up. I followed suit.

We lay on the beach, vomiting for what seemed hours, both passing out, and awakened to a flashlight in the face. The policeman asked what we were doing there so late at night. Ray was fast thinking.

"We hitched down from Boulder so that we can catch those waves and body surf before the Sunday crowd."

He knew we were lying, but we had made no trouble so he issued a strong warning that he'd better not see us here on his next patrol. We were gone, spent most of the night avoiding the few highway patrolmen who cruised on Saturday night.

Walking the fourteen miles from Santa Cruz to Boulder Creek, we saw lights approaching. Ray said to me, "Screw it. I can't walk another step." He stuck his thumb out and the red lights flashed. The next thing we experienced was the town constable grabbing both of us by the seats of our pants, hoisting us into the back seat, and slamming the door. "Where in hell you been all night. Who's Van Dyke?"

Meekly, I admitted to the crime. "Your dad came into my office 2 a.m. with your mom. They was mighty scared, wondered whether you'd been killed. If you was my kids I'd take you straight out to my shed. Fact, I might do that anyway. Don't think I'd get any resistance from your parents." He leaned to me, face to face. "If I ever see you two out past curfew I'm gonna throw you in the Santa Cruz jail and swoller the key. Got that?"

I felt his hot breath, looked into his one eye, the other covered with a black patch. I couldn't muster a word. Ray answered. "Yes sir, we're going to church today, communion, too."

He drove up our dirt road playing the siren full blast, dawn just breaking. The only words I heard were "Grounded, grounded," as my mother pulled me by my ear to the porch. "We'll talk in the morning," and they did. After church Ray was put on the noon bus to San Francisco. Few words were passed. We both knew that tough days lay ahead.

Carol returned the next Friday and I saw her down at The Junction on Saturday, my entire family with me. She came over and sat with us, lit a cigarette for my father, winked at me. My mother took Gretchen and Peter into the water.

Carol told my father that I was becoming a good diver. I told him that I had been surveying the place beneath the tree and felt that I was ready. I wanted him to watch me. I wanted everyone on the beach that Saturday to watch me.

Carol swam over with me while I climbed to the perch, looked below, measured the strength to push out over the ledge below. I could visualize it, the perfect dive, missing the ledge with room to spare, but when it got right down to letting go, diving, I stood frozen.

Carol looked up. "Wait I'll come sit with you." She climbed up, sat down next to me, this being the first time that we had any close contact, privacy since she left. "How about going to the dance at Big Basin with me tonight? I got a baby sitter. I'll pick you up about 8:30 p.m. down by the bridge. Let's get all dressed up."

"I'm grounded. I can't get out."

"I'll be there at 9 o'clock. Find a way to be there. This is our first night back together. Be there!"

I stood up, sized up the situation. The dive was easy compared to what I had to figure out for tonight. I pushed off, pointed my toes and split the water, two feet to spare from the ledge. It was anticlimactic. Walking across the beach, the lumberjack who had inspired me said. "Ya did it like a champ."

"Yeah, thanks, couldn't have done it without your encouragement." It meant little at that point in time. Dinner was slow. My father and mother sat in front of the fireplace, facing the only exit to the road. I excused myself and went to bed. "That was natural enough," I thought as I lay in bed. I sat up, looked in on the living room, saw my father slouched in the couch and snoring, my mother daydreaming into the remaining fire.

Stuffing blankets under the covers, I sneaked out the back door, crawled to the creek, and tried to make my way to the bridge. The moon ascended over the redwoods and I could see the bridge, the convertible waiting. Nothing else mattered. I was meeting her and we were going to the dance.

Climbing into the car, I kissed Carol fully. She returned the pleasure and said, "I missed you so." She was dressed in red, high heels to match, her hair flowing on her neck, lipstick and a little rouge emphasizing her features.

We danced. We kissed. We talked. We took a walk. The moon was overhead, opening the forest with light. Startling a deer, we moved further away from the dance, until just the faint sound of music softly serenaded us. The stars shone second place to the moon and far behind Carol.

This was the harvest moon. It was cool, but I felt none of it except joy and passion. We scraped redwood needles together, formed a mattress of comfort, lay down upon it, and scanned the universe, asking the impossible questions to each other. How far are the stars? How many? Is there an end, a beginning? How did all of this happen between us?

Turning from the stars and moon I bent, kissed Carol deeply, moved my hand over parts forbidden, and felt no cold lying there naked.

We were joined. We did it and dressed; walking down toward the outdoor dance floor, saw a lone car parked away from the others. The door was unlocked. We climbed into the back seat, did it again.

I tried again down at the bridge, but she knew that I was biting off more than I could and whispered, "I'll see you tomorrow down at

The Junction." She kissed me softly and drove off. Approaching the apex of the road, I saw lights on in the living room.

They knew. Walking down the steps to the porch, the outside light flashed in my face and my mother stormed out.

"You were with that bitch. You disobeyed us to be with that woman. You're not only grounded, but we are going home tomorrow. Wash up before you get into bed." She turned and disappeared into the one bedroom. Sobbing beneath my pillow, I swore that I would run away from home if she did not let me say goodbye to Carol.

The kids and my father, wanted one more swim at The Junction. My mother was cool, but far more pleasant than I had thought she'd be. We drove to the swimming hole, unloaded, ate our lunch, and Carol showed up. It was early afternoon. My father had forsaken lunch and sat across the river sunning himself. Carol approached somewhat sheepishly. My mother looked at both of us, told Carol that she wanted to talk and she wanted me present. Gene watched Peter and Gretchen as they played in the shallows. We walked down to the dam.

"Carol, I am taking the family back to San Francisco this afternoon. I want my son out of your clutches. Understand? If you try to meet him again I will slap a child abuse and contributing to the delinquency of a minor charge, take you to court, and write a letter to your husband's commanding officer. Do you hear me?" She bellowed.

I shrank inside, feeling nothing was left for me. My life was over. Carol broke into tears.

My mother walked away, muttering, "Better say goodbye to her because this is the last time you're going to see her."

We sat on a log, hanging our feet into the icy water. I dried her tears with a towel hung around my neck. We kissed and kissed. We both broke into tears.

"I'll hitch hike down to San Jose and see you. I'll leave home."

We kissed again. She looked up at me. "Hold me."

My father's car approached. We hugged and cried. My father honked the horn; my mother yelled. "Come on, we don't have all day."

Chapter 13

The Long Walk

Fall was not easy and it got worse. Unmotivated, fixating on the past summer, I flunked or got "D's" in all courses, except physical education where I excelled. I put everything into cross country running in the sand dunes, won one of the races against the incumbent senior, lifted weights in preparation for football the coming year. Spring arrived, new growth, poppies lining sidewalks and vacant lots. I longed for Boulder Creek, creating a plan late in May. It would be the last weekend, the Memorial Weekend, a three-day break from school. I quit smoking.

I told my father the plan, to walk from our 34th Avenue house as the crow flies to Boulder Creek. Lighting a cigarette, his lips pursed shut, he mumbled, "Talk to your mother." I agreed and told her my plan.

"I'll be back in San Francisco Monday night, take a streetcar from the bus depot. You don't have to do anything except say yes."

"How do I know that you won't meet that woman down there?"

"If I could I would. I just want to get away by myself for a time. It's important. I've been thinking about something like this for a while."

She agreed if I promised not to drink. Thursday night I was packed, could tell that my father was vicariously enjoying helping me pack, giving woodlore advice. He disappeared for a moment, came back with a rod case and reel. "This was my father's and he gave it to me.

I'm going to lend it to you, but you have to bring back a couple of trout for me."

Uncasing the rod, I pieced it together. It was beautiful, needed a varnish job, which I did immediately, set it down to dry the night.

"That's split bamboo from the Orient. It was put together by a rod maker friend of my father in Germany."

School the next day was like trying to climb Grand Coulee Dam with grease on my feet. 3 p.m. did arrive and I sprinted to my locker, put my books away, and rushed outside where my mother picked me up, drove me home, forced me to eat a full dinner she had waiting.

Glancing at my father's watch, which he had lent me, I traversed the sand dunes to Sloat Blvd. and 36th Avenue. I had started at close to 4 p.m. The Skyline Boulevard climbed to where I could look down upon the Pacific Ocean. Wind disheveled my hair, pelted my face with cold air. It was wonderful. I had not a care in the world. A deer jumped onto the road, stopped, peered at me, and was gone. I watched so many hawks riding the wind currents. It was so unlike riding in a car. I was part of my environment. Creating a rhythmical cadence, I hummed a Glenn Miller melody. Time erased, I picked up the pace, the Spring Valley Lakes on my right. Not a car had passed since walking the highway.

Low in the valley now, I felt coldness immediately descend as the sun disappeared behind the coast range of mountains.

The lake glassed off in isolated spots, like when you wiped water from windows, each little chop dissipating into smoothness, total silence, except for the clop, clop of my boots.

Dusk moved in slowly. I walked the landfill in-between the lakes created for the highway to pass, watched seagulls settle upon the lake's smooth surface. Deer appeared along side the road as I ascended to the top of King's Mountain, 4,000 feet from sea level.

Darkness came when I stepped from the road into deep forest. Finding a flat spot, gathering redwood green branches, I made a mattress to sleep upon, wondered about a fire, decided against it. Eating two candy bars, drinking water from a spring I heard in the darkness, I settled into sleep. It was deep sleep uninterrupted by dreams, a restful sleep from pushed to the limits physical activity.

Deep into the night I was aroused from sleep by a gentle licking upon my cheek. I bolted up, saw a form standing above me. I could see enough to know that it was four legged. Standing up cautiously, holding one of the redwood boughs in my hand, I scanned, some of darkness disappearing. Slightly accustomed to the dimness, I surmised a deer, but when it moved I heard a tinkling noise. It approached and nuzzled once more. Extending my hand, I moved my hand between its nose and ears. Oh so soft, I had never petted a deer.

Sitting down, wrapping the blanket around, I pulled my body in from that cold night air. The deer sat down on its haunches right next to me, so close that I could feel the warmth emanate its body, and smell the musky odor of its breath. I spoke in gentle terms, the deer's ears perking and relaxing. Was I dreaming? No, it was real for when dawn broke the animal was lying next to me. I petted it again, stood up, prepared a small fire, and ate. I had oatmeal so shared the uncooked portion with my new acquaintance. She was a doe and followed me everywhere, while I packed, cleaned up the area, bent to drink, fill my canteen. The doe gently drank next to my filling canteen. Every time she moved the bell around her neck tinkled. Walking back upon the road, the deer disappeared. I figured that there must be a ranch or house nearby and this had to be their pet deer.

The road dropped abruptly and moved eastward, throwing me off my crow's flight course. Into the forest I moved, checked my compass, and continued southward. Enveloped in the forest, I heard a tinkle, tinkle behind me, turned and there was my new friend. I figured that she had followed in the forest and as soon as I left the road she was there. We dropped into a deep canyon, at the bottom a small stream moved toward the ocean. The water was sweet to the taste and I refilled my canteen, moved upward to the other summit, broke out into a region that sickened me.

The redwoods were clear-cut for as far as I could see, all the way to the farthest ridge. It was hot and dusty, waste branches and trunks of huge redwoods strewn everywhere. I stopped, not hearing the tinkle, tinkle behind me, looked up to the ridge where the last tree line stood, and saw the deer on the edge of that forest where we had met last night.

She stood, pawed the earth, turned and disappeared back into the forest. I missed her for the next hour and then focused on what kind of progress I was making.

Good! I figured that I must be on the northern boundary line of the Santa Cruz Lumber Company. 1p.m, the sun beat down upon me with heated fury, sweat pouring down my face and back. Reaching the edge of new timber on the far ridge, I crossed a railroad track which extended in the general direction I was headed, stepped upon it, and walked, a cadence, miss the railroad tie, walk the next tie, on and on for hours, the sun on my extreme right side.

Picking up another stream to my right it got wider with each mile south. Noticing some holes, deeper than the regular runs, I climbed down for a closer inspection. These holes were formed from logs jamming, and then debris caught in the aftermath. Jumping from log to log, I bent and peered into the head of the pool. Partly shaded by debris, I saw trout finning, fish from seven to twelve inches. They flashed in the near bottom, feeding on something down in those depths.

Not resisting such an opportunity, I stripped to my underwear, rigged up my dad's pole, baited, and swung the egg out into the dark part of the pool. The line slowly sank. Not a muscle moved in my body. I watched the line sink. It changed direction, moved slowly up toward the logjam beneath the next pool.

Setting the hook, the rainbow cleared the surface, shimmered in the sunlight, and took line. The pole bent in grandiose manner, tired the fish in short notice, and I flipped it up on the sandy beach, baited and cast. Another fish. This one drove for the bottom, hooked up in the roots. I didn't want to lose my hook and edged myself into the freezing stream, bent and reached, feeling for the fish, hook, and line. I got the hook, but the fish was gone.

Wet from head to toe, I placed the rod down, and dove from a log back into that pool. I was an otter. I was a gull floating on the surface. I dove to the bottom, looked beneath the roots, saw more fish up against the submerged bank, became a beaver. Surfacing, I swam in large circles, free as that seagull whose system I had entered.

Drinking deeply from the head of that pool, I climbed to the next one. Sunshine covered its depths, but trout swam there nearer the surface. Cautiously, I sneaked up from behind, deftly as I could, threw the line forward. It landed softly, sank only for a split second, and a rainbow was in the air. This fish ended in my creel, too.

I put two hooks on, gambling that if they snagged up I could dive to retrieve them. Two fish at a time? Every cast for the next half hour I caught two fish at a time, all above seven inches, much better than Boulder Creek's average. Stopping at my twenty-five fish limit, I shouldered my pack after placing the fish in between fresh grass and creek watercress, walked the rails until far below me lay the mill.

Some time later I walked past the huge saws, stopped and peered into the millpond, a dammed up portion of this creek I had fished. Sunshine no longer touched this valley and I watched fish feeding on some kind of surface fly. They slurped, and flipped tails on some takes. I figured that I had a good two hours of light left, walked up to the lumber road, this one paved, and headed toward Boulder Creek about eight miles distant.

An hour later I was walking Highway 9 the road to Boulder Creek. Dusk approaching, I walked past the road off to Carol's cabin, stopped and looked at Carol's sign on the mail box by the highway, left the main highway, climbed upon the porch of her cabin. The windows and doors, covered by storm shutters, all visibility inside cut off. I returned to the highway and walked into darkness.

When I got to town, I shopped at John's store, signed a tab, then I hitchhiked to the cabin. I walked up to the cabin in darkness, flicked the electric circuit box to on position, and cooked dinner. It was warm in the kitchen, cooking, but eating on the cold porch was unbearable. I ate standing in the kitchen, and built a large fire. Tuning in the radio, I got the hit parade, listened to Tommy Dorsey, Artie Shaw, and, of course, Glenn Miller.

When I turned on the porch light I noticed that the screen door was partially open, off balance, but thought little of it, and descended into interrupted sleep, partially because it was so cold out, and the sound of the creek, the stars outside the screen, all reminded me of things of last summer.

Sometime later I dreamed that I had my feet too close to the fire, tried to pull away, but didn't move. Awakening, I felt a resistance to moving my feet. Grabbing the flashlight next to me, I shone it in the direction of weight. Two small eyes peered at me. It was a raccoon. I didn't move. It didn't move. We were at checkmate.

After considerable stand off time, the raccoon seemed to consider me no threat and turned back on its side, snuggling in between my feet. The animal was gone when I awakened next morning, Sunday. I had promised my mother I'd go to church, but what if I hadn't made it to Boulder Creek in two days? I rolled over until morning sun pierced the porch, had a wonderful solitary breakfast, cleaned up, and headed into Boulder Creek.

The town lay silent, no one walking the street. What a contrast to summer, when all the tourists came to swim, sun bathe. It was another hot day, but different than summer. I felt the pre-summer coastal coolness. It was nice.

Everything was dressed in green, and wildflowers were rampant. Nothing was open, not even John's store. The noon Greyhound Bus arrived, three passengers disembarked. I asked the driver what time it left on Monday night. He told me that it was a holiday and the run into Boulder Creek was dropped. "Too few people this time of year."

"What time do you leave this afternoon?"

"Not until 6:30 p.m. I've got to go down to Watsonville, Salinas, and then back here. Want a ticket?"

I purchased a ticket and told him not to leave without me. "Got a schedule. Can't promise nothing."

Well, I had plenty of time. It would only take twenty minutes to walk into town from the cabin, even if I didn't get a hitchhike. Moving down to the dam, I saw it no longer in place. The San Lorenzo River still was deeper than Boulder Creek, but it definitely was lower without a dam. It looked naked, the bare boulders exposed, the hip deep water where we had dove off the bridge. The log Carol and I sat upon dangling our feet was high and dry. Coolness touched me inside.

Walking the short distance to The Junction, I moved down to the beach. It was hot now, even the sand nearly as warm as summer, but the ledge where you climbed out was four feet above the surface. No one was down there so I stripped to my shorts, and dove. "Whoo!"

87

The summer water was warm compared to this. My chest felt as if it were enclosed in bailing wire. Sitting on the ledge, I looked deeply into the hole. Sand swished on the bottom and a steelhead shot under the protection of the ledge. I was happy that the fish was there, but taking a last look backwards, I saw change, that nothing was static, nothing remained for long in the shape you recalled it.

The bus pulled out of Boulder Creek at 6:31p.m. And I sat on the right side. Shadows covered the valley when we passed Carol's cut off, and I craned, but realized that perhaps, for me, those shutters would never come down again. Darkness descended and I made a wish on the first star.

Chapter 14

My Secret Gorge

The first weekend in June my parents took a trip to Fresno to visit some old acquaintances, chief amongst them, a dentist friend of my father. I took care of the kids and we had a ball, cleaning up the house only minutes before my parents reemerged. They entered tanned, and relaxed, and my father had a large package under his arm. I admired the tans, so different than the usual red burned ocean color. I wanted to be tan like that. I asked them where they had found such abundant sunshine.

"You think that Boulder Creek is great. You should have seen where we swam this weekend, the King's River outside Fresno, and then we took a long walk up what they called Dinky Creek. You think you catch fish in Boulder, try these for size." My father unraveled the newspaper over the kitchen sink and trout fell, trout from twelve to eighteen inches, beautiful, mixed rainbows and browns.

I couldn't believe my eyes. "I have to fish this place, what is it, Dinky Creek?"

My father said that he had set it up with this expert fly fisherman who promised to take us down into the "Gorge" the weekend of my birthday. He said that only about fifty people had ever gone down there, too difficult a climb, dangerous, rattlesnakes everywhere. He told us that some people who ventured down into the canyon wore stovepipes on each leg to ward off the rattlesnakes.

School closed and we packed up for Boulder Creek. No one had believed my story about the deer and the raccoon. At the cabin, the door still lay ajar, the screen pushed out in one place. "Have to fix that right away," my mother echoed. "Wonder how that happened?"

I brought up the raccoon and was laughed out. Rasputen set himself at the foot of my bed, his usual sleeping spot when he condescended to come home. Once he jumped out of the car he was gone, hunting, bringing all shape and forms of mutilated rodents. He sometimes lined the poor creatures across the porch, a gift to us for providing such great hunting grounds.

We went to bed early, allowing the fire to burn itself out. I slept soundly until I heard my mother scream, and I woke, a flashlight pointed at the bottom of my bed. The raccoon bolted through the screen, and stood his ground outside. Rasputen was up the nearest tree and I convulsed with laughter. "Didn't believe me, huh?" Rasputen slept on my brother's bed the rest of the summer.

It was the Fourth of July weekend, a three-day vacation for my father, and we drove into the night, reaching Fresno at midnight. We stayed at his friend's house, Vera and Cleo.

After eating breakfast, Vera got up and called a man named Lindy, the older man who was the fly fisherman. He came by for lunch and they all drank beer until late in the afternoon. Lindy told me that he would come by and pick us up Sunday afternoon. We'd head east and up into Oak Flat where we'd spend the night, getting up before dawn to descend into the "Gorge." He told me to get a good night's sleep, that I'd need all the energy I could muster. I slept fitfully and sat around the house most of the morning just readying my equipment, checking my leaders.

Lindy arrived, his 1938 Buick coughing and spluttering blue smoke. "She's perfect for getting up into that country. You'd ruin any other car."

Lindy talked about the "Gorge" like it was a loyal lady friend. "Never been skunked down there and you don't see no litter, no people. Only person I ever saw down there was a ranger and he was lost." He passed another beer to my father and lit a cigarette. I couldn't wait.

We set up camp, and I was sent to gather wood. "Watch what you pick up that it ain't no rattlesnake, plenty of them around here."

The camp was perfect, situated at 8,000 feet. We ate dinner, consisting of Dinty Moore's stew, some bread and butter, and hot chocolate. Lindy said that he wanted to walk up to the edge of the "Gorge", give us an idea of where we would be descending to next morning in the dark. The road was pretty much impassable, but what was left hung on precarious ledges connected by some bulldozer many years ago. I loved what lay before me, the huge Douglas firs, the mountain bloom, the purple blue sky, and the air, cold but bracing.

Reaching an abrupt turn in the beat up road, Lindy pointed. We stood poised upon an outcrop of granite. Granite spread the entire range, huge fir trees clinging tenaciously for support. The sun gone, its aftermath spread across the sky, punctuating the deep valley with dark shadows. A deer bounded, a huge mule deer, with antlers as I had never seen on the coastal deer. Lindy looked at us in confidence; it was his territory. "I get my mule deer every fall just before this place gets snowed in. Yeah, this is God's country." He looked over at my father who was lighting a cigarette. "No smoking in this country. A spark would make it an inferno. Don't even smudge it out on the ground." He pointed to the depths, a mile or more down the canyon. "See that stream down there? That's where we start fishing."

From up here it appeared to be a thread, spreading through the granite. I was skeptical. Turning, we headed back down to camp. An entirely new panoramic view opened, canyons, ridges, trees, and darkness blanketed us as we came to camp. Sitting around the fire I listened to Lindy talk about this country, the trout he had caught, lost, and how this was one place that would be here long after we were gone.

Near dawn, a warm breeze blew softly through camp. We stuffed everything we needed into our pockets and walked to the outcrop, staring into darkness. Lindy threw a hand full of rocks down the side and told us to continue that until light came. "Rattlesnakes everywhere and the rocks move them out of the way if you're lucky."

Lindy led, seemed to turn into a mountain goat. He didn't take steps like most do going down hill, but hopped down the slope both

91

feet together. We had set our poles up in camp and leading them through the thick underbrush they got snagged often. Some time later, as dawn broke, we came out of the forest and undergrowth to slabs of huge granite, some perpendicular, dropping hundreds of feet, others with small outcrops, handholds Lindy called them. "We have to scan for those outcroppings. Follow me across this ledge."

The granite, near perpendicular, stretched across to outcroppings of fir. We edged ourselves along this ledge not more than a few inches wide, hand in hand, leaning into the face, reached the firs, and rested. Lindy said that it was fairly easy the rest of the way. I looked down. It didn't look easy to me. We went in and out of small fir forests, climbed downward on our tails, slipped where shale predominated.

Poising a hundred feet above the stream, we looked into the pool. From our perch you could see trout moving deep in this pool, which was just being skimmed with morning sunshine. Lindy pointed down stream. "See where that narrow turn is about three-fourths of a mile distant. I'll fish every other hole, leaving you unfished holes all the way. Your father will walk with me. At that turn Dinky Creek drops into a hidden canyon, too steep for us to try. Besides, you'll have all the fishing you want by the time we get there."

Lindy skipped the first two holes and started fishing the third. I passed the first hole and started to figure my first cast. Huge granite boulders as big as a garage housed this stream, conformed it to drops, slices, side currents, deep pools, rapids filled with whitewater. It was not like gentle Boulder Creek. Casting into the end of that pool, I watched my salmon egg move with the current. The trout hit like lightning, jumped into a side current, sped upstream, fought to exhaustion. I had no net, but landed it on a small spit of sand. Fourteen inches of rainbow. I stuffed it into my creel, cast again, and landed another about twelve inches. Moving to the end of the hole, I cast toward the other bank, the egg bouncing off the granite wall into the stream. Another fish hit, and pulled to the bottom, jerked its head back and forth. It pulled steadily, but did not jump, and when I landed it saw that it was a Loch Leven (Brown) trout. It was skinnier than the rainbows and its markings more in a spotted pattern. I creeled it, excited, elated, three fish bigger than most trout I had caught. I sat down, and admired my fish.

Fishing slowly, I relished each strike, the jumping rainbow, the stubborn brown, and lost count of how many holes I fished. It didn't seem to make any difference whether I skipped a hole or not. It was great. Looking up into the sky, framed by the granite and fir, I thanked the being who had created all of this.

The sun rose higher and higher, got more piercing until I was bending at every hole to sip water. By the time I caught up to my father and Lindy, they were sitting on a ledge about twenty feet above a long and very deep pool. It was the one just before the drop into the next canyon. I had sixteen fish and ran to where they were perched, laid them out in the shade for Lindy and my father to admire. Lindy handed me his creel. Looking in I saw some trout that made mine look miniscule. I also realized why he had gone ahead.

"We saved this pool for you. Go to it," said my father. They sat back and I climbed closer to the water, stuck my head over and saw trout milling everywhere. They were big trout, like in the San Francisco Aquarium. I could see the hooked jaws on some of them. Quietly and as unobtrusively as I could, dropped my salmon egg into their midst. It didn't get near the bottom when trout attacked, tearing the egg off. I extracted the line, my heart sitting in my throat, pounding like a trip hammer, nervously attached another hook, put two salmon eggs on each, and dropped them into the water.

I had two trout on, doubling my pole, darting in different directions, sounding, sprinting up the full length of the two hundred foot hole. I held, played line out, gained three feet, lost five, but they slowed, and I brought them along side the ledge, but it was too far to the water to chance losing the fish.

Lindy yelled. "Move up here and edge them to the front of the pool. I'll climb down close as I can to the water. I'll get them." He did, climbed back up to the overlook granite, and flopped them down.

"Whoopee!" I screamed. These trout were sixteen to eighteen inches, fat, and one a brown trout had a hooked jaw. They did not fit in my creel so I strung them and my father said that he'd carry them. I went to rebait my hooks and Lindy looked at me.

"You've caught enough trout on eggs. It's time to graduate to a higher form of fishing. I'll show you how to rig a fly, and we'll practice cast from on this ledge. You can't get into trouble with your line up here." He demonstrated, let me try his rod, and in a short time I was able to get the fly far enough out that he felt I was ready. "I'll use your rod. I wanted to try it since I first saw you unfold it. They don't make those anymore."

Lindy said that we'd wait until about 2 o'clock when he thought there might be a hatch on the surface. It was hot, hot enough for a swim. My father and I stripped down to our birthday suits and dove off the ledge. What richness, such a lovely private swimming pool.

I felt that I had reached heaven without having to die. I swam up and down the pool's length, dove from different ledges, and climbed out, laid in the sun, and relished this very special moment, the sun drying my body immediately, the granite sharing its stored heat with my stomach. I dozed.

My father shook me, told me to dress, that we were moving upstream.

I practiced in a couple of holes, got the idea of utilizing the natural drift of the stream, and got a few hits, one trout coming right out of the water to smack the fly. Landing more trout, my total count reached twenty-two. Lindy told me to stop and wait until we got to that first hole both of us had left unfished.

A slight breeze ruffled the surface of the hole. Lindy edged closer, scanned. He turned to my father and me. "Look, see right where the water from the hole above bounces in. See the flashes underwater? They're hitting nymphs."

My father and I looked, but saw nothing. "Watch for the flash. Look, there are more of them. They're everywhere."

The pool came alive. The breeze whipped the water. We couldn't miss the flashes, tails slapping the surface. Lindy turned into a wildman, false casting, and then dropped his fly. It settled and was struck immediately. He let out a whistle, fought the fish, and hoisted it onto the rocks, cast again, another fish. I cast a little below the swirling water, hooked a trout, and landed it, a fourteen-inch fat rainbow. Lindy stepped back, motioned me. "Cast right where the whirlpool is." I put the fly fairly close to the mark and had a fish on, but it broke off.

"You got to snag soon as they hit. Watch your line. Soon as it moves strike."

I cast, hit a bigger fish than the first, and led it down to the far end of the pool so that Lindy could get back at it. Landing my fish, I handed the rod to my father. "Try it. They're going crazy."

My father caught the fly in a tree on the backcast. I climbed the tree, released it, and he tried again, this time hooking a fish which ran right up and wrapped around Lindy's leader. He cussed my father, but my father landed the fish. I dove upon it and held up a twelve-inch beauty. Counting my father's fish I had my limit. Lindy untangled the lines, cast again and again. It was over, just as quickly as if someone had blown a whistle.

We spilled the fish into a side brook, cleaned all fifty of them, laid them on moss, and admired the catch. Lindy said that the climb out was going to be hot so we had better cover the fish in moss. Beginning the ascent, I looked upwards. The mountain unfolded into eternity. Three hours later, spent like the fish, we climbed onto the road, paused in the shade, and allowed heartbeats to slow.

We stopped at Trimmer on the way out, a small bar, overlooking the King's River, watched a lone man, smoking a pipe, work the slow moving river.

I inhaled two Cokes, watched the man cast his fly back and forth, put the line out seventy feet. He landed two twenty-inch rainbows while we watched. Dusk came again. My father and Lindy downed their last beer, and we drove back to Fresno, me falling asleep in the back seat. We arrived at Cleo's and thanked Lindy profusely. He saluted us with a beer in hand and disappeared in a cloud of smoke.

My father sensed the let-down for me to fish Boulder Creek after the "Gorge." He came back the next weekend with a friend, a big, strong, heavily sunburned man, John. After introductions, John said that we were going to go abalone diving the next morning, early, almost before dawn. I told him that I didn't have a facemask or abalone iron.

"Don't worry. I can't swim. Where I am taking you the abalone are in knee deep water." Early next morning we were on the road to Santa Cruz. We drove by the Mission, and on up a foggy and winding two lane Highway 1. It was penetratingly cold when we walked down to the point at New Year's Island. As fog lifted slightly, followed by wind, we followed John out onto the reef. We walked all the way out to the island.

John said, "All you have to do is wade along these shelves, stick your hand under the reef cover, and feel for the shell. Tell me when you make contact and I'll pry it off with the tire iron." My father carried a large gunnysack, and I felt for the abalone. My third try and I felt the shape, covered with moss and stuck to kelp. John held the iron against the rock reef and pried, his hand suspended beneath. I saw the abalone drop into his outstretched fingers. He pitched it to Doc, and said, "Easy, huh, nothing to it. I'm ready for the next one."

I searched, found two indentations propped upon each other. These were in clear sight cleft to a piece of protruding reef. I grabbed the iron and took both of them with one deft movement under the abalone sticking to the rock. We wandered the length of the reef, only a few other hardy souls bent, fixed on purpose.

The gunnysack filled, we headed toward shore, feeling a surge, a swell creep over our backs. John yelled, "The tide's coming in. Move fast. I don't want to get caught out here." My dad and I swung the gunnysack between us and carried it up the beach, spilling the contents onto the sand. John measured with a tape, none under ten inches across the shell, a few above eleven inches, all pink abalone, possibly world records, but no one kept score in those days. I now remembered that John put the smaller abalone back, and the ones that weren't pink. Loading the catch into the car, we drove back to Boulder Creek. John showed us how to clean the shellfish, pound it until it was soft. He cut thin fillets and then used a hammer covered with a washcloth. Taking his share, John stood up, told us that he had a day off in a couple of weeks and that he'd come back down and we could go out deep sea fishing on the Stagnaro Barge.

"Wait till you do that. You'll scoff at your stripers. You'll need your own gunnysack to bag all the fish."

More abundance unfolding! We had the trout, the salmon, the abalone, and now scores of rockcod, flounder, halibut, cabezones, ling cod, to look forward to catching when John returned.

Chapter 15

Creating A Beach House

In June 1946, I graduated from Abraham Lincoln High School, my records depicted a seriously disturbed young man, grades a low "D" average. It was still Carol whom I missed, felt deep separation, and wondered whether she had been as involved as me. There had never been another woman for me. I had dates, attended dances, even went steady with a couple of girls, but Carol was the one to whom I had given my heart, soul, body, and mind. I thought of her daily, reminisced through Glenn Miller, Tommy Dorsey, and other big bands of the 1940's era, and drank myself into semi-oblivion. I was somewhat like the Yin and the Yang, working out to exhaustion, and then drinking it all down the tubes.

Trips to Boulder Creek were mostly in the hope that I might run into Carol. Now I could drive out to her house on the chance she would be there, and sit in the driveway until darkness or cold air drove me away. Swimming down at the Junction I pictured her just a few strokes ahead of me and sprinted even more crazily. Trips to Big Basin State Park where we had attended that Saturday night dance didn't help me. I had to come to terms with this deep aching in my heart or I might perish.

Upon graduation, I had received some football scholarships, Fresno State, San Jose State, Saint Mary's, Stanford, but my grades kept me out of all but Fresno State. In the fall I put my energy into making the freshman football team and pushed so aggressively that

I was moved up to varsity. Double practices daily kept me from thinking about Carol, but evenings before falling asleep I would look outside the dorm windows and wish upon the stars.

We had a week coming up without a game and the coach did not want us to get out of timing so he scheduled a practice game with Porterville Junior College. They had one really hot halfback who averaged ten yards a run. My coach had shown me how to stop this fellow and by half time he had made a few two-yard gains. We were beating them badly.

The kick off for the second half took place and I rushed down field, tackling the same back I had held to such a low gain in yardage. First down, and they exploded from their huddle, lined up, and the ball was centered. I broke through and was making the tackle on the halfback when I saw in my peripheral vision the other halfback, the one I had been holding to a near zero gain, cut behind me, kick his cleated foot into my back as I finished the tackle.

Piercing, burning pain pulsated deeply inside me. I came to on the sidelines with the team doctor examining my exposed left side. The pain dug into my kidney, tears filling my eyes.

The center lay on his side, injured somewhere in his chest, and our best halfback was being taped at the ankle level. This had suddenly turned into a dirty game.

The game ended and my pain had increased as I sat on the sidelines, but I was better off than the other injured men. The coach asked me to drive them to the hospital for X-rays. Arriving, I assisted each to the examination room. The doctor came out after finishing the X-rays and I asked him just for the hell of it to check me out. The pictures were read by the technician and passed to the doctor who told me I had some blood in my urine and an injured left kidney. "Go home and rest the weekend. Come in and see me on Monday. You'll be all right."

The pain was unbearable so the player with his ribs taped drove me home. I barely made it up to my room where I lay down. The pain got progressively worse and when I got up to urinate, there was a flow of blood into the toilet. I passed out on my bed. Sometime later, I think, my roommate came home, saw me, and called an ambulance.

The pain was so unabated that the doctor shot me with morphine before attempting another series of X-rays.

"Fred, you have a deeply ruptured left kidney. With all the bleeding I am afraid of peritonitis. We have to get your parents immediately to sign the papers. You're still a minor."

"I don't care. Give me more morphine." Again semi-bliss. I felt myself suspended above my body. I no longer cared for that body below me.

When they called my folks, my mother answered the phone and screamed to my father, "Doc, come quickly, Fred is in the Fresno Hospital and they cannot operate until we sign the papers. What will we do? We can't get a plane at this hour." My father grabbed my mother and they ran down into the garage, she opening the door and my father screeching rubber as he pulled out onto the road, stopping only long enough for my mother to jump in and close the door.

My father sped through town to Highway 101. It was a four-lane highway until San Jose and then became a barely divided two lanes. It was late and there were not too many cars on the road. My father told me later that he drove two hundred miles in less than three and a half hours, luckily not getting stopped even once by the Highway Patrol.

I saw my parents through tears and morphine, but I knew they were there. Before going totally under I heard the doctor say, "He's so young." I looked up and said feebly, "Don't worry Doc; only the good die young."

It turned out to be a four-hour operation, me hanging onto life. When I drowsily descended back into life, I attempted to sit up and felt like I had been cut in half, all fifty stitches stabbing me at once. That year three players had ruptured kidneys, one died, and another lost the kidney; with me they repaired the kidney, hoping that it would heal.

Time passed in between shots, and nurses awakened me at all hours to see if I was all right. My mother only left my bedside to get food. My coach and members of the team came to visit. I was weak and could not climb out of bed. Flowers from friends in San Francisco arrived daily and after three weeks I got the good news from my doctor that I could go home. He leaned over my bed and sat on the edge. "Fred, it's no more football." I didn't care.

The male nurse who wheeled me to my parent's car helped me stand and I tried walking the three or four steps to the back door, collapsed, and had to be assisted into the car. I knew then that this was no simple injury, that I had a long convalescence in store. The drain that had been inserted into my side was taken out that morning and I could see, sitting in the back seat, that it was oozing blood. The doctor had said to change the dressing when it became saturated with blood, that it would heal quickly and close if I got complete rest. In mid December the team left for Hawaii, without me.

Returning to Fresno after Christmas Vacation, my grades nose-dived and I all but flunked out. Called into the Dean's office, I watched him look through me as he said, "We cannot carry you, Fred. We'll pay your doctor bills, but you're just not making your grades. The doctor told us that you'd never play football again. I'm sorry, but you'll just have to look for another school."

I didn't finish the semester, visited the doctor once more and he said that I was doing fine, and the drain hole had completely closed. I returned to San Francisco, thirty pounds lighter, still so weak that I could only walk with a cane. Depressed, I spent hours in my room looking out the window to the ocean. I thought of fishing from the beach, but still had some stitches that ached when I made any radical move. The swinging overhead necessary for casting would not work.

A month passed and one day my mother came walking into my room. "Let's take a walk on the beach." She handed me the car keys and told me to drive. It wasn't easy. Even shifting gears took vital energy.

We walked from the car across The Great Highway and stood looking at a ferocious, January windswept surf. Whitewater marched across the beach to bounce against the tunnel opening at Judah Street. Foam, ten feet high, mounted in piles, was picked up by the wind and swirled toward the sky to disappear like bubbles blown from a wet soap dish. It would have been fun, as it was when I was a child, to run through the foam, but in my weakened condition I could only watch.

The air was piercingly cold, but felt good. I did manage to breathe deeply, and noticed there was no more searing pain for the stitches were nearly healed.

Driving home, I thanked my mother for forcing me out of the house.

Back in my room, looking out the large window seaward, I watched huge waves breaking long distances from the sandy beach, capping, tossing spume skyward. A thought formed: I'm going to get into shape like I never have. Becoming strong and healthy would dominate my focus.

The first day of my new life, I walked south from 34th Avenue until exhaustion caught up with me. I phoned my mother who came and picked me up. Walking a little farther every day, after some weeks I could walk from Noriega Street to Fleishacker Pool and back, a little over two miles.

In February the sun shone weakly. One warmer day, no wind, I took my sweatshirt and undershirt off, tucked them around my waist and began to jog. After about two hundred paces I slowed to a walk. Heading for the highway, I passed a little gully that looked warm. Sitting down, I faced the sun, then lay on my stomach enjoying the sensual warmth of sunshine on my shoulder blades until I fell asleep. Lengthening shadows and a chill awakened me. I decided this had been a perfect day. I would return to this place.

On daily walks to the gully I began to collect driftwood, which I propped into position as a windbreak to make sunbathing more comfortable. Amassing a considerable pile, I decided to build myself a more permanent shelter. By early March I had hand dug into the dune wall and lined it with vertical pieces of driftwood to hold the sand in place. I laid a floor of old planks supported on two long logs.

One day when the fog came in as thick as pea soup, I decided to cover a part of my retreat. I dug farther back into the dune, removing and replacing the pieces of driftwood on what was now a rectangular semi-tunnel. The next step was placing three large driftwood planks to make a ceiling. Then I searched for two days until I found a hatch cover, partially buried in the sand. It took another full day to roll push it closer to my place. I was ready to give up when a huge hulk of a man approached. "Need a hand with that cover?"

We rolled the hatch cover to the shelter, then grunted and strained until we had wrestled it neatly into place. I was afraid that the walls would collapse, but my newly found friend told me to push against the walls, supporting them as he shored up any spots where sand seeped. The walls held.

The man introduced himself. "My name's Stan. What's yours?" We worked the rest of the day building in seats to make for more comfort and added support.

Stan told me that he was a lumberjack, working only about six months of the year. He spent the rest taking bus rides around California. This San Francisco beach was his favorite place; he came back every year.

He said that he lived in a small rooming house down on Market Street, and carried all his money some seven hundred dollars tucked down inside his boots. Stan seemed to trust me immediately, but I was a little afraid of his ungainly size. Then, too, he was a wanderer, different from the regular run of the mill person. He was bashful, didn't say much, but early each day he arrived at my shack as though coming to work.

One day I arrived a little earlier than usual. I leaned forward to stash my wallet and bathing suit under the hatch cover roof when my hand touched warmth. I jumped back and saw a head rise slowly. A new man looked at me through piercing eyes.

"What are you doing here?" I asked.

"Just taking a nap," he insisted and smiled. "I got cold walking the beach. Walk it every day. Never saw this place hidden here. Real nice. You live here?"

The man stood up, moved toward one of the benches, sat down, and began rubbing his hands together in what appeared to be an obsessive manner. He talked verbosely, but not making sense, looking to the side and backward, as if he were being pursued.

Soon Stan arrived and the new man, named Ponce, quickly left. Stan told me he had seen him walking and talking to himself.

With the approach of March, more people came to the beach and the weather warmed. Jogging one day, I saw another runner, heavy set, in his early forties. He followed me to my little shack, talking baseball. His name was Bob; he had played some semi-professional baseball, but had no job.

The next day Bob showed up with a skinny, tense, little guy, whose hands shook as if he had cerebral palsy. Shaky Finnigan was bright and quick, a pushy fellow who had run for Councilman in the San Francisco Mission District, carrying 2,500 votes without even an ad campaign.

Bob, Shaky, Ponce and Stan became my regular visitors, making "improvements" on my place daily, but bickering, developing possessiveness, petty jealousies and personality conflicts. The scene at my shack was no longer much fun, and certainly not relaxing.

I spent more time jogging on the beach, lengthening my forays to three or four miles, and now jumping into the shorebreak after each run to cool off.

As long as I could remember, my parents had taken me to the beach. When we lived on 47th Avenue, my dad took us every Sunday to gaze in awe at the waves pounding the shore. I would fantasize that I possessed unbelievable strength that made it possible to swim to the outside break. I wanted to swim out beyond the waves, rest in deep water. Rarely did you see anyone even wading or dunking in the shorebreak back in that time. The Ordinance against swimming at Ocean Beach discouraged all.

This day I was running toward Fleishacker Pool, occasionally jumping over foam rushing up the beach, until at about Taraval Street I spotted something bobbing in the whitewater adjacent to Fleishacker. I got closer and thought it was a sea lion swimming in the surf, but it wasn't.

It was a human being, way out near the outside break, diving under waves, not losing ground, but seemingly working hard to swim in front of the approaching waves.

I thought of running over to Fleishacker Pool to summon a lifeguard; surely the lone swimmer wouldn't make it into shore. I saw him cascade down the face of a comber, bouncing in front of the whitewater, all the way to the shallow water where he stood up, bent over, and took off two green fins.

I ran up to him, elated. "What are you doing? Did that wave throw you in front of it? God, are you lucky you didn't drown. You know

103

people drown out there." I acted as if I knew something that he did not.

He smiled at me, an all embracing, friendly smile which set me at ease. Then he answered. "I just pau from body surf. You never body surf?"

"What do you mean, pau body surf?"

"Pau mean I finish. Body surf, you swim out to the first break, stroke hard, catch one wave, ride the soup, go out, do it again. I getting tired. I like shower. Come, I get dressed. We go eat. Time for lunch."

I only half understood, but followed him to the pool and shower room. He said, "You wait here. I come back when shower all through."

Minutes later he came dressed in a sweat suit, on his head a woolen cap, and then sat down, strumming an ukulele. I felt the music immediately. It spoke to me of the ocean, the surf I love to watch and to fish.

Cliff Kamaka was Chinese Hawaiian. He had come to San Francisco a few years ago on his way to a Mormon reunion in Salt Lake City. Cliff had been a Hawaiian swimming champion. In high school he had weighed one hundred forty-five pounds and now, after many hamburgers and milk shakes at the stand across from Fleishacker Pool, he weighed two hundred fifteen pounds, standing about five feet six inches.

"You like swim in the pool Fred? Go, I give you towel. Take hot shower afterwards."

"I didn't bring any money with me," I told him.

"Hey, money no matter bra, you my friend now. You swim."

Cliff introduced me to Eddie, his Hawaiian lifeguard friend. Eddie had just finished his daily lunchtime workout in the pool. He stood tall, lean, and strong; quiet, not unfriendly, but shy.

We all talked. Cliff tried to teach me a few chords on the ukulele. I failed miserably, but had fun. I really liked these new friends. I asked Cliff, "How about teaching me how to body surf? I've always wanted to swim outside the breaking waves like you did today."

"Ok, you come tomorrow. I take you out. You have fins?"

On my jog back past my shack I didn't even stop to see what was happening. I hurried home and looked for my Owen Churchill fins, tucked away somewhere from when they were last used during the previous summer. I found them, cleaned off cobwebs, and looked forward eagerly to the next day.

Borrowing my parents' car, I arrived at Fleishacker about 11:30 a.m. Cliff was chewing on a hamburger, a shake sitting half finished by his side. "Here, you like some shake? Give you plenty energy you going to need for swim out through the waves."

"No, I just had breakfast." It scared me to think he was eating just before going out to swim in such a treacherous place. I had been taught to wait at least an hour before going swimming. During this day, and a lifetime to follow, I learned that not everything San Franciscans had taught me was necessarily true for other parts of the world. To say the least, my belief systems were being eroded by my newly found friends.

We walked across the beach toward the shoreline. Cliff talked constantly, giving me necessary advice. Unless the tide was going out, after a wave broke the soup most often pushed a swimmer back to the beach. No need to worry about getting back in; rather how to get out to the waves on the outside reef.

Cliff pointed to a place where the water rippled. "Look, Fred, see how the waves back off there? They don't break completely for the water has washed out the sand and left the area deep. That's a rip. Follow it and you get outside quickly. Stay away from the sandbar for the waves that wash over it will push you back to shore. Follow me."

My heart pounded as I eased my fins on, inside waves breaking on me. I swam after Cliff and the first wave pushed me back to where I could stand. Cliff looked back and yelled. "Dive under the wave, grab the sand, let it pass over you; then swim hard. You make it out."

Ten minutes later and two hundred yards offshore, swimming in the surf, I looked back. I couldn't touch bottom. I had caught up to Cliff. He looked over to me. "Big ones coming. Dive, swim for bottom, hold tight."

I hyperventilated, dove deeply, straight down, bounced off the moving sand bottom. I grabbed sand; water washed under my chest. My breath waned. I finned hard, but the wave sucked me down, and again I bounced off the bottom.

All my San Francisco fear surfaced. I pushed hard off the bottom and shot two feet out into air, on the backside of the breaking wave.

Cliff looked into my eyes, recognized anxiety, fear, and laughed uproariously. "Ooh, that one mighty big dumper. We get all wiped out, but, hey bra we outside now. We catch waves, I telling you."

A wave approached. Cliff yelled. "Now, swim! When wave pick you up, put head down, hands to your side. You slide down face, bounce in soup; maybe catch one more and then we go in, tide changing soon."

I swam hard, missed it, and Cliff disappeared. I saw his head fifty yards inside, his arms stroking to get back out.

It was a lull in waves and I took advantage of my environment. Here I was on the outside edge of the breakers. It was peaceful, quiet in between sets. Looking shoreward, soup bounced in all directions, a cauldron on the inside; but where I now lay on my back with icy water pressing in, I could see the sky reflected on the glassy surface of sea. I experienced my childhood dream, swimming outside the breakers, and it was better than I ever fantasized.

A line of waves moved toward me at great speed. I put my head down and swam. The wave lifted me; I threw my hands down by my side and slid down the face, my peripheral vision seeing Cliff dive under me. Bouncing in front of the whitewater, the wave moved me, like on an escalator toward shore. The wave was so smooth, like a feather bed, and then the soup engulfed me on the inside double break. I bounced off the bottom and surfaced screaming with joy.

Running across the beach, I jumped into the shower at the pool, and let the warmth fill my body. I was stoked.

That summer I got a lifeguard job. A new and exciting way of life was opening for me each time I put fins on and swam to the outside break. A foggy day arrived and it was Cliff's day off, the pool mostly empty of people. I told Eddie that I was going to catch a couple of waves during my lunch break.

Reaching the surf's edge, I could not see to the outside break. I had really no idea of how big or small it was, but chose to swim out. The rip was running faster than I remember and soon I was somewhere out in that sea of foam and fog, completely disoriented.

I had figured on catching maybe two waves and had left my fins at the pool, just a brief body surf I thought.

In the space where I could see, a huge wall of whitewater moved through the fog. I dove deeply, but did not touch sand, the wave pushing me even more toward blackness, rolling me into heavy disorientation. I needed air, now, but the wave kept me in its clutches, churning me like spin cycle in a washer. Not able to hold my breath any longer, still deep beneath the surface, I sucked in foam and surf, throwing up under water. In complete weakness, not knowing up from down I gave up and floated helplessly. The next wave pushed me into deep water in the rip. I feebly broke through the surface, attempting to clear my lungs before I passed out, coughing up the foam, and getting a breath. It wasn't over yet. I tried to swim through the riptide toward the beach.

I was not making progress toward the shore, but moving sidewards and out quickly, so rapidly that I found myself back in the breaker line. The rip controlled my destiny. Fear drained what little energy I had.

Swim toward shore, move sideways, and back out to the line up, repeat, repeat. I was finished and gave up, floating aimlessly in the surf line, riptide, and my knees touched sand, solid land, three feet deep. I allowed the current to wash me further up to the shore and crawled out onto solid freezing cold sand. I lay there shivering, hovering on hypothermia. I could not stand up for a long time, but after what seemed an eternity, I staggered into Fleishacker Pool, Eddie running to support me and help me to the shower.

Three days passed before I could go back to the pool. Cliff came up to me and said that I had made it through what every surfer confronts one time or another. The fortunate ones like me, survive, the others drown and wash ashore days later if the sharks don't eat them. The surf was terribly bumped and choppy, the rip ferocious. We sat around the pool; Cliff spoke about Hawaii, his home, and its warm water, the huge waves of the North Shore. He said, "Some day we stow away on the Lurline ship, go Hawaii. I introduce you to my family, friends. We have plenty fun."

I told Cliff that I had to go back to college in September, but knew that some day I would have to go to Hawaii.

At the beach, I saw Stan one more time. He said that he was heading back up to the lumber land, and that the shack was no longer there. When I asked what had happened, he told me that Ponce and Bob had disagreed on an improvement. They had built an addition on top of the dunes somewhat blocking the adjacent homes view, and neighbors across the street complained to the police. Ponce was a runaway from parole and he was taken back to jail.

Bob and Shaky had begun to live in the shack full time, burning old rubber tires at night to keep warm. One day while they walked the beach, one of the neighbors from across the Great Highway threw gasoline on the shack and burned it down before they returned.

Those years long ago the beach was not a popular place and was rarely visited except for those few fog free days. There was one policeman who patrolled on horseback the six mile round trip from Fleishacker to the Cliff House at the entrance to the Golden Gate. The beach, unlike today, was a place of freedom, open space, clean white sand. On occasion a freighter would empty their bilges out at sea and the oil would wash up on the beach. Strict laws are enforced today, but rogue freighter captains still, on occasion, dump their oil before entering San Francisco Bay. Seashells and sand dollars used to fill the sandy beach, but many are now near extinction. Annual duck migrations blackened the skies in sheer numbers on their flight to warmer winter climes.

As long as you caused no major disturbance on the beach no one cared if you squatted there and built a shelter out of driftwood. The beach in its isolation and raw beauty had provided me with the environment for my kidney, my body and mind to heal. Cliff showed me daily that surfing was not a sport, but a way of life, a style of living I wanted to make mine forever.

Chapter 16

Board Surfing At
Pedro Point

Body surfing Fleishacker and Kelly's Cove (the Cliff House) was wonderful. I introduced my friends: Dave Devine, football buddy Ron Javet, my sister Gretchen, my brothers Peter and Gene to body surfing, and to Cliff Kamaka.

We went every day, but winter came and the water temperature dropped to the mid-forty degrees Fahrenheit. Wet suits had not been invented. Ron Javet had a new Ford. After we staggered out of Kelly's Cove, numb, on a mid-December day, Ron suggested we take a Christmas vacation trip down south. I had never been in Southern California, but had heard that there was warm water and clement weather even in the dead of winter.

We left on the afternoon that school let out for vacation. Charlie Grimm, a regular at Fleishacker and Cliff's closest body surfing friend, decided to travel with us. We left at seven in the evening, driving through the night, shifting drivers often.

About three in the morning, we could hear and smell ocean, but still could not see anything, but deep fog. It was not as cold as San Francisco, but that fog was just like home. Charlie started to make fun of the entire idea. "With fog like this how could it be really hot down here?" Charlie laughed.

Dawn broke as we rounded a slight turn in the two-lane highway that skirted the coast from north to south. I had just finished sixty-five miles of curved coast highway when we entered the sleepy little

109

town of Malibu. Stopping, we walked to the pier and looked out at the point break-the famous Malibu, a mere foot high.

After coffee, the only shop open at this hour, we headed south to Huntington Beach. This town was about three blocks long, in the middle of nowhere, just two motels. Charlie rented a room so we could all shower after body surfing. All, but Charlie, slept on the beach.

The next morning we ran down to the ocean's edge and saw that there was a wave that appeared to be about three feet plus, but it was at least two hundred yards out from the shoreline. It was hardly large enough to ride, but I had come five hundred miles and wanted to get wet. I tested the water, bent over, and touched again, then summoned my friends. Stripping to my bathing suit, putting on fins, I dove into the shorebreak, surfaced, let out a "Whoopee!"

Dave caught up to me, smiling like a Cheshire cat. "Just like a bathtub compared to Kelly's Cove."

We body surfed for five days, the night before leaving the police awakened us in the wee hours and made it clear that if they found us there again we'd be arrested for vagrancy. We got kicked out of Charlie's the second night, creating salty and smelly bodies, not being able to take a fresh-water shower.

The surf came up for our last two days, the water temperature sixty-five degrees, warmer than San Francisco in summer. On the last day, before departing, we took a quick body surf, and then sat in the sun soaking up the rays, all of us with a winter tan. We watched two guys carry surfboards out to the middle of the pier, drop them twenty-five feet into the water below, and jump. They paddled for a wave near the pier, caught it, and shot right through the pier, not touching one of the pilings. We had never seen anyone ride a surfboard and stood up, cheering. When the surfers reached the beach, we ran to them, filled with questions. How could you stand on a board? Was it really hard to make it through the pier? They condescendingly answered questions, and when they heard that we were from San Francisco, they walked away.

All the way up to San Francisco, my brothers and I spoke only of learning how to ride a surfboard. The next day we rushed out to see Cliff. He listened to our tales about the super warm water, and sat back, strumming his ukulele. "You guys think water warm there; you should come with me to Hawaii. Son of a gun, I show you warm water. Coming near eighty degrees, both winter and summer. You come Hawaii."

My brother Gene interrupted Cliff, "You know how to ride a surfboard?"

"I tried once or twice, maybe three times, but more fun to body surf."

"Does anyone around here ride a surfboard?" Gene asked.

Cliff sat back and thought. "Hey, I not see anyone ride up here too often, the surf too big, too hard to get out. But hey, the guys down at Pedro Point have a surf club."

Gene leaned toward Cliff to ask, "Who, who could teach us how to board surf?"

"This guy, Ted Pierson. He plenty good. Ted would teach you."

Gene called Ted and demanded that he teach us to surf. Ted was an intellectual loner, but the commanding tone of Gene convinced him quickly that we were not going to disappear.

Ted told Gene to meet him in Santa Cruz and Dave, Gene and I piled into Ron's Ford. We saw Ted down by the Santa Cruz pier and he said to follow him to a cove about four miles southeast.

Arriving, we looked down upon a lovely beach area, protected from the wind. Ted said that this bay was called Pleasure Point, a great place to learn because the inside waves were gentle.

There was a blanket of fog hanging just offshore and to the west, but it was warm and inviting at Pleasure. Ted explained the fundamentals; you wax the board on top. The skeg makes it so that you can hold an angle and turn. Watch the nose when paddling so it doesn't pearl dive. Feel the wave pick you up, move you forward and down the face; stand up.

Ted took Gene and Dave out first, catching a tandem wave, then pushing them into a wave and yelling, "Stand up!" They each caught a wave on their own, stood up, and fell off. It was my turn. Ron decided against it.

I was nervous, scared, and anxious. I was thinking, what if the board hit me in the head? I heard Ted yelling instructions into my ear as we tandem paddled. "Paddle, paddle," he screamed.

I saw the nose of the board slide forward, felt the push of the wave. Ted pulled me up from behind, and I was standing with his hands between my armpits. The board angled; I saw the kelp stand up straight as I slid shoreward. The shoosh of the water parting at the nose blended with the glassy sea beneath my feet. It was a two-foot wave, slow, but I was hooked.

We gathered firewood in the waning Sunset, started a fire in the cove, and Ted told us that riding a surfboard was not a sport, but like Cliff had said, "Surfing is not a sport; it is a way of life." He said that dogma filled with his own convictions. Piling more wood on the fire, Ted went up to his car and came back with a gallon of red wine. It was completely dark; the ocean was near quiet with an occasional wave breaking on the shore. The stars dominated overhead.

The wine touched me deeply in nerves I did not know I had. Life was perfect in this moment, Pleasure Point my newly found paradise. The fire burned itself out and we climbed the cliff to drive back to San Francisco.

Ted called early the next Saturday morning to ask, "Want to go surfing? I'm hitchhiking down to Pedro Point. Meet me early because the wind will come on shore from the west by noon.

By dawn I was huddled on the beach in glassy fog with Gene, my younger brother Peter, and Dave Devine. Ted arrived soon after. The way he explained it to us was that most of the boards that we were going to borrow belonged to some really cantankerous older guys.

They didn't like anyone fooling with their boards. Ted told us that if we saw any car approaching, to sprint to the beach and quickly put the board back under the pier house.,

It was gin clear, so glassy that you could see right to the bottom, but it was colder at Pedro than at Pleasure. I walked down to a lone cocktail lounge where the biggest surf broke. It was called the "Wander Inn." I watched the guys paddle the long boards out to the small left break in front of the boat launching area.

It seemed to bring back some memory to me, but I could not get in touch with it until l walked back to the boat launch and climbed up to where about a dozen rowboats lay, all of them in terrible disarray, as if they had been washed up on the beach. They were filled with old bait, sand, and oars hanging like broken limbs. Those boats caused me to flash to a day long ago.

I was six years old; my father was taking me fishing at Pedro Point. It was dismally foggy, rainy, and the ocean was chopped up. I remembered the ride down to the sea alone, getting seasick, filling the little skiff with fish, begging to be taken to land, all of the San Francisco fear of water coming up.

My flashback was interrupted by Dave screaming as he rode a long left slide from the boat landing area to shore. We did get the boards back where they belonged and I sighed a relief that we had taken Ted's advice. The owners arrived and I knew that they would have chewed us up and spit out our remains. These men were wicked in speech and threats. I did not want to test their physical prowess or lack of patience. This was a time when the bite was worse than the bark.

In time, however, in most cases their barks turned out to be worse than their bites. You did have to prove yourself before they extended a warm handshake. It turned out to be a toss up between which was more ferocious: the weather and sea at Pedro Point or the few inhabitants.

Those Pedro Point apprenticeship days have been lost in the past, but somewhere in a warp of time still lies the quiet farming valley of Pedro Point with its hardy fishermen, stock of big wave riders, strawberries growing right down to the sea, the occasional mountain lion raiding a chicken coop at night, a small stream where we gathered watercress, icy fresh water to drink, and seasonally caught huge King Salmon. We fished in the summer from paddleboards for halibut and rock cod, dove for abalone off the rocky point, and camped, when the land owner allowed it, in the field where Dick Keating Junior would sneak out of his house on the cliffs to sit by our fire and listen to stories that us big guys told.

Chapter 17

My Surfing Sister, Gretchen

Making up my poor grades from Fresno State College at San Francisco City College the time passed quickly and San Francisco State University accepted me into their teaching credential program. I was excited at the thought of being a real teacher. I even thought about coaching football and swimming. Life fell into a routine, a pleasurable and challenging time that I looked forward to each day with renewed vitality.

My father usually put things into perspective for me. He told me one day when we had taken a swim at Aquatic Park, a City and County project that created a nice recreation area right on the edge of the bay, that it was time for me to get a job and take care of my basic needs.

My father told me. "Your mother and I feel that you are completely healed from the kidney operation; we want you to live at home, but you have to justify your existence with a job."

My lifeguard job had ended due to financial problems in City Hall. They cut back to just Cliff and Eddie.

One day while checking the job bulletin board at State I came across an ad that read: Wanted : part time and full lifeguard position — Stinson Beach. Inquire Stinson Beach Fire Dept.

Calling the number, I asked about the job and was told to hold for a moment. A man named Anderson came on and asked me my qualifications. I told him that I had lifeguarded Fleishacker Pool.

He hired me. It was mostly a weekend job. I hitchhiked over to Stinson Beach just north of the Golden Gate. It was a tiny villa, maybe a few hundred people and Anderson was sort of the mayor, the police, fire, and beach maintenance man. He commanded a great deal of respect in the small community.

"Can you drive a jeep? I've been unofficially doing any lifesaving that came up, but I don't have time to safely watch the beach. Not many come over here to swim, but many of them come on the weekends and they aren't with their wives. Usually they show up on the beach in the afternoon, nursing a hangover. It isn't a tough job. You just drive up and down the beach, a three mile segment up to the Bolinas Bay lagoon, judge who should be told not to chance the surf, and keep an eye on those who do go body surfing. Pays a $1.35 an hour and you can use the showers and sleep in my office on Saturday night."

It was one of the best jobs I had in college. The only onerous part was that Anderson told me that each morning, regardless of the weather and water temperature, I was to swim out into the heart of wherever there was a riptide and determine how to bring a rescue shoreward. The water was rarely above fifty-five degrees Fahrenheit and I spent most of the day on the edge of hypothermia unless the sun shone. I didn't have a car at that time so it meant hitchhiking after a bus ride to the Golden Gate Bridge entrance, standing there trying to catch a ride and not attract the Highway Patrol who frowned on hitching. Once in Marin County I had to traverse the Coastal Mountain system to Stinson Beach. There were so few cars going to that beach town that sometimes I ended up walking the miles over the summit.

However, I loved the brief interlude into being nowhere, being lost in the ascent of a two lane winding road that when walked seemed endless. In between gusts of wind filled with fog, the quietude would settle and I could hear my heart beating. By the time I got to Stinson Beach I was in another world. I always had a lot of homework waiting at home and cared little whether I got to my destination or not.

When I did arrive, I had a job that could only be envied. I was being paid to wander a lone, and ruggedly beautiful beach in a jeep, and I got paid for body surfing and getting a tan, which was what I wanted to do more than anything else.

It wasn't always easy, though, and the inevitable happened when I was driving back from Bolinas and spotted a person flailing in the riptide. Racing, I slid the jeep close as I could, grabbed my rescue can, and dove into the surf. I sprinted. The person was a middle-aged lady and as I got close to her she reeked of alcohol. I told her that everything was going to be fine. She was drunk and panicky. I handed the can to her and told the lady that she was to hang on tightly and I would swim her back to the beach.

The woman shivered. She had very little strength and could not support herself, let go of the rescue tube, and sank. I surface dove into the depths, grabbed her by the hair and surfaced. She was choking on swallowed water down the wrong tube. I banged her on the back and went into a cross-chest carry, allowing the rescue can to swing behind. She was big and not easy to get to the beach, but I managed. She didn't thank me and stormed, as well as she could, up to Anderson's office.

After I got off duty I took a shower. Anderson called me into his office. "Fred, how come you tried to cop a feel off that lady?"

"What! She couldn't hang on to the can. I had to attempt a cross chest carry."

Anderson had turned his face away from me. "Fred, the lady told me that you grabbed her across the chest. She wanted me to fire you." He turned to face me, a grin spreading across his lips, and then he burst into heavy coughing laughter. "I'm surprised that an educated, experienced lifeguard like you didn't handle that better. Oh, excuse, me the pun on "handle." Lighten up. It's all in a day's work. Want a beer?" He reached for the cooler near his desk.

Back in school after the weekend, the class was interrupted by a call on the intercom. "Send Mr. Van Dyke to the office immediately."

"Oh God, am I being kicked out again. No, I thought. I was doing so well."

Stepping into the office, I was met by a messenger who told me to phone my mother immediately.

"Yes, I'll come home right away."

Hanging up the phone I ran to my parent's car, sped toward 34th Avenue and ten minutes later was climbing the stairs to our front door. My mother met me with a grim face. "They called me from school today and said that I should pick up Gretchen. She had not told us a few days ago that she had fallen rounding second base in gym class. Her fever is 104 degrees and the doctor is on his way. Come, look."

My mother pulled back the covers from Gretchen and she writhed in pain. Her right leg from the hip to ankle was covered with huge pus filled and blackened skin. Some had burst and oozed onto the sheets. Gretchen was semi-delirious.

I thought about my fifteen year old sister who had recently been crowned Queen of the May Day Pageant at Holy Name School. She had won the contest and now, in November, 1948, she lay before me gravely ill.

The doctor arrived, took one quick look, and told my mother that he was going to hospitalize her. "She has some broken blood vessels. I think that she is faking the pain a little."

My mother interjected. "Why don't you give her a penicillin shot?"

"It won't do any good, and besides I am the doctor and I make the diagnosis. I'll see her later after you check her into the hospital."

The doctor called that evening and said that it would be all right, that a night in the hospital with heavy compressing would alleviate the problem. He said that he had sedated her strongly and so we should not come until the morning to visit.

Just as dawn broke, the phone rang. My mother jumped out of bed and ran to answer. It was another doctor and he was a surgeon.

"Mrs. Van Dyke I have some bad news for you. Gretchen is infected with gas-gangrene. There is very little if any hope that she will survive an operation."

"Operation, what?" My mother cried into the phone.

"We must amputate her right leg at the knee. She can have a prosthesis, but her survival potential is nil."

"No, No, No, not my darling little daughter, my Queen of the May ."

"You'd best bring your entire family right now, You must sign the papers. The sooner, the better the chance for stopping this disease."

My mother, sobbing, tried her best to explain what was happening. My father was supporting her with his arm. She appeared ready to pass out. We all helped her to the car and for the first time did not fight over who got the side seats.

We sat until darkness descended. No news. My mother told Doc, my father, to take us kids out to get something to eat and that she would stay.

"We'll bring you back something, Billie," mentioned my father.

She broke down again. "I don't want anything to eat; I want my daughter whole."

When we arrived back, the doctor was sitting with my mother, holding her close while she cried her heart out. My father broke down. We all were crying and we found out that when the surgeon had amputated the leg at the knee that the gangrene had moved upwards internally, threatening her entire system. The doctor told us that he had to amputate the leg at the hip, a complete disarticulation. A hitherto untried method had been imposed: they X-rayed her complete body in hopes that it might kill hidden gangrene. The X-ray specialist told us that he'd stake his reputation on the fact that if she survived, she would have no chance of having children. In those days they did not use lead protection over the vital organs.

The next morning we all were in the waiting room. The doctor told us that there was little hope, but she was conscious. We could go into her room. She barely hung onto life for three weeks. Things got worse. My mother decided that the hospital food was not good enough to make Gretchen well so she prepared each meal herself at home, a long drive to the hospital. She drove like a maniac to get the food to Gretchen before it cooled. At 70 to 80 miles an hour through a residential district it was inevitable that she would pick up a patrolman. The policeman approached and asked what the rush was. My mother stuck her head out of the window and sobbed, "My lovely young daughter has lost her leg and is dying in the hospital." Gretchen had been written up in the paper by Art Rosenbaum, a top journalist, so as soon as my mother mentioned Gretchen's condition he knew all about her and said that he would give her a private escort to the hospital whenever she needed it.

Huge Makaha Surf, West Side, Oahu. A day worth cutting out from school. Photograph by Don James.

Waimea Bay, 1959. Photograph by Dr. Don James.

Pupukea, my back yard. Van Dyke. Photograph by LeRoy Grannis.

Waimea Bay, Van Dyke, 1959. I clearly remember riding this wave. Waimea Bay has taken more than a few lives, surfing Walmea challenges all survival instincts. Photograph by Bud Browne.

Makaha, huge point surf on west side of Oahu. A day worth cutting out of school, as my brother, Peter, told me. 1957 . Photo: Don James.

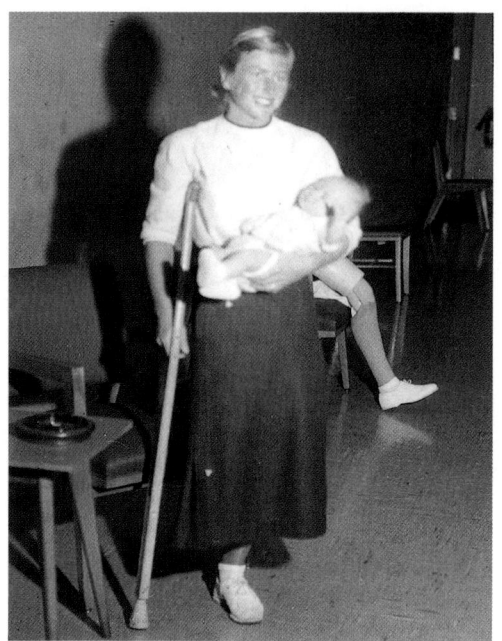

My surfing sister, Gretchen, with one of her five children. In the back her artificial leg. She rarely used it, although she could jitter-bug with the leg attached.

My surfing sister, Gretchen at San Onofre. It was Gretchen's favorite beach and she surfed it well. Surfing on one leg!

San Francisco open your Golden Gate. Photograph by Joan Marie Florence.

Checking the surf. Santa Cruz. 1960's.

Fred in Lanikai—ready to surf the Mokes! Photograph by Joan Marie Florence.

Standing in front of the Santa Cruz Surf Museum with my 11 foot, balsa wood board shaped by Dick Brewer. Photograph by Joan Marie Florence.

My first bass. I was 12 years old, in 1941.

Another Striped Bass, in 2001, 60 years later! Photograph by Joan Marie Florence.

Let's go camping, with my dad, Gene, and me
at San Francisco beach in the early 1930's.

Days of old. Our family's first car, a new source of freedom.

A popular view from the Santa Cruz Surf Museum—ocean, pier, and mountains. Photograph by Joan Marie Florence.

Santa Cruz, a paradise. Ice Plants bloom above Steamer Lane surfing spot. Photograph by Joan Marie Florence.

My parents, Doc and Billie. 1985.

Travels with Joan. Entering California
Joan and I are greeted by majestic towering redwoods.

San Onofre, 1963. Gretchen's favorite beach, where she surfed so well.

Wild California poppies.

Pedro Point launching ramp, a tranquil day, unlike my first experience there sliding down to huge waves. Photograph by Joan Marie Florence.

Pupukea, our beach home on the north shore of Oahu. Photograph by Joan Marie Florence.

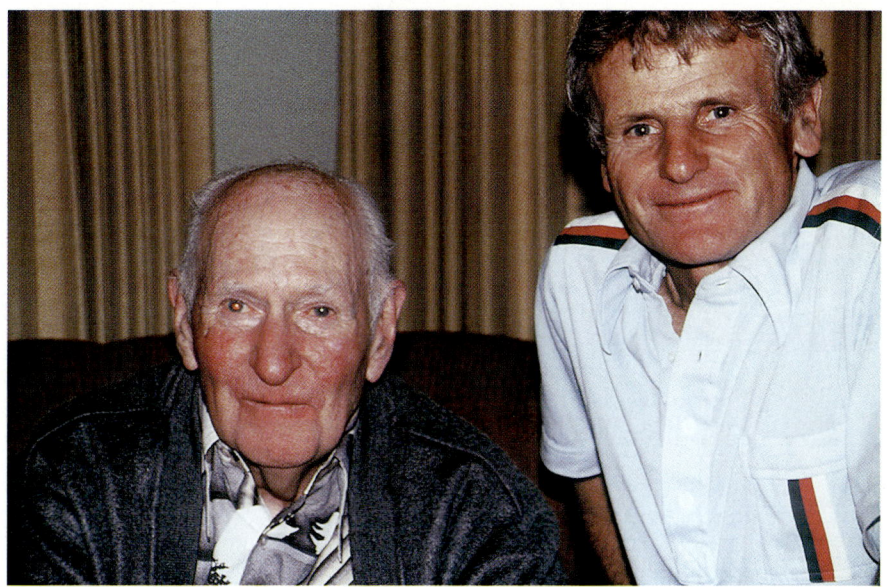

Jack Thompson, my mentor and dear friend, lived to almost 99 years. Photograph by Joan Marie Florence.

My loving wife Joan Marie, and me. 2001. Photograph by Cammie and Butch.

Muni Pier, Alcatraz, and Aquatic Park, where stalwarts, some in their 80's, swim without wet suits in 50 degree Fahrenheit water. Photograph by Joan Marie Florence.

The Place I asked Joan to marry me, but without the icy, driving rain, wind, and sleet. Photograph by Joan Marie Florence.

Silently, the whole family visited Gretchen on Christmas Eve to say a final farewell. I was the last to leave her side. Gretchen was heavily sedated. I bent over to kiss her goodbye and she grabbed me close. Tears filled my eyes; my throat and body contracted with spasms of grief.

Gretchen whispered into my ear. "Fred, I'm not going to die. I know it. Jesus appeared on the window ledge today, and he said I must fight to live. He said that I will swim and surf again, too!"

I stood up, wiped tears from my face, and vowed to her that I'd be there to help her do it. We drove back home to 34th Avenue. Every home on the street had a brightly lit and decorated Christmas tree in the front window, all but ours. Our home looked dismal as we pulled in front. Months passed, with many visits, consultations, specialists, more speculation by skeptical physicians' but we all could see that Gretchen was improving slowly, that she was going to make it.

Early in May Gretchen was dismissed from the hospital, returning a week later to have the last stitches removed, and then the question.

When can she swim again?

Her Doctor said, "Any time the weather looked right; give it a try, but be careful."

My mother left the judgment of when up to me. The day arrived, a perfect eighty-five degree San Francisco clear sky. I left college early and drove home, wondering if she would still be able to swim. What if she were lopsided? What if the stitch scars split open?

There was anxiety in all of us, except Gretchen. She was first in the car. We drove out to Fleishacker Pool. Gretchen walked toward the dressing room, using her new crutches, the empty space where a leg was so obvious. I walked behind her to make sure she was protected from stares of bystanders. Cliff, our lifeguard friend, stood next to me as Gretchen made her laborious way to the side of the pool.

I asked her if she wanted to start in the shallow end; it might be easier. She said, "No, if I'm going to swim it'll work just as well in the deep end. That's why you're here."

She dropped her crutches and hopped on the one foot, leaned forward, and dove deeply. We waited, and waited, and waited. She surfaced forty feet from the side, turned over on her back; you could not only see the smile of success, of happiness, but you felt it deeply. Everyone present was touched.

I looked over to Cliff. Tears streamed down his cheeks. I held my mother, and Gene and Peter dove in to swim out to Gretchen. It was a great day, a time of triumph, but just the beginning.

My parents moved to Santa Cruz, then to Capistrano Beach in Southern California. Gretchen went with them, ending up getting married and having five children, four of them avid surfers. Gretchen spent most of her time taking her children down to San Onofre, a secluded beach adjacent to where eventually President Nixon resided. She taught her children to swim practically as they were born.

Gretchen's husband, Chuck, gave her a camper truck so the kids could take their naps and live right on the beach until there father came after work, and then they barbecued dinner on the beach.

Gretchen got back into surfing the next summer, when I started by taking her out tandem. She got to the point of skill where she could stand in front of me on the board, and we even accomplished a few acrobatics.

Gretchen wasn't satisfied with that, so we wound up going into Dale Velzy's surf shop and ordered a surfboard to be made for her. She learned to surf at San Onofre. She could stand on one leg, making sweeping turns by dropping to her one knee, then supporting her weight on her arms, and dipping the leg into the wave. As soon as she got the direction, she would jump back to her standing position

Gretchen took up long distance swimming in the ocean. She would hobble down to the sea, crutch herself into water deep enough to swim and throw her crutches behind so the whitewater could push them to shore. My mother stood waiting and retrieved them. My mother stood waiting for a lot of things in protecting my sister. As time passed I noticed a resentment building in Gretchen. She did not like to accept help, but had to in some instances. There was a fine line set there and my mother took the brunt of it.

My mother and father never fully recovered from Gretchen's tragic accident, but it touched my mother most of all. She tried too hard to make it all perfect for her daughter, and Gretchen sensed it. My mother spent most of her day at Gretchen's home, picking up, rearranging furniture, washing clothes, changing diapers, bringing specially cooked dinners. It wasn't that Gretchen couldn't do all of these tasks, but rather the opposite. I saw her one day accomplish a task I could come nowhere near. She was out in the yard hanging up clothes when one of the crawling children got under her foot. Gretchen bent, picked up the child, stuck one crutch under her arm, and proceeded to bend again to pick up a diaper pail. She had spirit and inspired many.

The veteran's hospital, during the Korean War, would call upon her often to come visit a war casualty, an amputee. One occasion she wore her artificial limb and walked into the room of a seriously depressed vet who had lost his leg as far up as Gretchen's. He asked her why she had bothered to visit a half a man? "I might as well have been blown up. I can never live normally again." He ranted on about how his life was finished.

Gretchen smoked at the time, pulled out a pack of cigarettes, lifted one to her mouth, reached into her purse, and pulled out some matches. She pulled up her dress above the knee, exposing her artificial limb, and struck the match on her leg. The man burst into tears, convulsed, and my sister held his hand and said, "You'll walk again." Such was her spirit.

Chapter 18

Santa Cruz—A Paradise?

Dave, Gene, Peter, and I spent as much time as possible surfing in Santa Cruz. It was the better part of the protected Monterey Bay, warmer water, more sunshine, smoother surf, morning and evening glassiness like a sheet of oil laid out to the horizon. It was a slow moving town, almost all lumbering had ceased, the second growth Redwoods reached for the sky, and the chief industry was fishing. For us it was a surfing Mecca, although most of the best surfing areas were outlets for raw sewage. We were so heavily exposed that I think we built up an amazing immune system, although a few surfers did die of hepatitis. There was one doctor in town who was researching heart disease and prevention. He asked us to volunteer to be study subjects.

In Santa Cruz from about late October until February, the water temperatures sometimes dropped into the mid forty degrees Fahrenheit. No wet suits or hoods, we hung on the edge of hypothermia each surf session, and if you lost your board and had to swim to the beach, you were so cold that it took you a couple of hours before you could maneuver buttoning up your pants.

Doctor Sharp asked us to come into his office as soon after surfing as possible. We would arrive, dripping salt water, shivering, and stuttering. He'd attach all kinds of devices to our bodies and watch readings on his scope. His conclusion, after many such visits, was that we were experiencing almost non-detectable heart attacks, as many as a few each surfing session. He didn't seem to be concerned and said that we could continue surfing. Doctor Sharp looked upon us as creatures who had evolved into some kind of aberrant physical anomaly. To this day none of us has had a major heart attack, and most still surf.

With the advent of surfboard riding, body surfing was left behind, except to quickly get to the beach after a wipe out. We mostly surfed Pleasure Point and Cowell's Beach adjacent to the Santa Cruz pier. Inside Pleasure and Cowell's had very gentle breaks and the waves moved across the reef much slower. Outside Pleasure, when big, was challenging, and at the point of our ability, we chose only to ride outside on smaller days.

Steamer Lane, which was situated around the point from Cowell's break, so far out in the ocean, was another dimension in surfing. It had been named because of the Steam ships that passed outside the bay. There were three fairly shallow reefs, and as the waves got bigger they moved to the outer reefs.

The only inhabitants who took advantage of riding these huge and crushing waves were the sea lions. We'd drive up to the point and fantasize riding those waves. We didn't have the boards that could handle Steamer or the necessary skill at this point.

The full power of the Pacific Ocean lies just outside the point at Steamer Lane, consistently sending fantastic, glassy surf. Santa Cruz has always had a unique bay that protects a natural harbor while allowing both north and south swells to penetrate its reefs. Monterey Bay has Monterey on the south point and Santa Cruz on the north, a half moon bay indented inside the points.

In the late 1940s and 1950s balsa was used to build surfboards. The lighter balsa boards made Steamer Lane another surfing option. I experienced these waves almost alone, sharing swells with only a handful of surfers. It was not unusual to see a wave at Steamer Lane line up and move right through to the inside Cowell's break and onto the beach three fourths of a mile away.

Down at Pleasure Point there used to be a baby harbor seal who would sneak up in between sets and splash water in my face with a slapping of its tail.

Occasionally, I have been chased from the water by Killer Whales, during their migration. I'll never forget the day I was lifeguarding Cowell's Beach and a tribe of sea lions crawled right up onto the beach among the sunbathers. Two hundred sea lions were decapitated by the Killer Whales in one day. The sea lions shivered in deep fear right amongst the tourists sun bathing.

It was a real rush to bet who would have the guts to sneak up on the basking sharks and jump upon their back while they lay bathing in the sun.

Most of the time I camped in a station wagon or laid a mattress out on the cliff at Pleasure, a couple of army blankets and a single pillow sneaked from the sofa in my parent's home. Where we camped on the cliff is now the home of Jack O'Neill the inventor of the original wetsuits.

We used to leave our boards down in a twenty-foot wide crevice below where O'Neill lives. No one ever bothered them. Hardly anyone knew what a surfboard was. There were very few homes on the cliffs, and a house a half block off the beach was selling for anywhere from $4,000. to $10,000. I tried to get a loan for a place on the beach for $12,000. and couldn't qualify.

Up until about 1950 there was a surf club run by a bunch of really rigid old-timers: the Hicker, the Douger, the Chucker and the Wild Hook Gang as they called themselves with their leader, Dave Campbell.

They surfed just below Pleasure's inside break at a spot named by them, the Wild Hook. These guys, not unlike a motorcycle gang, rode the spot with complete abandon, not caring about the shallow reef and cliffs that, on a wipe out, destroyed a board at high tide.

We considered them weird, stodgy, for want of a better description, complete kooks. In those times there was still plenty of space. We rarely saw these fellows as most of them lived in San Jose.

I love to talk about Santa Cruz, reminisce about the reefs filled with fish and covered by abalone, the sunset in the redwoods, forested mountains behind Steamer Lane, or, a full moon covering the Bay. I remember one night in particular, the full moon rising above the sea, absolute glass from Santa Cruz to Monterey. The very last of the sunset disappeared, leaving an extreme coldness in the air, the water warmer than the air, an unusual phenomenon.

My friend Neil Frank and I used to frequently body surf Steamer Lane when the surf got too big for handling with the boards we had then. The 48-degree water without a wetsuit was a challenge to say the least. Of course, the seals rode the waves no matter how big they got, but just sit and imagine this scene: me on my surfboard and Neil body surfing, the last of the sun setting in the mountains behind, absolute glass, and I catch a perfect wave, skimming, effortlessly toward the face of a yellow moon rising from the sea; then behind me come Neil and a sea lion schussing, parting the wave like a cleaver with their chests.

The sea lion had popped into the wave as it broke behind me, followed by Neil, who finned in body surfing. It was one of the most magnificent surfing experiences of my life. And the climax came as I surfed around the point into Cowell's and a huge King Salmon jumped out of the water in front of my board, splashing water into my face. I screamed in joy and, in my excitement, dove off my board, it bouncing in the soup and me swimming in elation to retrieve it. I dove mostly to become one with that entire scene. The 48-degree water melted into the moonlight rising and was not even cold to me. It was a perfect moment and the reason I still surf in search of more of those perfect moments. You certainly do not find them on city streets or sitting in committee meetings. At that time, I had not taken acid or even smoked a joint, yet it was one of the purest highs in my life. How many human beings have been given that gift of nature?

The police knew all of us and allowed camping on the beach where we wanted as long as we behaved. Most of the time we did, while the old ladies who peered from behind curtains while we changed our bathing suits at Pleasure Point, delayed calling the police until they had finished watching.

In January of 1950 I had two days off from college. Hitchhiking a ride down to Santa Cruz from Burlingame, where I now lived, I was stuck on Highway 9 near Cupertino. Orchards of apricots and prunes stretched in all directions. There hadn't been a car for the past half hour except one farmer in a truck who turned into an orchard short of where I stood.

I wondered if I might get stuck for the night as sometimes in the past. That meant sleeping in an orchard or walking back to Highway 101 to catch a Greyhound bus back home. However, it was quiet and peaceful standing by the roadside, so silent that I could hear bees buzzing somewhere deep in the orchard.

Presently, the Santa Clara Valley is a series of criss-crossed freeways, and housing tracts that have just about eliminated the orchards. Smog hovers above the remaining open space. Auto noises dominate. An hour and a half later, and seven more rides, I arrived near Front Street in Santa Cruz, and walked the last mile to Cowell's Beach.

I couldn't find a cork for my hollow board and settled for a piece of newspaper wedged into the cork hole. I figured that it would keep the water out for longer than I would be out. I decided on surfing Cowell's and paddled for the point. Arriving, I sat up on my board and saw Dave sitting out at Steamer Lane. I wasn't really ready for Steamer, but saw the entire sea around Dave explode into the air as sea lions challenged him.

Dave was paralyzed, resigned to his fate. I paddled hard, waved my hand, and as I got closer shouted at a sea lion very close to Dave. It turned to me and charged, diving beneath the surface close enough that I could have reached out and touched him. Then they were gone.

We surfed until after dark, in caution, barely able to see the cliffs. On the beach Dave got a fire going. Thawing took some time, but long sips from a bottle of red wine helped.

We talked about the sea lions, which used to be far more possessive of Steamer Lane. At least we could ride now if harassment didn't discourage us.

The sea lions rode the waves when they were too big for us to paddle out. As long as I surfed Steamer Lane, the seals dominated. You had to clear the line up before relaxing into riding waves and the sea lions won their spot more than we did.

Since we had no wetsuits then, we would go to the Goodwill store and for fifteen cents find an old woolen shirt. The best one would be an old time woolen full body bathing suit, but when wet they got heavy. On a wipe out you had to abandon the suit to get up to the surface and escape from the engulfing kelp. Then there was a freezing swim to the beach. It was so cold that one swim usually finished you for the day. Now when I surf California I have a five-millimeter wetsuit and I can stay out three hours without getting cold.

We learned to avoid the cold January water by sitting high on our board and barely making any moves until the wave approached. We did not surf often in the wind, like today's surfers do, but went out most of the time a little before dark when the glassy surface of the waves reflected back like a mirror.

There was a guy we all thought to be a little out in left field, Jack O'Neill, who would show up in Santa Cruz on weekends and try to sell us on the idea of making a suit out of rubber and foam. We didn't buy the idea and stuck to our Goodwill bargains.

The few old-timers set rigid standards and were tough enough to enforce them. They taught us respect, love for the ocean not like the modern surfer who goes to a surf shop, buys a customized board, wax, wet suit, and turns on the store video to watch surf movies and get an up to date surf report. Many of the new surfers have been taught to go surfing by the media, to wear the proper surf clothes, listen to the hip surf music, and on the way to surf, litter their fast food cartons on the beach.

We went surfing to get away from society, the masses on the beach, any of the pressures that society imposed upon us. Surfing out at Steamer Lane was pristine, no sewer outlets, wild sea lions, crushing waves, offshore northwest winds blowing you over the back of the wave, an occasional eighteen foot Great White shark finning through the edge of kelp.

The contrast, after spending half the day surfing Steamer Lane, to paddle around the point into Cowell's beach was overwhelming. Rounding the point into more clement weather and surf, the smell of booze, cigarettes, and suntan oil filled my nose. If I were not so cold and tired I'd paddle back to Steamer Lane. Not unlike the Hell's Angel's motorcycle group, we did hear a different tune and distrusted salesmen, politicians, and considered anyone who did not surf a kook.

When still in the learning stage, I watched Chuck Foley, an old timer, perform on inside Pleasure. He surfed on a hollow paddleboard. Carving back and forth, standing on his board with tennis shoes, dropping his entire right leg up to the calf into the wave behind him, he executed a beautiful turn. I wanted to do that.

Chuck caught another wave as I paddled out in front of him. He finally beached his board and climbed the cliff, but the Chucker and Hicker threw rocks at me for two hours, if I even neared the shoreline. They convulsed in sadistic laughter. I was freezing and near exhaustion.

When the fog moved in, they allowed me on shore, the Chucker saying, "You never paddle out in the path of another surfer riding, but around the line up. You give first man on the wave the right of way; got it?"

Two hours of torture and freezing just to make those simple points, but I got it clearly and never broke those rules no matter where I surfed. Sam Reid, a Hawaiian surfer who moved to Santa Cruz, showed us the proper way to swim, catch a wave, and to get into swimming shape. He pushed us into rigorous training schedules when the surf was flat. Now many of the surfers can hardly swim to the beach when their board leash snaps.

Today, I have counted over a hundred surfers sitting out at Steamer and an equal amount around the corner at Cowell's. In the days of California abundance there was space stretching in all directions. Some of the better beaches were inaccessible unless you walked down steep cliffs, carrying your hundred pound plus surfboard. For the abundance of untouched beaches, you paid for it in the labor getting up and down. A ten to twenty-five pound board is somewhat standard in surf shops now.

One of my favorite memories of old Santa Cruz was the Rivermouth, which did not have the right sandbar every winter, but in 1952 it was perfect, and lasted well into June. We camped on the beach in caves that since have been covered and filled by tons of sand trapped by the Yacht Harbor breakwater. These days I would not believe my story if someone else told me about the caves.

It was a slowed down life on that clean beach with baitfish skipping on the surface and fog hanging outside; the water was not as choppy as Steamer Lane. A few fishermen cast from the cliffs above the sea. It was our northern Malibu.

Santa Cruz went into hibernation after Labor Day. You could practically have a picnic right on the main street in October. It was, for me, an exciting yet peaceful escape from the hyper-vibes of San Francisco. The air smelled as if the Pacific Ocean lay right in your front yard.

It was easy to live off the land, fish from the sea, and vegetables from my garden. There was little commercialism, no surf photographers, and no board manufacturers. Surfing is the in thing now, but when we started it was the out thing, and we liked it that way.

Now the abalone are all but wiped out; the salmon are near extinction, the land prices out of sight. Pollution presses in from all sides, especially the smog from San Jose, the Silicon Valley.

However, Santa Cruz still has the surf and the sea lions are coming back in force since they have gained protected status. Of course, the Great White Shark, which feeds on sea lions, is increasing in numbers, too, and there are more encounters with this monster of the sea, some deadly.

Give nature some space and it will eventually create an ecological balance, not one necessarily compatible with human beings, but we'll adjust to it in time.

Perhaps, with more foresight and public interest, involvement by local residents, the abalone, salmon, and trout will thrive again as once years ago.

Witness the change in Pleasure Point. When untreated sewage was being dumped into the bay, diseases like hepatitis were rampant. The sewer outlet has been moved from Pleasure Point to the west side. Recently, I swam with Dave Devine from the Wild Hook to Outside Pleasure. The ocean appeared in a pristine condition, cleared up, and through my goggles more beautiful than I had ever seen it, kelp swinging to and fro in the gentle swell.

Finishing that exhilarating swim, I sat beneath a redwood tree, second or third growth, but nevertheless as magnificent as its progenitors. I reflected on Santa Cruz as healing most of its wounds at some future date.

Chapter 19

Oranges, Oranges Everywhere!

The big wave riders all made fun of San Onofre as being a sanitarium, an easy place to surf, a place to feel like you were eight feet tall on each ride. However, they all returned time after time. Gretchen had fallen in love with the area from first sight.

Southern California was a great land of abundance right into the late 60's. Upon my first visit I remember the sweet fragrance of orange blossoms, driving through miles and miles of orange orchards. Aside from the multitudinous opportunities to advance in a field, to make big money, to develop untouched land that supported thousands of birds, snakes, (mostly rattlesnakes), mountain lions, coyotes, deer, and other species, Southern California had a raw beauty unique in America. It was the land of perennial sunshine, almost always having a mild winter. In the earlier years, the air was much cleaner, and you could see the mountains. That has all changed with the advent of thick smog. The strange phenomenon is that Los Angeles County has the most stringent anti-smog laws, and they are enforced, but there are still stifling amounts of dirty air.

Even at this point in time, Southern California has its natural splendor. The smog is overwhelming, but don't try and tell a Southern California resident that their city is unlivable. They'll answer that it is not their city, but the adjacent area. The water tastes like chlorine, oil, and dust, the freeways are packed at all times of day. Once in a great while a weather system will come together to form a

131

seemingly pristine environment, the winds blowing offshore, the sky so clear that you can see the island of Santa Catalina, the San Gabriel and San Bernardino Mountains. If fortunate, this may occur a few days out of the year. As soon as the weather pattern changes, the smog and all else are sucked right back into the Los Angeles Basin.

Gretchen moved to Southern California in time to experience no extensive freeway system and the joy was in the mountains and beach. My sister, after finishing her housework and shopping, would surf and swim everyday, even in the winter.

In those days, Southern California, for me, was the best that anything could get, the sunshine, the warm water, the abundance of animals that you saw daily. It wasn't like when the giant grizzlies bears roamed the Southern California area, but there was plenitude.

I spent a summer lifeguarding at San Clemente. The Captain of the guards asked us to get to work by 8 a.m. even though we did not go on duty until 10 a.m.

The first hour we speared litter and filled bags of it. The next hour we were to take a paddle, swim, run work out. At that time the sun was just beginning to penetrate the fog and massaged our exposed bodies to the warmth as the fog disappeared.

Lifeguarding could become hectic on weekends or when the Marines stationed at Camp Pendleton got passes. They would storm the beach, playing football, drinking beer, and then swimming out into the surf. They'd get caught in a riptide and washed toward the pier. Instead of using common sense and simply floating through the pier and coming in on the other side, the Marines would grab onto the barnacle covered pier pilings. By the time you got to them and pried them loose, blood streamed from their chests and arms.

The weekend would pass, and, if you were fortunate enough to get stationed at West Street you climbed down the steep cliff to a lovely, white, sandy beach. The wind rarely got into that cove and it was like being on a south sea island. Two lifeguards were always stationed down at that beach. It didn't have surf, but the water was crisp in comparison to San Onofre, and with severe tidal changes dangerous rips developed.

Mostly at West Street, the day was spent getting bronzed tan, taking breaks and swimming the length of the beach or going out to dive for scallops, which we would eat raw with lemon juice. It was like being paid to watch a private beach in the South Seas.

This morning was another perfection day. I was standing on Highway 101 hitchhiking to work. A man stopped to pick me up on the entry ramp, and I thought that I was definitely going to work today, but he dropped me off at Cotton's Point where I could see the surf. I stuck my thumb out for another ride and believed that I was still going to work. I walked with my thumb out and approached the Outside Trestle where the railroad passed, and you could see the surf. With my thumb still out, I stopped and watched the surf. No one stopped. After ten minutes, I thought that I'd just walk down to the beach and watch surfers ride.

This was Marine training land and they would arrest you and put you in the compound down at Oceanside. Everyone sneaked into the Trestle. It was about three-fourths of a mile to the sea. The swamp was tightly ensconced in trees, vines, and sand. You could not hear the highway from down in this mini-wilderness. Moving through the trees, trying to follow the overgrown, but well used trail, I noticed the fog moving from the ocean.

The fog settled in the swamp and visibility was less than thirty feet. I loved the feeling of remoteness, stealing away a day for myself in a very special place. I scared a deer grazing in the swamp. It bounded into the depths of the forest. The dew hung from the vegetation. It was almost warm in this protected hideaway.

A rabbit stared at me before showing his fuzzy, white cottontail. I soaked the special moment into my system, but knew that I should be at work. I wish that I were a deer, no problems, just graze and sleep in the tall grass all day, and best of all, no work. I needed this space to bask in it. I really did not care if I ever got to the beach on this day. It was perfect right here. I sat down in the little meadow surrounded by fallen and decaying logs. I gave myself time to daydream, to slow down and appreciate the grass beneath me. The foggy sky above was slowly clearing. I knew that if I did not get to the beach soon that the morning glass off would disappear and I would be confronted by the perennial west winds chopping up the sea. So what? I didn't even bring a board. I saw a squirrel cavorting to and fro, picking up little morsels. I thought that it would be nice to be a squirrel sometime in another life. I wanted to touch the squirrel and moved closer oh so slowly. The squirrel moved a bit closer to me, standing up on his back feet, and sniffed, but too late. I watched in horror as I saw a huge rattlesnake spring from the rotting log. It bit deeply and distended its jaw. The squirrel laid quietly half swallowed by the snake. The last I perceived were terminal spasms from the squirrel as it disappeared down the throat of the snake.

I was terrified and sprinted all the remaining distance to the open beach. I sat and watched surfers catch waves, but I was still with the squirrel. Looking back to the forest, I regurgitated my partially digested breakfast. I shook throughout my body, pulled sand up over me for warmth. I wished that I had simply gone to work. The fog lifted and my body warmed slowly. The next day I counted my blessings in having a good job, and that I, definitely, was not a squirrel.

Southern California fulfilled my dreams of warm water and abundance. It was extremely cold to skin dive in Santa Cruz, but here the reefs were loaded with fish, abalone, lobsters, clams, and porpoises.

A deeply guarded secret at the time was the mountains behind Southern California. You had to drive past the foothills and suddenly steep mountains covered with pine trees stretched to the sky. There were many streams and lakes, all abundantly filled with trout, catfish, and bass.

The sea level temperature in the summer stayed in the 80s Fahrenheit during daylight, while, up in the mountains, night temperatures could get to the low 30s. The forest closed in on you, bringing with it solitude, the air sweet. Gathering wood, and a campfire were allowed by securing a fire permit. Many of the streams are all but dried up now, and weekly fish plantings are necessary to partially satiate the droves of fishermen. These kids, who fish the lakes up by Julian, have grown up following the hatchery trucks that dump trout and eager fishermen wet lines fishing the trout out before the next plant. Now even air up in the mountains has become badly polluted.

In my most recent visit to Southern California, I saw condominiums line the cliffs, and the only access to the beach was with a key through a locked gate or knowing a friend who lived there. In fact, on that trip I noticed that all of the primitive beaches from Newport Beach to San Clemente were now tract housing, private acres with a gate guard to check if you were the right kind of person to enter. The increase in population put unexpected pressures on the ocean. The reefs were soon all but depleted of the resources I had taken for granted.

Crime increased in California. Special security measures were becoming more and more justified; gated communities abound. It is frightening to me to have moved from being able to leave your boards and belongings on the beach and not worry, to the paranoia, fear, and head turning necessary to protect your property now. So many people have guns, too, and are not reluctant to use them.

On that visit, I dropped by to see my sister and her family. We had some wine during dinner and I noticed quite a few times that my sister turned to her husband and winced. I thought that maybe it had been the wine, but Chuck asked me to go night fishing with him later down at San Onofre.

We cast our lines into the surf, stuck poles into holders, sat down, and reached for beer in the ice chest. It was a wonderful night and we looked up at the billions of stars overhead. Chuck broke the silence.

"Fred, you noticed Gretchen trying to cover up pain at dinner?"

"Yes, I didn't understand what was happening."

"The cancer has returned, and this time it is attacking all her organs. She doesn't have too much time and I'm glad you came to visit. I don't know what I am going to do with five kids. Your mother has been wonderful, but the strain is telling on her, too."

"Can't anything be done?"

"Not according to the tests. They say that she is terminal. As a last chance ditch I am going to send her to Mexico. There's a doctor down there who is doing incredible things."

We packed up and went back to Chuck's. I told Gretchen that I knew and she burst into tears.

"I don't have the strength to swim anymore. I take the drugs and sleep."

I returned to my home, deeply depressed, saddened that such a spirit was coming to an end. I thought of all the tandem rides we had at San Onofre, the fun, the suntans, and fish barbecues on the beach.

The regulars at San Onofre respected the special privacy of that area. The people who loved Gretchen protected her own need for anonymity. They all had gained special spirit from their acquaintance with her.

Gretchen didn't feel like swimming and that was the one thing she told me that made her feel normal. In the ocean her handicap disappeared. She could compete as an equal swimming or surfing.

My mother called me and told me that the Mexican trip had changed nothing. Gretchen's health had deteriorated and she was in the hospital on life support systems. Two days later my mother called again, "Fred, my darling daughter died today. She called out for me and I held her. She died in my arms."

My father took the phone and told me that my mother was sobbing and that he would take care of her. His voice was cracking and I told him I'd come immediately. I remembered all the love my mother showered upon Gretchen. They had the mother daughter struggles, my mother attempting to cover up all references that Gretchen was anything but normal. I burst into tears thinking of the insensitivities that Gretchen faced.

People stared when she chose to use her crutches instead of the artificial limb. With the limb she was able to jitterbug, but she preferred the crutches to the bulkiness of the artificial, and, when it was hot she'd perspire and create an irritation where the limb met the disarticulation at the hip socket. No one knew the pain she endured to be able to walk like regular women, no one, but she told my mother and me.

Sometimes she would rip the leg off in anger, taking layers of skin, which could become infected. When that occurred she would not use the artificial leg. Eventually she stuck the limb in the closet and stayed with the crutches mostly.

Her husband, Chuck, acted much like my mother, lying down the carpet of protection. In my heart they both have angel stature in my eyes.

The funeral took place on a lovely day, the sun shining, very little wind, just like she would have liked it. Chuck handled the burial ceremony, and we returned to Gretchen's home. A lot of people were there that I didn't know and it was a touching affair, but I became claustrophobic and wandered out into the backyard. A thunderstorm moved across the sky in the direction of where Gretchen had been buried. I followed it with disinterested feelings. The sky blew up right over where she was buried, and the bolt touched ground, exploded, and I felt Gretchen ascending into the thunderhead to heaven.

Since it was such a beautiful day, I decided to go down to San Onofre and ride one more wave for my sister. Paddling out, I turned and stroked for a wave close to shore. Suddenly, I was tandem and Gretchen lay in front of me, helping me to pull down into this wave. I jumped up, bent over, and helped my sister to her foot, as so many other times. Lost in the moment, I didn't see the beach coming up and smashed into the sand, Gretchen disappearing, maybe, forever. That wave might well have been the climax of my surfing. Gretchen did not disappear forever as I had felt in that wipe out together, but has visited me many times since dying. She comes through me when I surf, work in the yard, visit San Onofre.

Some years after Gretchen's death, I went camping up at Shasta with my brother Peter and two of Gretchen's children. Her oldest son wanted to borrow my fly rod and attempt to catch some trout. My first reaction was to say no because this was my choice rod, but I couldn't say it as Gretchen intervened by saying and appearing in my psyche, "Don't be so stingy. Let him use your Rod." He went off with the rod. After thirty plus years she still visits me in dreams.

Chapter 20

Santa Cruz Beckons

It was time for me to face the world on my own. Gretchen dead and my parents living in the San Clemente area, after receiving my California General Secondary Teaching Credential, I was left with the puzzle, where to live? I knew one thing for sure; I wanted to teach in a community where surfing and fishing were near. Sending out letters to Southern California, Santa Cruz, and remote Northern California, I received a few interested letters, but most were inland. One letter from Boulder Creek High School interested me. I made an appointment, put on a suit and drove there. The interview went smoothly enough, but the Superintendent thought that I was very young. He told me that these kids were mostly from lumberjack families. They were tough. I told him that I had a cabin up by the Forest Pool and that I had taught swimming there for years. He seemed interested in that portion of myself.

"Mr. Van Dyke, you do realize that we need a full time coach and seventh grade teacher. Let me look at your records and then I will get back to you."

Filled with elation by the thought that, at least, there was an opening, and what area could fill my needs more than Boulder Creek, an easy ride to Santa Cruz surf?

Some days later the phone rang. I lifted the receiver cautiously.

"Mr. Van Dyke, please."

"Speaking."

"This is Mrs. Hicks, Doctor Haskell's secretary. Could you come for an interview with Doctor Haskell on Friday morning?"

I almost dropped the phone, but spoke as nicely as I could.

"Yes, I'd be happy to come."

Nervously sitting in the waiting room, Mrs. Hicks smiled and told me to follow her. She opened the door to Doctor Haskell's office, and I saw him sitting behind his desk. Standing up he extended an arm.

"Well, Mr. Van Dyke, I think that we could use you, but it would not be in the capacity of just being a teacher. Your credentials qualify you in many fields. That is what we need in a small school like Boulder Creek High School. If we offer you a contract would you be our Athletic Director, football, basketball, track, swimming coach, physical education teacher grades seven through twelve, teach a seventh grade class, four periods in the morning, science, English, math, and social studies? Also, after practice sessions, you would have to drive the team members home."

Dr. Haskell added, "If a basketball game ends late, the custodian, who also drives the regular kids to and from school, won't clean up the gym because he has to be on the road early in the morning. That would be a job occasionally. I spoke to some of the Board Members and they said that they could offer you $3,450 per year. Think about it. Mrs. Hicks will give you a contract as you leave."

I drove to Santa Cruz, contract in hand, parked at Cowell's Beach, and read the contract through two times.

"This will have to wait. That surf looks good out there"

Paddling my board to the Cowell's Point, I sat and waited for a wave. The fog was lifting, the sun penetrating, and massaging my bare back. It was the perfect moment.

I thought out loud, "I'll take the job."

Catching the first wave of the set I rode all the way to the beach, feeling connected to everything. One elderly couple walked the beach. I greeted them and smiled ear to ear. I had my first full time job starting in September. During the week, in 1951, no one came to the beach. It was all mine, to bask in the sun, pull the sand up around my chest, to fantasize about my new job. On the way back to the cabin, I dropped the contract into the mail.

The summer passed like it had never begun. Entering the teacher's lounge, I met my colleagues to be. There was Ralph, my football and basketball assistant, Winona who taught the eighth grade, and Barbara, the girl's physical education teacher. The others melted away to their own classes after the meeting.

During the summer, I had managed to sign up five games of football. On the first practice fifteen kids showed up in uniforms that I had scrounged out of the closets in the locker room. When close-teaching a skill, I could smell tobacco on most of them. Gene Meschi, whose father owned the only meat market in Boulder Creek, was huge for fifteen years old. He was cocky and I called him on it during the first practice. He sneered at me, hands on hip, saying I couldn't make him do anything he didn't want to do.

I knew that if I didn't tame this kid that I would lose any chance at discipline. I walked up to him, and looked up at his smug face.

"Maybe you didn't understand when I called you cocky. What I meant was that out here I am the boss. You do what I tell you to do. If I say jump, you jump, and if I say jump and salute you do it. Got that?"

He bent over and laughed right in my face. Something from the past, maybe just the moment, the rebellious challenge, and I snapped. Punching him hard and deeply in his solar plexus, he doubled.

I rabbit punched him behind the neck, and yelled.

"Turn your uniform in and get out of here."

Telling the rest that they should run four laps and shower, I headed for my office, sat back and thought. The first day and I'm fired, I know it. I pondered my stupidity, the loss of composure expedited by a fifteen-year-old punk.

That night I fell asleep in front of the fireplace and awakened to the alarm, rushed off to be at school early. I sat in my office and waited for the summons to see Doctor Haskell.

Filling my grade book with the new names, I heard a faint knock on my office door, expecting it to be the Superintendent.

"Please come in."

It wasn't Doctor Haskell, but rather a very shy and quiet Gene Meschi.

"Coach, can we talk. I told my father what happened yesterday, hoping that he'd come to school and see to it that you're fired. He said that if I didn't apologize that he'd take me out to the wood shed. I'm sorry. I want to play football. Will you consider taking me back onto the team?"

I answered after some deliberation.

"Gene, I'll have to think about it. I'll let you know this afternoon in P.E. class. Now you better get off to class." Maybe I hadn't lost control. Maybe it was the only way that a twenty-two year old punk teacher could survive in such an environment.

We worked hard at practice and the night of our first game arrived. Playing under lights for my kids was a really new experience and I think they reveled in it. The Watsonville stands were filled to capacity, while a few parents attended from Boulder Creek. Doctor Haskell was there with his wife and six year old daughter. He stopped on the way to the stands and shook my hand.

"We'll be all right with a one touchdown win, Fred."

The coach from the opposing team had five complete strings of substitutes, and when they were ahead by forty points, he began sending in substitutions one after another. My kids were pooped by the half time, and that's when I hit them with the fact that they could not excel and smoke cigarettes. Second half was a continuance of the first, but far more brutal for he brought his starting line up in again.

We lost sixty-six to six. Doctor Haskell came by after the game and said, "Well, Fred. Looks like we're going to have to get ready for that next game now that the cobwebs are cleared." We had two severe injuries and ended the season with no wins and eleven players.

Basketball was a bit more encouraging. I had two full teams, mostly the same who played football, and won five games. Track fared better and we had a fast hundred-yard man who won continuously, and when swimming arrived, I coached the best diver in the league. He won everything. All in all, I was feeling that I worked and cared more than the kids did, and I was missing a lot of surfing time.

When the school year ended, I was called into the office.

"Doctor Haskell wants to see you. Sit down and I'll inform him."

I figured that he was going to compliment me on having handled a tough job very well, give me my first year evaluation. I sat full of confidence. Mrs. Hicks came back and motioned for me to enter

141

the Superintendent's office. I walked in smiling deeply, feeling great that summer vacation was ahead.

"Mr. Van Dyke, I want to inform you that the Board of Directors has voted not to renew your contract."

I sat down, floored by the news. The cleaning the gym flashed past my mind, the long traveling games and me with not enough money to buy a hamburger, while the kids stuffed themselves after a game, driving the school bus after practices, and not getting home until late at night, never knowing when dinner would take place or if it would. I felt like walking over to Doctor Haskell and punching him in the nose.

Doctor Haskell continued. "However, the parents, the Board of Directors was extremely pleased with your classroom and physical education classes. We are willing to offer you a new contract to teach P.E. and classroom. If you read the contract you will see that you get a $150. raise."

He sat back much satisfied with his philanthropy.

"If I understand what you are saying, I will teach the four academic classes and one of P.E.; is that it?"

Doctor Haskell answered, "Yes, that is the way it appears."

My mind raced to afternoons surfing with the sea lions, sunning on the beach on those lazy afternoons while most everyone else worked.

"Let me run this past you Doctor Haskell. I'd volunteer, without extra pay, to be the football assistant to the new coach you will hire, if I can leave for home after my last P.E. class when the football season ends."

"That sounds good to me as long as I don't get reports of you surfing before the school day ends."

Driving home, I was ecstatic. I was burned out on being Athletic Director, Head coach, and general handyman because the custodian had a union and I didn't. Now my last class would finish at 2 P.M., which meant I could be surfing in Santa Cruz by 3 P.M. Arriving home, I looked around. The place was falling apart, the screens ripped out by the raccoons. The fireplace heated the inside of the house, but out on the porch where I slept, it was mighty cold without any heat. My parents lived in Southern California. My brother, Peter, was in Korea fighting a war, and Gene lived in Cupertino, his father in law owned a huge apricot and prune orchard.

My parents agreed to allow me to sell the house. I sold it to one of the Directors from school who was in real estate. He bid $1,500. and I looked at it as sort of job insurance, accepted the money, and moved to Santa Cruz at Pleasure Point. My friend Dave Devine was married now and had a job teaching at Watsonville, lived two blocks away from me. Santa Cruz was a small town, maybe 25,000, tucked away in remoteness. For under two dollars you could get a fulfilling Italian dinner at the Santa Cruz Hotel.

Far better than the hotel was to be invited to Dave Devine's home. His wife, Diane, was a fantastic cook, specializing in Italian. Everyone contributed, abalone, salmon, red wine, freshly baked sourdough French bread. We all helped in preparation. These were my best friends, the people I surfed with at Steamer Lane and Pleasure Point. I cannot remember since those days any dinner get-togethers spent in such harmony. We were all surfed out, having spent four or five hours in the water. I was frozen when I climbed into the shower, warmed some, and put on a cashmere sweater to attend dinner. Santa Cruz, in the winter, got very cold at night, especially when it was clear and all the heat escaped into the atmosphere. By the time Diane announced that dinner was ready most of us were pretty well satiated with wine, but it didn't cease and a new bottle of dago red was passed around the table. After dinner, the fire was stoked up and we told job stories and of course, surf bravado.

The salmon and steelhead still entered the San Lorenzo River. One afternoon during a physical education class, one of the shadier kids took me aside. "We're going steelhead fishing tonight. Wanna come along? I've got to warn you that it's damned cold and we won't get started till after midnight. We'll supply you with the steel leader you'll need. Coming?"

I'd rarely turn down a chance to fish and I figured that these kids knew the river better than me. I didn't understand the part about the steel leader, but figured they had some new kind of extra strong leader. "Sure, I'll meet you at the school parking lot."

It was also a good way to get closer to this kid who had bugged me since the beginning of the year. Arriving at the school near

143

midnight, I didn't see any of the kids. Oh, oh, I thought, fell for the snipe-hunting trip. A few minutes later, I saw two warmly clothed kids walk toward me from the direction of the river.

"We don't park in the school lot. We're down the road a piece. Let's get started." He handed me my steel leader and a flashlight. "That's all the equipment you'll need."

I grabbed the pitchfork and realized what this fishing was. I could hear the kids snickering as I caught up to them. "Coach, we're just testing to see if you got balls. No limit on these fish, if you ain't afraid to spear them"!

I was damned if I did or did not. I thought about my fly-fishing, how I had joined organizations to protect salmon and steelhead, how I delicately released most of my fish. Out of the darkness I heard one of them splash from the creek, head up the bank, and mutter. "Goldurned, coach, I got me a ten pound female son a bitch filled with eggs. I'll sell the eggs to Meschi's old man. Come on fore it begins to get dawn."

For some reason I missed all my jabs, and when we climbed back to the road, I saw that each of them had a hefty load of steelhead.

"Duck into the bushes. Here comes that god-damned game warden. Quiet now. He don't know nothing."

He slowed, searching with his spotlight. My heart beat like a hummingbird's

"Let's get to our cars. That bastard game warden is half way to Santa Cruz by now. Here, coach, take this smaller one, just right for you. You're sure a crummy fisherman. See you tomorrow."

I didn't want to leave the fish to rot so picked it up and took it home, watching my rear view mirror all the way to Santa Cruz. The kids had told me that Mc Dermott could smell you if you were hiding, but they bragged that he had never caught any of them. Although conscience ridden about that fish to this day, it sure tasted wonderful! In one way I was glad that I had accepted the invitation. It showed me that I didn't want to get close to those students.

I was becoming adept at riding Steamer Lane, it being my favorite spot. I took off on the shoulder of a twelve-foot wave, making it to the bottom, turning, and wiping out.

Driven deeply into darkness, I stroked to reach the surface, tangled in kelp, and stuck my arm up to the elbow in some deep ledge in the reef, nearly wrenching my arm out of its socket. Surfacing out of breath, I felt that I could handle most any surf after that. A month later I still felt deep confidence in having handled that wipe out.

Driving up to Boulder Creek, I arrived in the school parking lot, walked into the office to pick up mail, and saw Doctor Haskell, a smile splitting his otherwise tight lips. He approached me, offered the morning Examiner newspaper, and said.

"Fred, you think you have waves in Santa Cruz? Look at this picture of surfing in Hawaii."

I grabbed the paper from him and peered, amazed. There was this front-page photo of a mountainous wave at a place called Makaha Beach on Oahu. There were three surfers stacked like tiers, one above the other. It appeared, to me, to be twenty feet high.

Handing the paper back to Doctor Haskell I said, now a deep and sardonic smile upon my face, "You just lost yourself a teacher."

I resigned in June. A job teaching at a private school in Honolulu had grabbed my attention, and I applied.

Dr. Fox, the President of the school, seemed to like me and hired me to come in August.

He asked me one question at the end of our interview in Palo Alto.

"Do you surf?" We have a couple of surfers on our faculty and I don't think that I want to hire another one. They're always cutting out."

"Well, I've tried it, but it is not a serious part of my life. I don't think cutting out of school will be an issue."

In the meantime, I had not resolved my feelings for Carol and played the same old nostalgic tricks on myself. I got married, but my heart belonged mostly to Carol. There was no other woman for me. Much time passed, and my marriage collapsed and I was attending San Jose State College, doing graduate work. An unturned stone lay before me. What had happened between Carol and me? I always wondered if I had been used, the only one around with all the men in the service over seas? Had she loved me? I had to know. One day, in between classes I thought, why not?

I found the number in the phone book and dialed. A man answered.

"Can I speak to Carol?" I asked.

I told him that I was an old college friend passing through and wanted to say hello.

The man answered very abruptly.

"Carol is dead." He hung up.

Calling Vital Statistics, sobbing over the phone, the lady in the office was empathetic.

"I'll check for you sir. Hang on."

Minutes passed, seeming like eternities pushed together.

A voice filled the phone. "This lady committed suicide last August, an overdose of amphetamines. I'm sorry. Was she a relative?"

"No, my first love; my only love. Thank you." I hung up. I cried. I swore to never love again. I was devastated when I knocked on my brother Gene's door in Cupertino.

His wife opened the door and said:

"Fred, what are you doing here? I thought you were going to State."

"I am. Remember me talking about Carol? Well, she's dead, committed suicide."

I fell into Betty's arms, sobbing. She tried to comfort me, but I was beyond and she led me to the front room couch where I collapsed.

"Will you just leave me alone for awhile?"

I sat and reminisced, the first time I met Carol, swimming at the Junction, walking to her cabin, how I fought my dread fear of a mountain lion attacking me on that lone and dark road, but desire dominated reason.

Sitting on the living room sofa, I remembered the dances at Forest Pool, Big Basin, and my mother destroying our relationship on one fateful day. The front door opened and Gene walked into the living room.

Betty beckoned to him that she wanted to talk in the kitchen. Gene said, "Hi, what are you doing here?" He moved toward Betty. She closed the door and told Gene what had happened. Gene brought me a beer and sat down next to me.

"I'm sorry, but I don't know what to say."

"There's nothing that I can do or say to bring her back, and I blame myself partially. I was going to visit her last summer and put it off until school was in session, and then forgot about it. I waited one summer too long. I can see her diving from the ledge, smell her perfume as we danced. I'm losing it."

I burst into tears, grabbed my beer, chugged it down, and asked Gene for another.

Gene said, "You don't need more beer. I know what can help you to get through this thing. I'll be right back. I'm going out into the shed."

He returned a few minutes later, holding what looked like a cigarette in his hand, bent over and lit it. He handed it to me. I looked at him and reminded him. "Gene, you know that I don't smoke anymore."

"This is a joint and it'll fix what's ailing you."

I had never smoked a joint. I had never used any drug, but alcohol, and that didn't help to solve a problem.

"No, I don't want to touch that stuff. I don't even want to be in the same room if you're going to smoke it. I'm going to take a walk in the orchard," I said.

No matter how deeply I moved into the orchard, I could still hear the noise of cars speeding on Highway 9. Things had changed from those times hitchhiking when I took a chance on being stranded there. I noticed rabbits running, attempting to evade me. Some time ago, the orchards were far larger. Many of the acres had been sold off for new housing tracts. It had pushed the rabbits closer and closer.

One rabbit ran from behind a tree, looked at me, jumped three feet into the air, and fled, only to meet face to face another rabbit. They displayed heavy anxiety, like something was pursuing. I saw it as an introduction to what we human beings were setting up for each other. We lived in more and more crowded cities, filled roadways until gridlock took place each day. I knew that the orchard farmers were being issued out, similar to the rabbits. We created concrete culverts where rivers used to flow freely, destroying the flora and fauna once present in abundance. The orchards became either freeways, tract housing or shopping malls.

147

It was no longer relaxing or replenishing to my soul to stroll in the orchard. The whole thing was coming down and most people considered it progress instead of unnecessary and greedy growth. We resembled the lemmings in Alaska, but disguised it with our coats and ties.

I returned to my brother's house.

"Fred, I want to talk to you. I've got a plan. Me and some of the surfers have taken LSD. I know that it will help you to put Carol into perspective. Here, read this book. It's written by Timothy Leary. He's a Harvard professor who has turned his students on to LSD trips. The essence of his philosophy is, "Tune in, turn on, and drop out.""

I wanted nothing of it, feared losing my job if I did, feared having the police break down Gene's door and take us to jail.

We had dinner and I sat down in front of the fireplace and began reading the book. I wandered back and forth from Leary's rantings to Carol. Somewhere around midnight I finished the book.

Maybe I should try LSD. My brother was still a teacher and he had done acid a lot of times. I called Gene into the front room and asked him to tell me about what happened when he took LSD.

"Fred, you would really have a good trip. You go to the mountains, alone, every summer. You have a deep appreciation of nature. You would see the wonder, the beauty of nature as you never have seen in your most remote wilderness."

"All right let's do it, right now."

"No, No, No, slow down. Betty is planning a picnic tomorrow in Big Basin Park. The kids will come and we'll give you the acid and you can trip in safety. You should not take it in a place where it can be threatening. The mountains are perfect."

We left early the next morning, entering patchy fog as we descended into Big Basin from the Highway 9 summit. Gene paid the day fee and we parked. Moving out of the car, Betty let the kids run ahead of us. Gene pulled out this little pill, and I was unimpressed, thinking that maybe it would act as I heard tranquilizers do. The pills were handed to me with some orange juice. I swallowed them and asked Gene when this thing was supposed to happen. He said to be patient, that it might take an hour or so.

Skeptical, I told them that I was going to jog ahead and catch up to the kids. Betty told me that that might not be a good idea. "You see, your brother thinks that you are a totally straight, coat and tie man. He wants to blow your mind. Instead of a regular 250 micrograms Gene wanted to give you 3000 Micrograms. I was afraid that you'd die or at the least end up in the nut house. I made him cut the dosage in half."

I calculated in my mind. Hmm, that is about 1500 micrograms, six times a regular dose. Oh well, I'll take a work out run and forget about the whole thing.

Ascending the mountain, I felt great, having worked out on the road, five to ten miles a day. Arriving at the summit, I looked at giant Redwood trees almost down to where the ocean lay, which was covered with fog. It was warm and the sun felt good. I lay down and looked up at the gloriously, blue sky pierced by first growth Redwoods. The perspiration from my forehead evaporated and my armpits cooled. The two boys caught up to me and sat next to me. Kurt, the youngest, sat in my lap.

"Tell us about your surfing adventures Uncle Fred."

I was saved by the arrival of Gene and Betty who asked simultaneously, "How's it going? Notice anything?"

"No, I don't think that I am the type that gets affected by drugs.

Kurt looked up at me. "Uncle Fred, how far is the ocean away?"

Thinking that I had seen something that wasn't there, I asked Kurt to repeat his question. He looked up at me from my lap and repeated the question.

I looked down his throat, past his esophagus, and saw deeply into his stomach.

"Whoa, what's happening?"

I heard Betty say to Gene that it looked like I was beginning to trip.

Placing Kurt on the ground, I stood up and walked closer to the overlook. The fog had lifted and the ocean undulated as it always did, waves throwing up white caps. It was two miles to the ocean, but I felt like it was right in front of me.

"Wow!"

To the north I watched a giant Redwood tree swing back and forth in the breeze. I admired trees for their beauty. Suddenly and determinedly the tree bent toward me, nearly touched the soil in front of me, and said.

"Hi, Uncle Fred."

"Far freaken out."

Words that I had never uttered issued forth as if I had always used them. They immediately became my vocabulary.

"Man, this was heavy stuff."

I knew what all these terms meant, but have never tried them as they were so foreign to my character. I dismissed that kind of lingo as hippie stuff. I was a respected schoolteacher with a graduate degree. Most of the hippies were drug smoking, drop outs without ambition.

Gene held a dollar bill in front of my face.

"What do you think of that? You work for bills like that every day."

I laughed hard.

"How about your college degree?" Gene grinned. I cracked up, laughed until I got cramps in my lips and face. I lost track of time, the day, the year, the century. I was tripping deeply now, moving back through all of evolution, arriving at nothingness, disappearing.

I became God floating through the universe, earth somewhere billions of miles below me. The nothingness moved toward boredom. Ascending back to Earth, forming into a single cell, multiplying, dividing into millions of cells, I took the form of a swamp creature, and climbed as a reptile onto land, transcended and flew as an eagle surveying all that lay beneath. Evolving ceased when I became a man, a very old, gray haired man, who delivered the sermon on the Mount, born as Jesus, and moved into Fred again.

I had a brief contact beyond myself. It was Gene who brought me back. He was smoking a joint and that created paranoia as I had never known.

"Get rid of the joint !" Betty screamed at Gene. Her angered tone hurt me deeply. Dissolving to tears, I asked them why they did not love each other?

Betty answered, "I'm sorry. How are you doing?"

I was fading again. My entire body burned. I saw the flames leave me, climb the trees, and disappear. I looked behind me to fog and thought that I'd deal with that some other time. I wasn't ready.

Peering into the ground, I saw China and all of its people. I felt all the wars that had ever been fought. I saw the bankers choking people out of their money, tying them into unsolvable debts. "Flow with everything. Don't fight. You'll glide through, trust me."

I made it. The feelings changed. I was sitting atop a mountain covered with Redwood trees. It was wonderful. I touched the sky and it touched me back. I looked through myriads of kaleidoscopic rainbows cascading into my eyes, colors, expanding contracting. I was drawn to these undulations, leaned forward and left the cliff. I flew effortlessly, each color unfolding into a newer and more beautiful universe. I had another contact with my brother, the reality I had transcended. Gene held me above the rocks below by the scruff of my pants.

I experienced unfathomable beauty, love, joy as I had only been told by the nuns was heaven. I was in heaven and in tune with the entire universe. Dissension, chaos, was not in this dimension. I think I fell asleep for when I awakened the fog had moved further up the mountain. I felt that a great deal of time had passed.

I contacted with Gene, and he told me it was time to go down the mountain. "You've seen a lot of things today. You have broken civilization's taboos, seen through hypocrisy. Come here. I want you to listen to something , the heart of this tree before we descend to the Park."

Placing my arms as far as I could reach around the trunk, I buried my head against the bark. Remember, I was also a science teacher. I listened to the Redwood's heartbeat and felt it pulsating.

I experienced the terror of all the Redwood trees that had been felled, every single bit of slash left by the unseeing, unfeeling timber industry. I assured the tree that it was safe in this park domain. It thanked me in deeply moving and pulsating vibrations. Far out, I thought.

My brother asked me to follow him slowly.

"Sometimes you really get burned on re-entry. Some don't make it. You had the best acid going so I'm not worrying."

I could not imagine anything adverse happening. Everything was so perfect, so beautiful, filled with wonder in my universe. I told

Gene, "I want to look down to the ocean once more and then we can descend."

"Betty and the kids will be waiting at the car. Go ahead, but hurry."

I didn't like being rushed in my state. I resented my brother attempting to set boundaries into my world. Climbing to the ridge I looked down, saw the long fingers of wispy fog slowly moving up the mountain. I sat in awe, searching. An image took form, half in the fog and slowly emerged. I could not focus clearly and squinted. The image moved closer to me and broke out of the fog, as pulsing energy. A woman, I thought Carol at first, but as she took shape, I could see that it was not her, but the most beautiful woman I had ever encountered. She walked toward me and became more defined the closer she approached. The woman had blonde hair as Carol, but seemed beyond earthly beauty, beyond Carol's spirit. I knew that this was the woman I had always fantasized, my dream woman, the one I had searched for, and it definitely was not Carol.

She was the mate I wanted for life. I reached out to touch her and the fog enveloped, taking her with it.

Cold fog covered the mountain. I ran into the fog, but could not find her. I heard Gene summoning me and moved toward him. We walked down the mountain together. Nearing the bottom, my brother hugged me and said, "Just stay cool. There's a man coming up the trail. Just pass him and we'll move on to the car. He may appear weird, distorted, but let it go."

I didn't know what he meant. The man stopped next to us and wanted to know if he was on the right trail. I looked down and he asked me a question. His face was strange to me. I did not want to say anything to him. My brother answered for me and the fellow moved upward.

"In a short time you will handle conversation with others. You're still re-entering. You've been a long way out of the structure that we always thought was the only one."

The searing flesh roasting on barbecues reached my nostrils, taking me back to cave man times. Husbands and wives screamed at each other, babies cried. It was dinnertime and they did not want to be kept waiting. I almost panicked and ran back up the mountain.

These anxiety filled voices seemed foreign to me, and set off a chain reaction of fear. They acted like dangerous people, and I feared they might sense the differences between us and attack.

Gene asked, "Are you all right with this?"

"It's really weird. I was a part of that. I believed in that kind of life. I lived it. There were no other possibilities. Yes, I'm all right. I'm better than I ever have been."

A lot was going on inside of me. My values had done a 360 turn and Gene said not to worry.

"In a couple of weeks you'll forget most of it."

I knew that these insights and changes, so abrupt, would follow me through life. I would not forget a moment of it.

We arrived at the car and Betty told me that she had a roast she would put in the oven when we arrived home. The thought of food turned me off, but by the time we drove into the Cupertino orchards I was hungry. After dinner I fell into a deep sleep and, as far as I know, dreamed of nothing. The next morning I did not get up to do my usual jog. Occasionally, during the day, I had quick flash backs into the trip.

Nothing would ever be the same. I did not feel as driven as before the LSD. I was calmed out and the world appeared more beautiful. I walked in a lovely dream world, a world I was to find out conflicted with all that was civilization as we know it. I found people avoiding me.

I could not keep my mouth shut. Whomever I encountered I felt compelled to share my trip with them. I truly felt that all the wars and chaos in the world could be solved if everyone took a hit of LSD, especially the leaders of countries. However, I realized that many people were on bum trips and LSD accentuated where you truly were in life.

I wanted to turn on my Superintendent of schools. I wanted to stop all pollution, to put a moratorium on taking any more Redwoods from the Santa Cruz Mountains. I saw how wonderful existence could be if we only looked into the past and tried to simplify, help each other. I only felt beauty, joy, and peace. What was considered by crass developers and politicians as progress was really greed and corrupting the environment. They did not seem to differentiate between real progress and uncontrolled growth.

Slowly, as my brother had said, I returned more to what is considered the norm. I did not put on the coat and tie unless it was a formal occasion, but Redwoods would never be the same for me. When I drive through a Redwood forest I am fascinated by how they pierce and punctuate the sky. I haven't seen a Redwood tree bend and touch the ground, greet me, since LSD, but don't dismiss it as impossible.

I became more interested in sunsets and sunrises. I appreciated a moth in flight, didn't swat mosquitoes for a long time. I stopped eating red meat, rationalized fishing at times.

My dream of stopping pollution and saving all the remaining Redwoods went the way of lumber trucks spewing out toxic diesel exhaust. Private land owners sell their Redwoods to pay taxes. I learned a lot from Nick, Betty's, father that was never taught in college. I admired his life. He gave to the Mexicans who worked for him seasonally. Most returned and worked harder for Nick than the other orchard owners who did not care for the Mexicans, looked at them like you would a tractor or bulldozer, necessary equipment.

When I visited the orchard, lunchtime was a special event. Everything stopped from about 11a.m. until 3 p.m. It returned to quietness with only birds singing and the trees swaying in the west wind. Nick started the barbecue, and while he waited for the coals to be just right, sat back and looked to see if his wife was near. Determining that she wasn't, he handed me a water glass and asked if I would like some homemade wine. Reaching behind an apricot tree, he pulled out a half gallon of red wine, pouring into my glass, stopping about half way to the brim.

I assured him that I could enjoy a full glass.

He grabbed my arm and told me that his wine he knew like it was a child of his. "I crushed the grapes with my bare toes, tasting the juices that flowed out, coming to the cellar early in the morning and late at night to test whether it was fermenting into alcohol. I never worked out a method to determine how strong the potion would be when ready. What I am saying to you, Fred, is that you should fill the remainder of your glass with water. Try it and if you feel you need more you are my guest."

I laughed, but did what he had suggested, noticing immediately, upon the very first swallow, that I needed a reality check. Three sips later and I knew that I could get into deep trouble drinking this wine without water mixed. I melted into the chair I was sitting upon, and felt orgasmic like nerve endings in my toes, fingers, head, and body pulsated sensually.

Sitting in the shade, listening to Nick speak about the old days in the orchard when deer, bobcats, mountain lions, hawks, and many other animals roamed, I felt at home.

Noni, Nick's wife, carried a tray full of vegetables and sirloin steak, placed the food next to the barbecue and Nick stood up, ready to perform a work of art. We ate, the vegetables from Noni's garden, and the meat handpicked at the little market in Cupertino.

Never have I enjoyed and tasted food like that since, nor the hospitality of both of those old country transplants from Yugoslavia. Until Nick was forced to sell out, acre after acre to pay taxes, a way of life in the orchard just about disappeared. As long as any of the orchard remained, Nick shared his abundance with all who visited. Nick passed on, but the heritage of orchard life lives on in Gilroy where Betty, Peter, Kurt, and third son Eric work the new farm.

Each of them gives love and care to their trees and vegetables as they learned from Nick. Nick had told me, while we drank wine, that he wanted his grandchildren to be near the earth as he had. Nick had come to America with little more than the clothes on his back and built, through hard work and love for the land, a thing of beauty and stability. Every time I drive on the freeway where his orchard used to be, I slow down and think of all that has been lost. There are drive-by shootings, graffiti, gangs, drugs, hold ups, smog, a water-well level that has dropped over a hundred feet, and the best topsoil in the country under housing developments. It is thought of by some as a better way of life.

Chapter 21

Hawaii Calls

Mid August, 1955, landing on the island of Oahu was exhilarating, peering through the window, seeing the reef and ocean, such a contrast of colors that sunglasses were a necessary protection. As beautiful as my first sight of the island was, it missed the grandeur of the Redwoods. Looking to the mountains from the other side of the plane I saw mountains, stark, perpendicular, covered with greenery, mostly shrubs and some trees, rainbows spreading toward the sea. The stewardess opened the cockpit door and the humidity rushed in, engulfing my lungs, the heavy fragrance of plumeria flowers, and I felt squelched. This was not Santa Cruz with cool ocean breezes that cleared sinuses.

I had a feeling that I had made a mistake, but then I decided not to judge first impressions. It would be a big change, but maybe the warm water and consistent surf would make up for the lack of a Redwood forest when I looked shoreward. Two weeks until my car would arrive on the boat passed at a snail's pace. I swam in the Punahou pool, but I had not come to Hawaii for swimming. The principals loaded my schedule so that I had very little free time. Beginning work at 7:45 in the morning and finishing around 6 p.m. I really had only enough time before dark to swim in the school pool. I liked my new job, but felt depressed over the lack of surfing.

One of the faculty men was a beginner surfer and offered to drive me to Waikiki. On Wednesday our teacher meeting finished at 4 P.M.

We shoved the boards in the back of his woodie Ford station wagon and headed to Waikiki. Parking was easy right next to the beach unlike these overly crowded days when you have to feed meters just to surf.

I paddled out to Queen's surf. It was about 3 feet, but well formed. The water felt like the warmth of a lukewarm bath. I felt like I might begin to sweat. I could not believe the difference from Santa Cruz and 50 plus degree water. I did not know whether I like it.

One thing I did like. There were only 4 people surfing at Queen's, unlike the 100s who surf there now. The two local guys were a joy to watch, turning, climbing the face of the wave, and deftly kicking out over the backside of the wave.

My turn! I lined up a right peak, paddled forward, felt the wave surrender its energy. It was like riding the face of a windowpane, the wave so clear, so smooth. The sun set and we caught a wave to the beach, me expecting to shiver as I did in Santa Cruz. On shore it was totally pleasant. I could grow to love this.

Paddling back out, I saw my new friend catch a wave, slowly climb to a standing position, dig a rail and fall off. I retrieved his board and paddled it back out to where he was swimming shoreward.

Surfing Waikiki, I compared it to Cowell's Beach, the same gentle easy swell, fun to ride, but not challenging at four feet. I had to experience Makaha and the North Shore.

My car arrived the second week I was in Honolulu. I picked it up, drove back to Punahou where I had a small Quonset hut on the tropical, lavishly groomed campus, and grabbed my board in the carport. It was early enough in the afternoon to drive to Makaha, about an hour distant.

The drive was a new experience for me. Most homes on or near the beach at Waianae were falling apart and front yards, as a general rule, were littered with old cars, garbage, and children right in the midst of it, playing, laughing, and oblivious to the environment. The closer I got to Makaha, the more laid back the people seemed to be. When I stopped for juice and filled my gas tank, I asked the attendant to check the oil. He was very friendly and cleaned my windshield, something that rarely happened in Santa Cruz.

Handing him money, the attendant smiled and said, "Not too much surf lately. The winter come and, ooh, the surf gets big. I surfed this morning. Pretty good, about three feet. Have fun brah." The friendliness and accepting attitude of me a stranger changed my feelings about going back to Santa Cruz. I immediately liked local people, at least the ones that I had met. The local people showed me a different and more slowed down way of looking at life, much like Cliff and Eddie.

I drove on and the road became more desolate, fewer homes, but the mountains were outstanding, reaching right down to the sea. I felt like I was in Utah when I looked to the mountains and in Mexico ocean side. It impressed me as a desert in the middle of the Pacific Ocean. Makaha was hot, the sun penetrating every nook and cranny. I had to get into the ocean.

There were five people out surfing and the gas station attendant was just about on the money with his size analysis. The water reflected the sky in aquamarine and the clouds in a flat opalescence, ever changing, mostly dominated in azure. Walking to the water, I looked to the horizon. Life, the sea, as far as I could see reflected quietness, solitude, and a world slowed down without the paraphernalia of living in Honolulu.

I rode wave after wave, glassy, the water so clear that I could see the fish swimming on the reef. From the surf, I could look back into the Makaha Valley, eyes ascending the sheer cliffs, and watch the trade winds push puffy, white clouds down into the valley. This was the pure essence of being one with the sea. I knew how the ancient surf kings must have felt. At this particular moment, I was in paradise.

Walking up the beach, my board tucked under my arm, I passed some local people barbecuing on the beach. There were spears stuck into the sand, and facemasks lying on the sand. "Hey brah, you hungry? Here, have this piece of aweoweo. It's one of the best fish on the reef."

Putting my board on my car, I chewed on the fish. It was delicious and just what I needed after so long surfing. I went back to the barbecue fire, sat down, and asked when the big waves came?

"No worry, brah, they come. Ooh, not many ride those big ones, only the experts. You looked good out there. You living out here?"

They kept on pushing food my way. I was filled. A local lady sitting nearby handed me a beer. The sun set in a glorious show of kaleidoscopic, reds, greens, and blues. The local lady sitting next to me told me to cover my eyes and wait till she said to look where the last of the sun was disappearing into the shadowed sea. "Now, haole, look !"

She asked me what I had seen. I said nothing, but that the sun had disappeared. "Whoo, haole, you miss the whole thing, the green flash just as the sun disappears, and then the sky explode with the last light. Next time, maybe."

Settling into teaching, the days passed, and I did not get much time to surf, much less than when I lived in Santa Cruz. However, the surf I did encounter was more exciting. The waves came to the Hawaiian reef without any encumbrance to slow them down like the seven hundred mile relatively shallow areas off the coast of California called the Continental Shelf.

Thus the waves broke harder, stood up more perpendicular, and moved over the reef with nothing to slow their progress, making the California waves seem slower.

My brother, Peter, came to the islands on an extended surf safari. I was sitting in my home correcting papers when the phone rang.

"Fred, I'm renting a house right near Makaha and I surfed fifteen feet point surf today at Makaha. The predictions are that it is going to get bigger tomorrow, and it's supposed to remain glassy. This could be the surf of your lifetime. Meet me at Makaha near dawn. There were only five guys out today."

"I can't, Peter. There's no way that I can swing it."

Calling the other science teacher in the Junior School, I begged him to take my classes. "Put them all in with you; I don't care what you do, but please say, yes! I'll give you fifty dollars."

The amount I offered was a small fortune for then, but I knew that Peter was right. Why had I traveled 2,500 miles? Why had I given up the security of the Boulder Creek job? Why had I left my friends? What about my sweet deal with the swimming lessons at Forest Pool?

I thought all of these questions out in my mind as I drove in breaking dawn to Makaha. When I arrived, the sun had not risen above the Waianae Mountains, but it was a clear sky, almost cool.

Parking on the edge of the sand, I turned off my motor and looked seaward. I saw bodies sitting high on their boards at least three-fourths

159

of a mile outside the regular line-ups. There were some small waves breaking on the inside reef where I had surfed.

Searching the horizon, I saw undulations moving toward the surfers. They rose into huge ground swells spaced evenly apart like they had been engineered that way. The first of these swells passed under the surfers who appeared to rise up to the sky. The second wave I saw two surfers paddling, one picking it up immediately, the second surfer a bit late, but standing up and dropping. He spun out about half way down the wave and his board flew up into the sky, landed in front of the giant wall of whitewater, and bobbed to the beach.

I ran across the beach and retrieved the board, placing it well above where the waves covered the beach. Seeing two surfers tandem on one board, I grabbed mine from the rooftop, and sprinted to the sea. Paddling out through the momentary channel, I realized that I had met these surfers at Waikiki, Buzzy Trent and John McMahon who were both experts. I asked them what had happened as we sat in the channel.

John McMahon said Buzzy had fallen through the air and folded his knee on his board as he landed on the tailblock.

"The board hit him on the head, and he's a bit out of it," said McMahon.

I asked if I could help?

"Nah, we're all right. Get out there and surf. There are some twenty-foot sets. Your brother is already out. At dawn he caught a twenty-foot plus wave and wiped out. Lot of guts that kid."

It seemed I paddled forever, and I could see the point where the few surfers sat, but it didn't seem like I was getting closer. Instead of paddling across, which would have been quicker, I saw a huge wave approaching and paddled straight out to sea. It passed under me, and that moment, I knew that there was no other way to the beach, but to catch a wave. I came closer to the point or it came closer to me. My focus was on getting to where they sat. I thought that maybe they would tell me something to make it all right, but when I arrived, I saw that everyone else seemed focused in their own world. My brother said hello, and then screamed that he had caught the biggest wave he had ever seen and wiped out on it. He did say one unconsoling thing.

"It's supposed to get bigger as the day progresses."

I sat near Peter, but nothing was said. I thought of what period I would be at school, and how easy and far away all of that life seemed. I was out in the middle of the ocean, and I did not know for sure if I could handle this surf or if I wanted to do it. My mind was fixated on survival. Peter caught a wave and disappeared somewhere down the front of the face. The other surfers paddled and huge swells passed under us.

I thought. This is it. This is why I came to the islands, to ride the biggest waves in the islands. This was put up or shut up. The other choice, to lose my nerve, freak out, meant death by drowning.

A wave approached. The other surfers paddled for the horizon. I heard one muttering that it was too big. I stood my ground, judged what to do and when I realized that I could not make it over this giant even if I wanted to, I leaned forward and paddled, looking backward in peripheral vision to judge for the last paddle which would put be careening down the face.

The board held; I stood up and looked down a mountain, seemingly no bottom in sight. Turning very slowly as I dropped down the face, I saw the channel one hundred yards ahead. The slow turn put me too deeply into the wave to make it even near the channel.

Abandoning all thought of surviving the upcoming wipe out, I gained a full angle and catapulted across the smooth face. This was my life in the now, no future, just this beautiful moment, and I saw the wave caving in front of me. I was not going to make it through the bowl of the wave. It had me trapped on all sides, but I was riding this small oasis of unbroken wave where I was still out of the grasp of the tons of soup descending upon me.

The wave closed, its force driving me down into depths where my eardrums felt like they would blow up. It was as close to what I imagined being stuck in a giant Maytag washing machine was during spin cycle. It finally released its grip and moved shoreward to smash my board on the sandy beach or on the lava rocks near the point.

I knew that I was running out of oxygen, that I was at least twenty feet beneath the surface and if I sprinted for the top my air would be used up more quickly, but if I didn't I would surface into the next wave if there was one.

The bubbles that formed the wave of my life dissipated into gin clear ocean, and I surfaced with no other waves descending upon me. I had survived my first huge Makaha wave and the three-fourths of a mile swim to the beach seemed like I was in a sanitarium, taking a warm salt bath.

Body surfing the shorebreak to the beach, I retrieved the board at the point, no dings, and headed to my car. Walking across the beach there were a few tourists. I looked back at the ocean and kept moving, tripped over two people sunning themselves, a man and a woman. I peered from behind my board to Dr. Fox who said very loudly, "Why aren't you in school?"

I saw that it was my boss, that I was undoubtedly going to get fired on the spot, and looked more closely. I had met Mrs. Fox at parties, and this definitely was not Mrs. Fox.

Looking Dr. Fox right in his eyes, I asked, "John, introduce me to your friend."

Excusing myself I walked to my car, fastened the board atop, and Peter and I drove to his house, which was about a mile toward Waianae.

"Thanks, Peter. This was the day of my surfing life. I don't know if I'll have a job tomorrow, but it was worth it. I'll see you this weekend."

Walking back to class the next day, I ran into Dr. Fox who said that he had never seen such big waves. He told me that I had to have a screw loose somewhere to ride such waves, but that was it, never a mention of the fact that I had cut out, done exactly what he was reluctant to hire me for, but did I ask questions? No! The universe was on my side that day.

Summers passed. Each winter a pattern had been established that when Sunset Beach closed out we drove around Kaena Point to the more protected Makaha side. It was most often somewhat smaller than Sunset.

This day Sunset was totally closed out, but glassy. We decided on Makaha, driving by Waimea Bay. I saw that Greg Noll, my friend, had stopped and was checking out the point. Parking on the cliff overlooking Waimea Bay, I asked Greg what he was doing. Makaha would be twenty feet on big sets and glassy smooth.

We had always checked out the Point at Waimea Bay, but it was so far out in the ocean that we saw it as a narrow peak, too close to the rocks inside.

Greg said that he was going to paddle out and check it more closely. He asked us if we would retrieve his board from the rocks if he wiped out. He seemed to shrink in size paddling to the outside. It was a distance we had not calculated correctly.

Greg had pioneered many other areas that had never been surfed, including Molokai, Maui, and Kauai.

A wave approached from around the point, Greg positioned himself, and took off. His board stood absolutely perpendicular, and he dropped straight to the bottom, appearing to stop, and looked up behind himself.

Before the wave engulfed him we realized that this was a bigger wave than we had ever ridden at Makaha. Watching his board bounce in the soup, we fully expected to see it crushed on the rocks near the point, but there was a horrendous riptide inside, and his board drifted into a large channel. Greg swam, head up, and saw his board sitting. Climbing on, he paddled back to catch another wave.

We were stoked, frantically waxing our decks, and standing in the shorebreak waiting for a lull so that we, too, could get out there and surf this new spot. At the size of the Bay, it was not easy to get out and I watched three out of five surfers lose their boards attempting to paddle over the fifteen-foot shorebreak that was breaking one hundred yards offshore. The other two made it beyond and paddled toward the point.

Size and distance are very deceiving on the ocean. I waited what seemed to be a long time, probably four or five sets, and then I saw my chance. All movement except the abatement of the last vestiges of foam were disintegrating when I ran down the beach, jumped on my board, and sprinted to get beyond where that shorebreak loomed. I was running out of breath as the huge shorebreak wave threatened to break on top of me, but I pushed my board over the top and dove deeply. Luck was with me and when I surfaced on the other side of the wave, my board was sitting there.

If not, I would have been washed down to the southern boulders that protruded menacingly. Waimea Bay is a narrow, beautiful, white sandy beach bounded by cliffs and boulders. You don't want to lose your board.

Paddling slowly, conserving energy for when I got to the line up, I watched a surfer drop into a wave, shoot for the shoulder. He made it, but the next rider was Greg and he didn't. His board was swept by the riptide into the channel again. I caught up to Greg's board and paddled it to him by gripping a foot around his skeg.

"Van Dyke, this surf is so bitchin. It's a twenty-foot peak that's so freaking hard to even make the bottom that I've fallen off twice, but that channel saves the board. Bitchin!" he screamed.

The line-up lay one-hundred-and-fifty yards off the point. Greg said that you lined yourself up a bit south of the Catholic Church near the point, and look up the Waimea canyon on shore. Reaching the outside position, I allowed a few waves to pass under me and looked to the canyon. The wave appeared to me to drop off quickly, nothing like the long line almost unmakeable at Makaha.

Moving closer to the shoulder I waited. Those who had caught waves paddled back to try again. I took advantage of no competition for that fortunate moment and lined up on an approaching wave. It didn't threaten me like those huge walls that descended at Makaha.

Paddling hard, and watching the wave form behind me, I took two more strokes than usual, stood up, and looked down from atop, what I thought Mount Everest must appear to be. Held on top for that split second of indecision, I stepped forward on the board and dropped through space, skimming the bottom of the wave, and climbed the perpendicular face, kicked out over the backside, and screamed in release.

We all caught waves on that first day that Waimea was surfed, wiped out, swam to the channel to retrieve boards. As I took-off on my last wave, I caught the nose of my board at the bottom, looking up at what appeared to be a drive in movie screen, experienced for that split second the perfection of that wave. Time stopped as I looked up to the crest throwing out to engulf me. I was safe in that time capsule. I felt like a movie that had been stopped on one frame, accentuating droplets of water in the wave, sun reflected to my eyes, seeing my board dug deeply into the wall of water, and then the frame exploded forward wiping me out, holding me down for what seemed an eternity, searching for my board and not finding it.

I was caught in the rip, moving toward those killer rocks. Greg paddled by me on his way to shore, and yelled, "Swim back out and come in with the soup." I did that, fighting the rip to get back in the soup and a huge set moved toward me, broke, and the soup did wash me into the beach was the biggest surf that we had ever surfed. We did not have the proper boards to ride Waimea successfully.

Our boards were stiff, didn't respond quickly, and the most important problem was the steepness of those waves. Getting into the wave was like taking a one stroke take off on a three foot wave, a negotiable stunt, but try it on a twenty plus wave that stands straight up and the first thing that happens is you find yourself backing off, rationalizing that you were at too critical a part of the wave. Moving into deeper water didn't help. What did you do when standing at the top of the swell if you pushed forward a second too late? The board drops out from under you, board and rider free falling through the concavity formed by the wave jumping too quickly. This was a usual pattern until we streamlined the foam boards and increased their length, improved the scoop and rocker, created a lightning like paddler with a skeg that held in on the steepest waves.

The remainder of that day we drank beer and discussed board shapes, ideal weights, and rails to hold turns. The wipe out showed me that I was not in the kind of swimming and holding my breath condition that was vital to survival.

The next day, I arrived at school early so that I could take a swim work out before school. I set my goal on a mile swim, four times a week with surfing on weekends. Punahou's swim coach, Steve Borowski, former Olympian, helped me by teaching me better form, and introduced me to Interval training, which consisted of setting a distance in which I sprinted, rested ten to fifteen seconds and then was off on another sprint. Quickly, I worked my way up to twenty, one hundred yard sprints which was a little farther than a mile.

Four weeks later I felt stronger than I had ever, and the skin diving I had done during the summer put my lungs and body in such shape that I now could take a wipe out and sit on the bottom for a minute and a half. I was ready.

Punahou School where I taught became an oasis for me. If I didn't surf, the pool was there, the track, libraries, cafeteria, and interesting teacher friends. There was a weight room, gymnastics, handball courts, and a number of tennis courts. I never had to leave school. It was a self-contained campus, but I wanted to surf the biggest waves rideable in the world and did.

Teacher friends told me that there was a new lady who taught in the sixth grade, an English teacher named Joan, who coached synchronized swimming after school. Everyone I met said that she would be perfect for me. I wasn't interested, still recovering from two divorces, and feeling that I had put Carol into perspective, all I wanted to do was work out and surf. I didn't enjoy having two marriages fail, but the truth was that as hard as we tried we were not meant for each other. I had three children and they suffered the marriage break up far more than my second ex-wife. Both marriages I found myself to be incompatible with, even though we sought professional help. I was a surfer striving for big recognition and that did not help to cement both marriages solidly. At the time I was quite immature.

One of the more elderly English teachers who worked with this lady told me just to go over to the pool after three thirty in the afternoon. She told me that Joanie would be there. I couldn't miss her, blonde hair, blue eyes, lithe, supple, and intelligent. It sounded like a set up and I forgot about it.

Some time later I had to go to the locker room to pick up some running shoes. On the way I noticed activity at the swimming pool and walked over to see what was happening. Closer to the pool I heard Debussy's music playing. Entering the pool, I noticed nymphettish forms in various water positions, toes pointed, reached to the sky, the body hidden by three feet of water. My thought was that these young ladies could probably take horrendous wipe outs the way they held their breath.

Turning to leave, my peripheral vision was obstructed in a sun-splashed miasma of reflected rainbows. I focused and this blonde lady surfaced. She stretched, lifted herself demurely from the pool and told a small group of girls that the least water splashed the better. "Now you try it," she motioned. The elderly English teacher had been right; Joanie, was lovely, but so young, couldn't have been more than twenty-two, but I also thought, that's good.

The girls surfaced on the other side of the pool and looked back to Joan. They needed instruction and I saw, which I am sure no one else at the pool witnessed, Joan not walking around the pool to the other side. I saw her walk across the water on bare feet. She didn't sink. I watched her for some time, bending, reaching, demonstrating how to porpoise, raise hips above the surface, hold, and dive, all in tune to the music. Seeing this lady perform was like a major flashback from my acid trip. The girls she worked with seemed to love her. They did whatever she demonstrated.

I knew ! I knew for sure that this was my dream woman, the one I had seen materialize out of the fog on my LSD trip in the Santa Cruz Mountains. It mattered not that she was nineteen years younger than me. I left without introducing myself, walked into a coconut tree, and had a difficult time finding my car keys. I was in love, love at first sight.

After dinner, I called Helen Matthews, the English teacher. "Helen, Helen, why weren't you more forceful? I'm in love and I only know her first name. What's her last name, and you have got to help me by introducing me to her. I always work out in the pool during lunch. Couldn't you talk her into walking over to the pool? You don't have to tell her that I want to meet her. Just come by and get a little sun. She must like sun."

"All right Fred, I'll give it a try. I don't see myself as a Cupid and I don't have arrows, but I'm glad that you think she is beautiful."

"Don't worry about arrows. She pierced my heart on my very first sight. I don't care if I surf. I want to be with her."

Finishing my tenth interval sprint, I hung on the side gasping for air. The apparition I had seen yesterday was walking with Helen to the edge of the pool. She wore a purple mini-skirt which fluttered delicately just below mid-thigh.

Helen yelled at me, "Fred, I want you to meet a friend of mine, that is if you can take yourself out of the pool."

Helen was cynically sarcastic and never missed a chance to jibe me. Climbing out of the pool, I was pumped, my chest heaving, water dripping from me.

Helen grabbed Joan's hand and put it into mine. I nearly fainted, the warmth of her fingers locking in mine, the tender skin, her blue eyes focusing on me.

"Joan Marie Florence, I want you to meet my friend, Fred Van Dyke. He teaches in the eighth grade at Bishop Hall. He's a surfer, but don't hold that against him."

My tongue-tied, my heart beating out of control, I stuttered, "I watched you teach synchronized swimming yesterday. You're great and I could tell that the girls really like you."

"Thank you, that's nice."

My heart palpitating, I said, "Well, I have to shower and get back to class. Good meeting you." I felt like I was standing on my head.

Joan was so beautiful. I felt like a voyeur when I watched her in the mornings, mini-skirted, flowing blonde curls, stride down the path past my classroom.

Maneuvering in the teacher's lunchroom, I managed to end up sitting right across from Joan. She spoke first. "My boyfriend tells me that you are a famous surfer. He hero-worships you and wants me to introduce you to him."

Boyfriend I thought. That's not good. I should have considered that possibility, but in my lopsidedness I overlooked that detour.

"Why don't you come over after school. Michael probably won't get home until after you arrive, but we can listen to music and talk. He usually surfs and hangs out with his friends while I am at school."

What was happening? She had a boyfriend with whom she obviously shared a home. Where do I fit? Was there a place for me? Did she even think of me at all? "Where do you live?" I asked.

She gave me her address and said that she'd be home right after school because she did not have swim practice on this day.

Driving to her home, which was a short distance from school, I blocked out that she had a boyfriend. Knocking on her front door, I heard Joan moving toward the door. She opened it and stood there bikini clad. My groin shifted, but I pulled myself together and entered, sitting across from Joan on a sofa. She came toward me, records in hand, and sat down right next to me. "We can't pick music if you are across the room from me. What do you think of the Grateful Dead.?"

Looking at the cover of the music, I also could not overlook that she leaned toward me, her breasts hanging precariously in balance. A bead or two of perspiration slipped down my forehead.

She noticed and asked. "Is it too hot for you in here. Afternoons are sometimes overwhelming. Can I get you a beer?" She moved toward the kitchen. Soon, beers in hand, Joan handed me a beer and sat next to me. The alcohol struck my brain immediately, the sweat on my forehead evaporating, and me flowing into deep relaxation.

The music was good and we sat. Joan got up and put on, my request, a slow nostalgic song by Karen Carpenter. She touched my hand. "How about dancing with me? I love to dance and Michael could care less."

I held her, enough room between us that you could drive a semi-truck. She said that I was a good dancer and my face heated. The music ended and we returned to the sofa and our beers. "Can I get you another beer?"

"Yes, I think just one more. I'm going to swim later."

"Oh, could I go with you. I love to swim."

We finished the beers, and I said that we could go in my car. She wanted to go down and swim next to the Outrigger Club at Waikiki. There was a small sandy beach and a channel that went out beyond the reefs. We sat in the waning warmth of the sun and talked about working out and school, mostly school.

"The sun is going to disappear soon so let's do it."

I thought, as I stood up, "Yeah, let's do it."

We swam into the setting sun. She was a beautiful swimmer, having trained under the best in the swim field. I had trouble keeping up with her and arrived out at the channel marker winded. She swam toward me, head high, and out of the blue, said, "Why don't you kiss me?"

Bashfully, I turned my cheek, and she grabbed me by the neck and softly kissed me deep into my heart. The water cooled, but not around me. Walking across the beach to the car, my cynicism toward women disappeared into the warm air rising toward Diamond Head. We drove back toward her house, and she broke the silence. "You know; you must have noticed in my behavior that my boyfriend and

I are not doing that well. I don't kiss every good-looking guy with blue eyes like you. I try, but Michael seems more interested in his boyfriends and watching games on television."

We arrived at Joan's house and I noticed a car in the driveway. "Michael is home. Why don't you come in and meet him? I know he wants to meet you, you surf hero," she mockingly mused.

Meeting Michael, I experienced a serious time warp. Through him, I saw that they were both very young, and that I was coming in on some time, space invasion. It did not stop my feelings and when Michael offered me another beer, I politely refused. It was time for me to leave.

Joan and I swam often, down at the beach and in the valley pool below her home perched on the hill. I met her for dinner as often as possible at, what I considered, the more romantic restaurants in Honolulu. Joan loved it and once in a while we ate at a hotel on the beach, and danced after dinner. Our relationship was falling into more and more romancing, the once prominent swim workouts fading into the background.

Big surf moved north with the low-pressure systems and the end of the school year arrived. Joan and I were getting closer, but she still lived with her boyfriend and he was suspecting more than swim workouts.

Joan sent me a note to my classroom requesting that I come up to her room after school. Arriving, I sat on one of the mini-tables in her sixth grade classroom. She sat at her desk correcting papers.

"Michael suspects us. He keeps accusing me of being a Star you know what. I've got to stop seeing you until I get this straightened out. I can't play it both ways."

My heart, my hopes plummeted. Dropped out of the clear blue, I dejectedly drove home, grabbed my surfboard, and went to Waikiki, paddling out the channel we had swum in together, kissed for the first time. I paddled into darkness, coming back to reality when I sensed that I could very well attract a shark in those depths.

I didn't realize how far out I had paddled until I found myself resting about every two hundred yards on the way back to the beach. I went home, drank four beers, and fell into a deep sleep.

I saw Joan Marie at school, but she avoided eye contact, and continued on her task what ever it was. School closed for the summer. I spent most of my time surfing the South side of Oahu, which received a summer swell. Day after day, surf, swim, paddle, run on the beach, home, a few beers, and fall into sleep, interrupted often by horrendous nightmares. My life had fallen, in such a short time, into near complete disrepair. I had to create diversions to keep me motivated to get out of bed in the morning.

One night, in deep sleep, unimpeded by nightmares, I awakened to my phone ringing. Joan was on the other end, sobbing. "Come over, please, right now." I looked at my table clock. It was three in the morning.

"Are you sure you want me to come at this hour?"

Arriving at Joan's door, I knocked. I could see her in silhouette through skimpy curtains. Opening the door, she fell into my arms, covered by a nightgown and a bathrobe.

"Michael had told me that he was taking me to California with him, and three days ago I found this note when I returned home from shopping. "Sorry, Joan, but I don't have time to explain. I'm going to California with my friends, see you in a couple of weeks. I'll call from the airport when I get back." That was it. He hasn't phoned. I didn't think that it was real, but I know now that it is."

"Why didn't you call me sooner?"

"I didn't want to bother you and I didn't send you away with kisses."

I told her that it was all right, that I cared for her a lot.

Joan held me close and whispered, "Would you stay with me for a couple of days? This is not the safest neighborhood."

I believed in prayer. I believed in God again. "Of course, I'll stay," attempting futilely to hide my elation. We sat and talked until near dawn. She said that she'd meet me in the bedroom, and I climbed into her bed, pulled the sheet over me.

Before entering the room she switched off the lights and cuddled against me. I felt her firm body resting against mine, and she was stark naked. I kissed her and moved my hands all over her body, searching and finding deep warmth. We made love past dawn and fell into sleep, folded in each other's arms.

171

The Hawaiian sun forced us into wakefulness and we ate breakfast in the kitchen, which remained cool. Joan suggested a hike up into the forest. Walking at a snail's pace, we kissed and kissed.

Returning down the trail, I told her that I was going to the mainland soon to pick up a new car in Oregon where there was no sales tax. "Would you consider going with me? We could camp from Oregon to California."

She said that she couldn't because Michael would probably be home before we left.

I told her that the car was ready and waiting. I just hadn't thought about going yet. We could leave as soon as I made reservations.

"All right. I need to have my head examined. You're nineteen years older than me. It's crazy, but those blue eyes. Yes, I'll go."

"Whoopee," I screamed and looked in the yellow pages for travel agents. Calling one, I made a reservation for the next Friday. Joan wanted to lie down after our strenuous walk, and I thought it a great idea. She awakened in me energy I thought had begun to wane.

I kissed her goodbye as I had to go over to my place and pack. I was gone about three hours and missed being with her, returned with two bags, and a fly rod. I was ready.

Chapter 22

Travels With Joan

The airport was hot and our plane delayed for an hour. Checking in our bags, we walked and sat by a pond with carp swimming. In this quiet oasis, except for the occasional jet revving its engines, we found a pleasurable interlude. I looked into Joan's eyes and saw that she was on some distant planet. I wasn't far behind, and we gathered the momentum to move to our departure gate.

Fastening seat belts we felt the surging power of jet engines as we moved to the take off point. Gunning for take-off, the plane moved at breakneck speed, and Joanie reached for my hand and held tightly while we left the ground. I had never had a woman cling to me as she did. I loved it.

We were struggling against strong head winds, and it was early the next morning that we arrived in Portland, Oregon. Unlike my arrival in Hawaii, when the door was opened, the pungency of pine trees, and Douglas fir filled my nostrils, and there was no humidity to suck my energy. We walked hand in hand to the baggage counter.

Summoning a cab, we went to the downtown Ford agency and I showed my receipt for pick up. The manager was overly solicitous and assured that all had been checked carefully as we climbed into the Pinto. In the garage I reversed slowly to turn and head out the front door, stepped on the brake and nothing happened. I slowly glided into the back wall, Joan asking what was wrong?

"The car, the new car, doesn't have any brakes."

The manager and a mechanic rushed to us. "What happened? Did you misjudge?"

"Yes, in buying a Ford. There aren't any brakes. Explain that in a new car?"

"Don't worry, sir. We'll have it all ready in two hours. Can we buy you lunch?"

We ate lunch and wandered down the street to a bridge where it crossed a river. Climbing down near the stream, we sat down. The sound of cars passing over the bridge disappeared, the river riding smoothly over rocks and submerged logs, like there was no beginning or end. It was a wonderful place and we both fell asleep until coolness, the sun disappearing behind a giant Douglas fir that hadn't been caught by the logger's saw, blotted out the remaining warmth.

The car finished, we drove out of the agency, checking the brakes carefully. Some distance down the road, I noticed a sign that said Illinois River next right.

I turned and told Joan that we better look for a place to camp. Passing through a tiny town we drove along and picked up a small creek on our right. There were blackberries growing down to the water's edge. The road narrowed to a barely passable two lanes. There were bumps, curves, and tiny bridges that criss-crossed the creek. The sun was slowly dropping behind the coastal mountains.

Coming around a curve in the road, I saw a sign that read, "One mile, Blackberry Camp."

We found a campsite right above the river, a lovely place with a barbecue pit and grill, a picnic table, and green grass interspersed with blackberry bushes. Unloading the camping equipment, I told Joan that I was going to look for firewood. There was very little wood near our campsite so I wandered building pile after pile to pick up on the way back. I checked out the stream and saw six to seven inch rainbows finning in the currents.

Gathering my piles of wood on the way back to camp, I smelled a fire. There were no other people camping. Coming out of the brush my eyes did not believe what they saw. There was a fire in the barbecue pit; Joanie had collected blackberries, which lay on a paper plate, and flowers, freshly picked, adorned the camp table. The crowning point came when I noticed on the other side of the car was a blue tent I had never seen. It was Joan's Girl Scout tent, a two-person abode.

Joan had gone back to that small town while I hunted wood. She looked over to me. "Fred, would you please go into the ice chest and open that bottle of Chardonnay? Thanks."

I poured drinks and we sat near the fire while salmon roasted in tinfoil. Two glasses of wine later, and Joan got up, walked to the barbecue, and picked up the tinfoil, which was stained with charcoal marks. She brought it to the table with two paper plates and two forks. "Fred, please bring the bottle of wine. I'm ready for a refill."

Returning to the table I saw two neatly placed, side-by-side, filets of salmon, green peas, and a watercress salad picked from the stream. "I am flabbergasted. What next?"

"Wait until after dinner and I'll show you what is next."

By the time we climbed into the tent the air temperature had dropped to near freezing. However, the tent was warm and cozy, and lying next to Joan, both of us naked, conserved all the heat in our bodies. We slept gloriously, wrapped in each other's arms.

The next morning we waited until sun touched our camp before venturing out, and ate berries with health bars. Breaking camp, we moved westward, lost the paved road, went over a mountain range and dropped into a valley with the Illinois River running through it. We arrived early in the afternoon, the sun burning hot, and the terrain extremely rugged and primitive.

The Ford held up well even though there were some bogs and deep chuckholes. We found a camp near the river and put bathing suits on to swim.

The sand warm, we lay in it and covered our bodies. It was sensuously delightful. We saw a couple of fishermen up stream a goodly distance.

Joan Marie looked at me and I knew what she was thinking. I followed her into the icy river, probably twenty-five degrees colder than Hawaiian water, but so refreshing. We swam, dove off rocks, did synchronized swimming stunts, me a sad second to Joan. It took me back to Boulder Creek that winter a long time ago when my brothers and sister sneaked down to the creek, swam and jumped off the cliff. I wanted to share swimming at the Junction with Joan.

We were in and out of the water until the fishermen approached. It was time to gather wood, put the tent up, and get ready for ice-cold cocktails, followed by dinner.

We followed what little there was of a road and it finally became paved. I noticed ocean smell and felt excited, but the closer we got the deeper the fog enveloped. Parking the car above the ocean, we ran to the beach, shoeless. It was a wonderful beach filled with white sand, no people, and driftwood strewn everywhere. Finding a sand dune pit we lay down and the wind moved past us carrying huge wafts of fog. Cuddling beneath the sand canopy, it almost seemed warm, at least in comparison to standing in the wind unprotected.

We walked, hand in hand, and made wishes, secret wishes, mine that this moment would never end. Running out of beach, we headed back to the car and searched for a place to eat breakfast. We stopped at this restaurant overlooking the sea. It was a fisherman's hang out, but I noticed that there was some surf breaking on a distant point. It looked good, but my interest lay in Joanie.

Body surfing occupied a split second thought which disappeared when Joan grabbed my hand under the table. We drove the coast and the fog lifted, leaving a clear, blue sky and a piercingly cold west wind.

By the time we reached the California border, bathed in Redwood trees and ferns, it was beer o'clock and we both had a deep nostalgia and love for California. We stopped just inside the boundary from Oregon.

Sun shone through the perpendicular Redwoods, casting majestic shadows into the forest. We toasted our having been fortunate to be born in this state. Joan found a huge Redwood tree that had fallen, we thought, during a horrendous windstorm. Standing together, the trees were protective for each other, but when the timber cutters came, they left little or no protection from the fierce winds of winter. Rain softened the soil and the Redwood trees fell.

Was this another token gesture from the lumber people who must have known that by leaving a few giant trees, that the wind would blow them over eventually, and then they would have a good excuse to go in and haul out the trees?

For some reason they passed up this giant that had crushed everything in its path falling to the ground. Golden rays of sunlight filtered through leaf mosaic patterns, which mottled the forest's musky scented floor. New growth in green fern fronds reached toward the light, these delicate hints of new life to fill the gap laid down from the gigantic tree, formed tiny dew drops which slowly dropped to earth. The sweet scent of new growth permeated all. On closer examination of the fallen trunk, there was further evidence of sprouts growing from the crippled Redwood tree. Redwoods do this to continue propagation of the specie. A single fallen tree will fill out the space lost with these sprouting trees, sustaining itself off the father or mother tree, and, in a short time baby Redwoods will issue forth. The lumber companies do not keep up with the regenerative powers, and I was told by an executive in the lumber company that they often replant clear cuts with Douglas fir, which matures more quickly.

Its diameter was so round and large that we could not ascend it until we climbed the roots at one end. Running the length of the tree trunk many times, we laid back winded, and melted into the forest. Silence predominated, except for the intervals of lumber trucks, which noisily sped through the forest to the mills, spewing out their fetid and stinking diesel exhaust. I wondered if most human beings were born with some penchant for destroying beauty or could it be an aberrant gene?

The lumber trucks broke the magic spell. Joan stood up and looked down to the end of this fallen giant. She ran its length again and stopped. I caught up to her and she fell into my arms, crying for this wonderful tree, which had been growing before Christ, had been born. Silence descended, so silent that I watched and heard the movements of a yellow slug on the bottom side of the tree, felt the wonder of this forest before it was ravaged in man's insatiable need to destroy.

Joan and I hugged in silence, in awe, in respect and love for this moment that was given to us. The sacredness of this cathedral of Redwoods touched our souls, our essence of being. Another diesel truck, loaded with bleeding Redwood trees, sped by and broke our reverie. We moved back to the car, taking a few photos on the way.

We drove in silence for a long time, partly because of the Redwood wonderland, that is, what was left of it, and in our common bond with California.

We both had noticed the immediate changes upon crossing the border. Besides the magnificent Redwoods, which are pretty much limited to California, there was a definite change in the vibration level. Oregon, although excitingly hypnotic, had a rawness, a fierceness that did not exist as we entered our home state. We both realized that it was like a line had been drawn on the border, a line of clement weather, a drop in wind, the sun more penetrating, a dream land in which stark beauty and wonder existed.

Stopping at Jedediah Smith Redwood State Park, I cracked two beers, and we chose to sit under the highest Redwood tree to have our first picnic in California. The fog had long ago cleared, and the sun penetrated our sweaters, which we discarded. We had descended into the land of milk and honey; the harshness up the coast in Oregon disappeared.

Capturing the moment, I lay back against the tree, looking ever upward until the sky was blotted out by Joan bending over and kissing my lips. There was nothing, but us, and we were both snugly and securely tucked back into California, and we took full advantage of the moment.

We found a camp on the Smith River and prepared for evening. Unlike the weekend upcoming, there were very few people in the campground. We spent the last moments of daylight building a fire, and setting up our tent. Squirrels descended from high up in the trees, begging for food. They were cute, but all they wanted were the sunflower seeds we scattered. As the light dimmed, deer came out from hiding, and walked right through our camp. Darkness descending, we heard coyotes in the forest.

This was more than just picking up a car, more than traveling with Joan, more than camping, more than the love I felt toward Joan. I realized, even though much had changed, fewer Redwood trees, more drought conditions in streams, dangerously threatened anadromous fish populations, and a growth boom that was putting more pressure than the environment could handle, I cherished being back in California. It was my birthplace where life had begun for me.

Early next morning we arose just after dawn, took a walk along the Smith River, and I pointed out trout finning beneath the surface. There was a huge splash and I looked to see water settling back. The next time that took place, it was right in front of me, and I watched in awe, a huge steelhead trout, its pink stripe catching light. It careened up stream, doing a series of flashing jumps into the air.

I told Joan that spawning fish come in fresh from the sea with sea lice clinging to their gill covers. They jump to clear the lice. The steelhead usually does not die at the end of spawning. It sometimes swims back to the sea spent, or it will stay in the river until the next heavy rains. I told her of the steelhead I had caught during the summer when trout fishing. Of course, she asked the difference between trout and steelhead and I answered that they are rainbow trout that go to sea to grow and mature, then return to spawn. Some argue that they are evolved into a separate species.

Whenever I landed a big steelhead, I saw it as a huge and beautiful rainbow trout. They almost always had pink meat like a salmon, mostly because they fed on crustaceans. What breaks my heart is that at the time I was born and until after the Second World War, coastal streams and rivers had large runs of steelhead. Water pollution, over fishing by both commercial and sport fishers, use of rivers as agricultural water sources, and dumping waste, cattle stomping the spawning grounds, has led to the near demise of native, wild steelhead. I felt that Joan had heard enough of my tirade, at least for now.

We moved down the coast, watching surf break upon beaches without a soul present, except for our peering as we drove. At that time, there were so many desolate beaches filled with white sand, kelp, and rotting timber that had washed down the streams into the sea. I didn't know about the dioxins and other poisons dumped in the sea by the lumber industry, and assumed that this northern coast was semi-pristine. Sometime later, when surfing became popular up there, the surfers experienced unusual diseases and conditions, chief amongst them dioxin poisoning. The abundance existed, but one took one's health in one's hands by entering the ocean.

179

Even in the mid-seventies nearly all the streams had dangerous bacteria present, most deleterious, Giardia, an organism that brings on flu like conditions, nausea, and diarrhea. If not treated, one can lose enough weight to put themselves in serious jeopardy.

I turned left onto Highway 299, and moved inland, the temperature rising rapidly, passed a little farm by the road and got out to admire the vegetable garden.

Walking across the lawn goats approached us, one a baby. They were quite friendly and we fed them leaves from foliage. The goats seemed to enjoy cavorting around us for they would charge, jump into the air just as it appeared they would ram you, and then nuzzle up, wanting more leaves to eat.

Early afternoon we passed Trinity Lake, decided to swim, and turned around, finding a parking spot in the shade. It was hot here, a lovely lake, cool enough to support large populations of fish, mainly trout, bass, catfish, Kokanee salmon, and other species. We swam a long distance to the eastern shore, climbed out and lay in the sun.

The beauty of living, for me, is to run, swim, surf, fish, ski, eat nutritious food and move like an animal oblivious to a beginning or ending of life. A man once told me that was a good way to live. You didn't collect moss, and if you forgot about age, who knows how long one could live in optimum health. You rust faster than you wear out.

Joan Marie and I experienced abundances of love, exercise, fresh air, warm sunshine, and our bodies and minds reflected it.

When you feel that good, when you are so high, when the endorphins kick in, you have to watch who you smile in front of, for a lot of people don't like to see happy and smiling faces. Joan and I realized that together and guarded our actions when deep in a city or with hostile appearing people.

However, this day was glorious and we basked in it, far away from the nearest people.

I lay next to Joanie soaking up sunshine when a single cloud threw its shadow over us, dropping the temperature by degrees. Another cloud climbed high into the sky and we swam back to our car, me hoping that the lightning would hold off until we got out of the lake.

Drying off, we both felt a chill in the air, and drove toward Lake Shasta. In the distance we saw lightning streak the sky, followed by huge claps of thunder. This would not be a good night to camp out. Stopping at a roadside cafe, we walked in, sat down, and pondered what to do tonight. It started raining. I saw two highway patrolmen sitting at the counter drinking coffee. Walking up to them, I asked if they knew of any place isolated from the main road. They both appeared puzzled, but then one said to his fellow patrolman, "How about that camp at Shingletown?"

They told us that this was what we were looking for and that it was reasonable. Thanking them we followed their directions and came to this camp sign nailed to a tree, "Shingletown 2 miles right."

It was an unpaved road and had filled with some puddles. The lady in the office was very friendly and asked me about my wife and whether she was interested in antiques, postcards, quilts?

The office was large and filled with unique paraphernalia that you would not find in a regular store. Upon entering, a multitude of fragrances charmed your senses, peppermint, chocolate, lavender, and coffee. Bunches of dried flowers and herbs suspended by brightly colored ribbons hung from the rafters. Large glass canisters held all kinds of candies, lemon drops, licorice, mints, butterscotch, caramels, and assorted jellybeans. Flowered tins waited to be filled with aromatic teas. Baskets of pastel colored soaps of varying shapes and scents rested on worn wooden shelves. The light, mellow, was illuminated by multi-colored stained glass lampshades. Old black and white photos, partially bleached brown from age hung amongst framed advertisements for Burpee seeds, Gold Medal flour, Morton salt, and colorful packing crate labels from California fruits and vegetables. This kaleidoscope brought smiles and filled our hearts with joy.

The lady told us that she had owned the place for many years, but that her husband was getting too old to do all the work necessary.

"We hired this young fellow and he does the hard work now. I'm going to give you a log cabin right on the stream. It's private through our part, and if your husband fishes, he can keep five trout. There's also a lake at one side of the stream and the fishing is good there, but we plant them. The native stream trout are the best."

For fun and in fantasy, I opened the door to our cabin, picked up Joan, and carried her over the threshold. It was a token gesture hint that I wanted to be with her. She caught it and handled my pushiness with grace.

We brought necessary items from the car, but the place was fully furnished with all the necessities. The fireplace had a large buck's head mounted above it, the log walls neatly chinked.

The storm cleared fast and behind it high pressure filled, allowing the late afternoon sun to enter our room. Joan said, "Why don't you use that pole you've been carrying? I'll watch and see how it's done."

"Not a pole, a rod. I was hoping that you'd want to go to the stream with me."

Setting my rod up, I showed her each step, and then stepped into the stream. I didn't have wading boots, but I was excited, having not fly-fished for a year. She stood in the background, framed by Douglas fir trees and lush greenery.

My first cast was pure luck. I was trying too hard to impress Joan, but the fly landed right under an overhanging bank, and caught a perfect drift. The trout hit so hard that it flew into the sky.

I played it carefully, as it jumped two times, and then slowed enough so that I could lead it to my net. Lifting the net skyward, I grabbed the fish and held it up for Joan to see. She had her camera ready and I cast again, this time landing a trout about four inches bigger and fatter than the last.

I breathed hard in deep excitement, pulled out my knife, bent, and cleaned the two fish. They were pink meated and firm. Joan took a picture and said, "I didn't know that you had ballet dancing skill."

"What do you mean?"

"You move like a dancer when you cast. It's so graceful to watch."

I tried nonchalance, but failed, my ego threatening to burst.

Joan cooked the fish to perfection, placed a salad next to them, and waited to toast a hearty merlot breathing next to our plates, the table all neatly laid out with flowers, candles, and, in the background a local music station adding the crowning touch.

Igniting the wood in the fireplace, we sat in front of the hearth and sipped brandy. The fire died to embers and we took the mattress off the bed and set it in front of the stone hearth, lay together, and fell asleep to the fire designs on the edge of the chimney.

It was so cold when we awakened that we didn't move out of the warmth of woolen blankets until the sun shone in through the windows. We thanked the lady on our way out, and said that we would be back when time permitted.

"We'll be here;" she handed me a business card.

We decided on the coast again and drove over Highway 36. The road climbed and dropped, curved around itself, some places so narrow that I would stop to allow a car to pass from the opposite direction. A lumber truck called upon all of my driving skills to negotiate, especially on a corner. A sign said to honk your horn on curves. It reminded me of the old dirt road that led into the Indian Creek Lumber Mill outside of Boonville.

It was an exciting road whereby you never knew what to expect at a turn, a huge grove of trees, meandering stream steeped in watercress, clear cut forest, clean and well manicured log houses tucked in the forest.

This road was another sequence in time, lost away from the hustle and bustle of freeways, cement culverts to move what was a meandering stream to the sea into only a flood control project. I lost frowns and squinting on this road.

Approaching the coast and Highway 101, the scenery changed, far more clear cut forests, bulldozers resting in areas next to the road where the underbrush had been removed. I opened windows for the air had warmed considerably, an unwanted change from the road we had traversed.

Coming upon 101, traffic streamed by. I had to wait minutes for a clearing to turn left. Once upon the highway it was easy to see what public relation ploy the lumber companies used. For miles Redwoods lined the highway. Joan and I stopped a few times to view and walk beyond the noise created on the highway. It was shocking to realize that these buffer zones of trees only extended a couple of hundred feet beyond the highway. Behind this zone lay tons of tangled slash, debris left by the lumber companies after abandoning the land to move to another virgin Redwood forest.

The Avenue of the Giants, a grove of virgin Redwoods, renewed my enthusiasm. We stopped and gazed upward, so perpendicular these trees that our necks ached. We didn't escape the diesel fumes from the lumber trucks passing or the noise of their motors invading this cathedral of sacred trees that have, in some cases, grown for over two thousand years.

The Catholic Church destroyed my illusions about religion. I had been a choir and altar boy. I watched priests chug a lug wine in the vestry. When I was ten years old, the church tried to teach me that my cat had no soul, and that it was a mortal sin to love Rasputen, my faith weakened. The Redwood forest and the surf stood as my belief in God.

I did understand the need to cut trees for building, but I also could experience the wanton greed that these lumber tycoons displayed. They will not be satisfied until they cut down the very last virgin Redwood. Their pompous and contrived rhetoric only masks their deliberate intentions. The lumber companies will replant forests only if there is a sufficient profit margin that will make them richer. Otherwise, they abandon the area and the people dependent upon their living on lumber harvest.

I asked Joan if we could head over to the coast, a few miles west, and try to get away from this tourist trap. I needed to find solace, space, and I wanted to camp on a remote beach tonight. Joan thought it a good idea.

The road, paved in a few parts, meandered through deep and almost impenetrable Redwood trees. They were second growth and the healthiest trees I had ever seen. I thought that they must have been cut before the beginning of the century. This was state land and safe from the axe, at least for the time being. Their crisp green leaves and auburn red trunks covered with some shaggy, lime, green moss appeared as an ancient forest in miniature.

I felt the wonder of those trees having been left alone, and the immediate recovery. It acted as food for my soul when we arrived at the coastline, covered with fog, and the trees followed us right to the sandy beach.

The beach seemed to expand indefinitely, but we could not tell for the fog cut off all, but a couple hundred yards of visibility. The fog held the wind to a gentle lull, causing the beach to seem fairly warm. This was the beach I wanted.

Unloading, we set up the tent, and dug a small pit to build our fire. It was to be primitive, the barest of necessities, food and drink. However, we needed a fairly large supply of wood to keep a fire burning until we crawled into the tent. Removing our shoes, we ran up the beach, quickly warming with a slight perspiration issuing forth. We moved about a half-mile and I signaled that we would collect our wood on the way back to camp, that is after Joan reached into my jacket and asked for a hug. Silence, except for the washing back and forth of surf gently, filled our world. Driftwood lay in abundance and we piled it around the fire circle.

Joan wanted to ready the fire pit and I broke larger pieces of wood into pit size. We had no table to sit at and eat, but Joan settled that problem by asking me to push two logs together, and then she laid flat pieces of driftwood across the logs, spreading a red and white-checkered tablecloth. I hung a Coleman lantern from a nearby shrub, and we were ready.

There was probably a half an hour of daylight left. I walked to the car a few yards distant, and returned with a bottle of California Cabernet. Digging Joan's Swiss army knife's corkscrew into the cork, I pulled the plug, which popped out.

Igniting the fire, Joan filled the plastic wine glasses, and we toasted finding such a perfectly isolated beach. Darkness descended and I filled the glasses. Joan lifted the top of the ice chest, reached in, and brought out two tightly sealed tinfoil packages. She told me that it would be a one-foil dinner for each of us, no dishes, and one plastic fork for eating.

I asked, "What's for dinner?"

She said to wait and see. "Drink your wine."

Ten minutes later, to avoid getting burned, she used a washcloth to remove the tinfoil from the dying embers. Joan watched me unfold the tinfoil, fork into the middle, and raise the deliciously aromatic morsel to my mouth. It was gourmet on the beach, garlic, vegetables mixed, and a potato covered in melting butter. I didn't know what the solid particles were, and asked Joan what was the food that looked like meat?

"Just enjoy it, and would you pour me another glass of wine?"

Finishing that wonderful dinner, I lay back and looked up into the sky. A few stars broke through the fog and I felt the air-cooling. Standing up, I picked an armload of wood and placed it on the embers. In a few minutes a fire roared and threw off concerted heat. This was the life, and how did I luck out to travel with Joan?

Fog moved in thickly during the night and we awakened to a chill morning with condensation soaking everything. Hanging the clothes, tent, and sleeping bags to dry, we ate breakfast which was a mixture of sunflower seeds, almonds, raisins, swallowed with some orange juice and vitamins. Joan enjoyed sipping a cup of good coffee in the morning mist.

The clothes semi-dried, we packed the car and headed inland, retracing along the unpaved and unnumbered highway to Highway 101, fog persisting back into the Redwoods. Driving, we wanted to get into warm weather. I knew that the beach was still there and when I came back to visit again it would probably be much the same.

Passing Albion, another childhood memory flashed. I recalled the time when Jake Pesula, the man who owned the lumber mill on Indian Creek outside of Boonville, had invited us to visit his folks ranch up Albion Creek. My father drove our 1934 Chevrolet over the rough and pothole filled road to the Pesula's. The ranch was huge, and they owned most of the land for about two miles up the creek. We unlocked and relocked gate after gate and finally arrived at their home, a dog sprinting and barking to meet us. He was friendly and we petted him as if he were our own. Sheep wandered everywhere, and there were a few cattle.

One of Jake's younger sisters, a little older than me, offered to show us the land, the barns, and the creek. My mother told her to stay away from the creek. Jake said, "Don't worry about the creek. We'll all go fishing when the sun begins to settle."

The girl, Anna, took us down the cow path and we stepped in cow dung. She told us that sometimes they used it for a fire. "In fact, I think we should all gather a few dry cow pies. It'll make my mom and Jake happy."

We were barefooted and I saw the first cow pie that looked dried out, ran to it, and scooped the pie up with both hands, not knowing that you were supposed to first of all test its hardness with your feet. If it held then it became fuel. The soft inside layer oozed through my fingers.

"Ee yuh, you stink," chided my brother and sister. "Don't come near me," giggled Gretchen.

Gene stepped backwards and a sloppy one oozed between his toes. Quickly, we had enough of collecting organic fuel. We raced back to the farmhouse and were confronted by a herd of cows using the road to get home for water. We were terrified as the cows moved forward mooing and moaning. Anna walked up to the lead cow, grabbed a Redwood plank, and whacked the cow across the fanny. It took off, followed by the entire herd.

Jake came into the living room where we were sitting drinking hot chocolate. My father and Jake held quart size jars of beer. "Time to get groceries for dinner. We're all going fishing."

Jumping in the back of an old pickup truck we bounced down the rickety trail to the creek. The water was gin clear, and reflected the waning sun's rays.

Jake led us on a muddy trail to the river. "Fred, you stay here with your mother, brother and sister. Doc, Anna, and I are going to go up stream. We'll be back in about an hour. I'll set up three drop-lines for you and leave a can of worms. Be quiet and watch your line for strikes."

I didn't want to run into those cows again and settled into fishing. I saw trout moving in the quiet pool, but nothing touched my bait. Gene came and sat next to me. "Do you think they'll remember us? Daddy and Jake were drinking a lot."

Feeling a tug on the end of my drop line, I pulled back. The water exploded, a rainbow trout jumped, its side turned pink to the last of sunshine, flopped into the water, and headed upstream. I ran after it, and the fish jumped again, my mother entering the place where the trout now rubbed its mouth against a snag.

My mother ran to my side and helped me horse the huge trout onto the bank. She extracted the hook and hung it on a branch, the trout still shivering and attempting escape. My mother said, "You're quite the fisherman. We should head back to the house because it's going to get dark in a few minutes." I carried my fish proudly. She said that it was almost two feet long.

Wild rainbow trout swam freely in all the streams from San Diego to Alaska in the nineteen thirties. People lived off what they caught and hunted. It was a time of great abundance. The gold fever had leveled off and people turned their interests to making a living in the growing cities. Wildlife was left pretty much alone, and the small amount of hunting and fishing offered little threat as in today entire species are threatened with extinction. Although we all had tightened belts, feelings were good and a handshake had meaning as strong as a lawyer's contract.

Walking up to the house, I noticed that none of the men were back. I placed my trout in the sink and part of the tail hung over the top. Jake's mother made much ado about my fish.

The men arrived, carrying sacks of fish. Anna had stayed down by the creek petting a baby fawn. Looking into the sink, I saw trout upon trout, fat, but none as big or beautifully rainbow striped as mine. Jake and his mother cleaned the fish and Jake's mother lifted a huge frying pan off the wall. The fragrance of freshly caught trout simmering in the pan wafted over the kitchen and into the dining room.

Soon the table was set and we ate, had strawberries and freshly churned whipped cream for dessert, and settled in front of the fire. I noticed that it had been dark for a long time and Anna had not come home. I asked Jake's mother where she was and was told that sometimes Anna would not come home until the wee hours of the morning. She loved to be with the wild animals that lived around the ranch.

Her mother told me that when she was younger she would disappear from the fire and one night they watched from the front porch as Anna approached. It was a full moon night and her mother saw that she was being followed.

Coming out of the bushes behind Anna, a huge mountain lion followed, moved right up to her, and they sat down together. Anna petted it and her mother yelled. "Come quickly, the lion will kill you." Anna stood up, petted and hugged the lion one more time. The lion disappeared into the brush. The entire family did not understand Anna in her camaraderie and love for all of the animals. Apparently the animals trusted her for she wandered freely over the land.

Returning from my memories, I told Joan that I wanted to show her a fairy tale forest where I had spent my tenth summer, slept outside most of the time under a star filled sky, and listened to the animals, mountain lion, coyote, some unidentifiable. I wanted to return to the virgin Redwood forest that Jake had allowed us to stay for a summer, on a platform with two tents, with our cat Rasputen, the place where I had learned to swim, and catch trout on bent pins with worms for bait.

Passing through the south edge of Albion, I saw that it had not changed greatly, still maintained the fishing village environment, but was overrun with tourists. I asked Joan to see on the map if Highway 128 went all the way to Boonville? I knew that once in Boonville I could find the old lumber road that moved up past the one room schoolhouse.

Boonville was hot, not a wisp of a cloud showed. Entering the road to Indian Creek Lumber Mill, I recognized the landmarks. The old school house still stood, but was somewhat dilapidated. I checked the speedometer to register the beginning mileage for the nine mile trek.

We ascended into oak trees, and then down into a valley where a stream meandered. The road went right down to the creek and a load of gravel had been dumped in it and raked smooth. The water still threatened to squelch the motor, but didn't.

"Whoopee, the first obstacle overcome."

Across the creek, the road curved upwards. We climbed and I remembered how you had to hug the outside of curves so that if a lumber truck came around the corner they had the safer inside. I remember that my mother hated driving over this road. The horn was honked as you approached a curve, although I doubt if the driver could hear over the roar of the engine.

Leveling off on the ridge you could see the coast enclosed in fog, and then we descended into a deep and wide valley, the road curved more so. A mile into the ascent I had expected to enter the magnificent virgin forest I remembered. Two miles into the ascent and a few oak trees stood appearing in disarray. We touched the bottom of the road, dust spewing behind and I looked for the lush valley of childhood.

I figured that there must be another ridge to climb and then we would drop into the fairyland of giant Redwood trees. There wasn't and I knew that we had arrived at the Redwood bridge where we camped that summer in 1939, nine miles right on the nose.

I felt cold chills up my spine, and my hands perspired. I stopped the car, walked down to where the old Redwood log lay and wondered if that rattlesnake den existed. I was so taken aback that it took me some time to realize that the creek had dried up, that just about every Redwood tree had been cut down, and dust hung on the limbs and leaves of the few trees that had not been taken. They certainly were not the giants I had run under, explored, caught trout, and jumped from that bridge into a roaring creek. It was all gone. I had never really believed in sin, but looked at Joan who had tears streaming down her face. "This is a sin," I shouted. "Let's get out of here, I never should have come back."

Some time later we stopped at a little tomato farm on the Eel River. The old man who came out to meet us asked where we were going. "San Francisco," I answered.

"How about delivering a couple of boxes of tomatoes to my son who lives a few miles south on 101?"

Joan answered, "Sure we'd be happy to help."

The man told us that his wife had died recently, and that he had bypass surgery last year. "Feel a lot stronger. No one ever told me that smoking caused heart disease, but I quit. I'll load the tomatoes in your car and you can take as many as you want. You won't find tomatoes like this in the big city. I sell to local people, restaurants. Go ahead pick one and taste it."

Before departing, we each ate at least three of these huge ripened on the vine tomatoes. It took me back to the produce men who, with horse and buggy, sold fresh vegetables daily in San Francisco. We dropped the tomatoes off with the man's son. " Your Dad, he's sure a sweet man," Joan smiled.

"Yeah, he's quite a character. People like him around here. Thanks for being honest."

Crossing the Golden Gate Bridge, I looked oceanward, the orange sun setting in the sea as lingering clouds burst into hot pinks and mauve. We drove across town on 19th Avenue, and turned onto Lunado Way where Joan had spent much of her childhood. Joan teared again, and I came close. San Francisco is a special place filled with so many memories. You go up and down on the hills, descend into valleys, my emotions gravitate as the hills and valleys, and whenever I visit, I always say to myself that I could live here happily. Leaving Hawaii never affects me in the same way, although the aloha spirit is special, too.

Chapter 23

San Francisco
Open Your Golden Gate

Having never met Joan's parents, I felt anxious, but it is compounded when driven home to me that there is such a large gap in age between Joan and me, and such a short gap between her parents and me.

However, that is my paranoia for Joan has told them that I am a colleague from school and that we work closely together on our school curriculum, and are just good friends.

Paul and Bobbie are gracious when we meet, and Joan's mother apologizes because I will have to sleep on the living room couch. I struggle through the first night but things loosen up after we all take an early morning walk on Ocean beach. By the way Joan's mother looked at me when I walked next to Joan, I knew that she felt that our friendship was more than what Joan had shared. Should I disguise my feelings?

San Francisco gives Joanie and me the gift of a fog, wind free day. It is glorious in the City by the Bay if you catch one of these days. They occur most in September and October, the Indian summer. It is so warm that I suggest we take a ride down to Pedro Point, about fifteen minutes south of San Francisco.

I hadn't been to Pedro Point in many years. Driving over the hill, we looked down at the beach, a half moon shaped white, sandy beach. It was far from crowded, but there were a lot more people than when I learned to surf there. A stop signal at the area where the treacherous

Wander Inn surf sandbar was gave me a chance to look at the valley. It hadn't changed that much if you blotted out the housing development that extended deeply to the beginning of the coastal range. If you hiked over the hill, you looked down upon the Spring Valley Lakes. Fences and riders on horseback kept all but the bravest and adventuresome out. There was justification for this; it was the San Francisco water supply source.

As a teenager I had taken the challenge with my buddies, climbed the fence, and sneaked down to the northern lake. The water, crystal clear, reflected the mountains and sky in a dramatic manner. However, we were there to attempt to catch the huge bass and trout that resided in the lake. We saw plenty of fish feeding in the shadows made by the sun moving over the mountain. None of us got to wet a line for out of the shrubbery galloped a horse, a man balancing a shotgun across his hips, and chaps to maneuver the brush.

The rider was mean, cussing at us and his horse, and rode on our tails as he pushed us up the hill and rowed thorns. "If I ever see you punks in here again, I'm throwing you in jail. Now git! We did not have any protection from the scrub brush and got scratched within an inch of our lives. Two days later our reward for this bravado was an itchy dose of poison oak. I didn't go back, but still fantasize the fishing that exists there. I've heard that the city officials go in and fish from one of the speedboats that are on the lake, but as teenagers that did not surprise us.

The signal changed and I drove to the southern part of the beach where now lay a Safeway market, a large parking lot, and lots of people. We camped there in the fifties, and had a fire ring about where I stopped for gas. I remembered Dick Keating, around nine years old, would sneak down from his home on the hill, roast marshmallows, and listen to the stories we told in front of the fire. The boat ramp was still there, much as it was when my father had taken me fishing and I got so seasick.

Pedro sea air, fresh as a rose, drifted into our nostrils. It was sweet, mixed with some pungency from dried out portions of bait left on the ramp and kelp tangled, twisted in the shorebreak. I liked it, the sea and beach without the overly washed out sterile Clorox odor. Pedro was much as it had been, and that was amazing, it located about twelve miles from San Francisco, an oasis, a blessed pocket amongst the spreading disease of urban growth.

When I surfed Pedro a few shacks still existed, worn out bleached boards that in places warped inward and outward. Joan and I sat in the sun, leaning up against an old rowboat. Seagulls swarmed above cackling, waiting for a hand out which we didn't have. A small seal popped up in the kelp and stared at us.

"I wonder what the water temperature is? Certainly not Hawaii."

Joan answered, "Let's change into our bathing suits?"

The car was parked above the shacks built into the cliff. It was a narrow strip of land where you could see San Francisco and Mount Tamalpais in the distance. Changing, we walked down the many steps to the ramp, jumped from it onto the sandy beach. Looking north, I saw some waves breaking on a sandbar about where the Wander Inn restaurant used to be. Now there was a parking lot, bathrooms and outdoor showers, the water cold. "Let's jog up to the showers. That should warm us up sufficiently." Dipping our toes into the sea, relatively speaking, it felt good. "Come on Joan. We can wade out to those small waves and body surf." We jumped over the first wave, avoiding getting the water on our bodies, but the second one rose higher, and we were forced to dive under it and swim out the other side, like at Fleishacker, but smaller surf.

Joan yelled, "Ooh, that's a rush !"

We body surfed waves and Joan wanted to get some distance swimming. She suggested that we swim back to the ramp instead of walking. It was low tide and we had to swim beyond the kelp. The sparkling sea was clear and I could see the reef, the fish that swam, and I was back to that first day at Fleishacker, swimming outside the breakers.

We swam stroke for stroke, climbed over the exposed reef, and I gave Joan a hoist to the dock. We both shivered, and I grabbed a hose used to wash down the ramp after cleaning fish. Before I could turn it on, a voice from one of the houses above us emphatically urged, "Come on you Hawaiian icebergs. We have a hot shower. Come, use it."

I looked up and thought I knew the fellow, but just could not place him. "Dick Keating, remember me at the camp fire when I was a kid?"

"Of course, you're not nine years old." I introduced him to Joan and he hugged both of us. We showered and came into the living area.

A woman sitting on the sofa looked up, "Hello, I'm Dick's wife, Penny. Dick went diving. He'll be back soon. Won't you stay for dinner, that is if he gets anything to eat?"

Looking seaward, we saw Dick's skiff anchored near rocks at the point. We didn't see him for a long time, and then he surfaced. I put the binoculars on him and saw that he surfaced with an abalone held in his hand. Penny offered us some red wine, as Joan was still shivering some. I covered it up better than she.

Finishing our glass of wine, I looked at Joan. "Why don't you call your mother. I'll go over to the Safeway and by the time Dick warms up we can all sit down and have a drink."

Closing the door, I heard Joan ask, "Penny can I help in the kitchen?"

Arriving back, there was activity in the kitchen. Joan was putting together a salad from ingredients out of Penny's garden, Dick pounding abalone, and a large ling cod lay on the cutting board.

Watching Dick move onto cleaning the fish, I gazed in awe. He cut the head off, filleted the two sidepieces, pulling all bones out, and turned the filets so he could skin them. Cutting them into four pieces, he handed them to Penny. I opened the merlot wine and poured. We sat outside sipping, and waiting for the green flash after the sun descended below the horizon. Everyone saw it, but me. I lived most of my life on the beach, watched the sunset from a surfboard or a porch, and I did not believe that there was such a thing. We talked of old times, of what we were doing with our lives, and darkness filled the beach. What a day; what a meal; what a night!

Dick was a very self-reliant person, balancing fishing, diving, and building surfboards. He went out into the ocean in his eighteen-foot skiff, mostly alone, unless he would invite someone like me. The sea in the winter off Pedro Point turned ferocious. Dick had to feed two children, a wife, and himself, a string of dogs and cats. He fished under the most adverse conditions when commercial fishermen like himself sat in front of a fireplace. He was adept beyond reason, balancing in a boat bouncing up and down on huge ground swells, steering with one hand, and slowing when he hooked a fish, leading it to the gaff, hoisting it aboard, and revving the engine to hook another fish.

Salmon season was the most profitable and the easiest because the sea was somewhat calmer than winter and, certainly, the air warmer. He not only challenged the sea in fishing, but also surfed as a champion, being invited to some of the most prestigious meets in the world, paddling out alone to the huge surf that pounded the rocks out on the Point. This was before leashes and a wipe out meant a long swim in that freezing water.

Dick shaped, glassed, and sold surfboards to an elite group of people who hero-worshipped him. To this day he is considered one of the prime surfboard shapers.

Penny follows Dick on those cold-water dives. She gets her share of abalone, surfs some, but is trying to get a teaching degree while balancing children on her lap. She is a community asset, and spends a great deal of time working to keep Pedro Point much as it was. She has had huge successes, meeting with high-ranking officials, and supplying the facts in a non-threatening manner. Penny is a writer and contributes articles to the Pacifica newspaper. In her spare time she works in the garden and runs on the beach with her Doberman.

Both of these superior human beings prefer to live simple lives, and gaining large sums of money has never been a goal for either. I feel they are richer than Rockefeller in zest, outstanding health, positiveness, and love. Just recently they and a few others who have homes on the beach secured rights to purchase 3 1/2 acres of that precious land fronting the beach. There purchase is at the southern end of Pedro Point beach. Purchasing those acres secures that part of the beach for as long as they hold the deed. No development!

We left the Keating's and drove up to San Francisco, arriving at Lunado Way, the light on in the front window. Joan's mother met us at the door. We retired to our respective sleeping areas, and I dreamed that Joan had sneaked into the living room and was kissing me. I awakened to the Doberman licking my face; Joan smiling as she drank a cup of coffee.

Paul handed me the morning paper, and Bobbie brought a steaming mouth watering breakfast to the table. I was hungry and took at least my share from the plate in the middle of the table. Paul looked at me, then asked me, "What are you doing today?"

"I'd like to go over to Stinson Beach where I was the first lifeguard. Also Mount Tamalpais is a memory for me of childhood. Would you and Bobbie like to accompany us? We could make a picnic lunch."

Paul replied that he and his wife had to go to work. Joan and I did the dishes, showered, separately, and left for Marin County. Recrossing the bridge, we drove a few miles to the coast road, and moved up toward Mount Tamalpais. Such a breathtaking view from the top, we couldn't resist taking photographs. You could see the fog threatening to move inland, but hanging offshore like swirls of cotton candy. It was not as warm as yesterday, but quite pleasant sitting in the mountain top amphitheater. We walked past the sign warning of rattlesnakes, stopped and got into the kissing mode, and continued up the mountain. Golden grasses undulated under foot and the air smelled fresh, with a hint of warm oak.

Checking for snakes where we sat down, we scanned for special memory spots, and focused on the John Muir Redwood Park. It lay two thousand feet below, and Joan said. "Why don't we visit the park? I haven't been there since high school."

Curving roads I was used to from driving the school bus when I worked in the Santa Cruz mountains, but this road went beyond, and it was narrow so that two cars passing from different directions was dangerous. It was still too early for the onslaught of tourists as we paid our fees at the park and looked for a place to leave the car.

Joan grabbed a sleeping bag from the back seat and we found a grassy spot in the sun and lay down. It was comfortably warm in our clothes, and the huge trees staved off the gentle breeze.

Joan spoke first. "In high school my girlfriend, Elsie, and I used to skip school on days like this, find a protected spot, and lie in the sun. It was such a wonderful escape from pressures in school, and we never got caught."

Then I recalled my own days of truancy: *My friend, Ron Javet, and I planned a fishing trip out to Lake Merced on opening day of trout season, May 1, 1946. Ron had a car and he picked me up at three in the morning so that we'd be assured of a rental rowboat. Standing in line we nearly froze, the fog sitting right onto the ground, but we got one of the first boats. Finding a little cove, we dropped anchor, and baited our hooks. The fog was so thick that you could not see the shoreline.*

Ron set the hook on a trout and it jumped immediately, but it was so foggy that we could only hear the splash. He fought the fish to the boat and I netted it, holding up a twenty-inch rainbow striped fish. The fish was put on the stringer and we settled into fishing again.

We both caught our two trout limit and were back at the landing as the fog lifted. Holding our fish hung by our sides, we walked up to the car.

I lifted the trunk, and bent to place the fish in there, the wonderful sensuousness of the sun penetrating my back, and was interrupted. "How about a picture of you two with those fish? They look like the biggest brought in this morning." We proudly allowed pictures to be taken, and then the man asked us what our names were. The man was a reporter and knew of Ron and me from football games as he was the sports writer for the San Francisco newspaper.

We tried to melt back into school the next day, but never got past the principal and attendance lady. "So, how are your colds this morning?"

"Oh, they're fine. Can you give us a pass for having been out yesterday?"

The principal, Mr. White, handed me the newspaper and told me to open to the sports page. Peering at the picture of Ron and me, my stomach dropped and bounced on the floor, Javet's cheeks turning a bright crimson.

"Yes, we'll give you passes, but you know I think the custodian is out sick today and we need the bathrooms cleaned. You could help us couldn't you?"

"Yes, mam," we chimed, and headed to our chore, passing the custodian on the way.

Joan stood up. "We'd better head back to San Francisco. I want to shop at Petrini's Market so that I can fix dinner tonight." We picked up the sleeping bag and put it in the back seat.

The traffic was backed up on the Golden Gate Bridge so we had a chance to enjoy the view. I talked to Joan about before the bridge had been constructed. Architects and engineers around the world had looked skeptically at the possibility of ever completing the bridge, and they thought that it would never support the weight or stand against the ferocious riptides, currents, and winter floods that exited through the Gate.

·

Looking toward the open sea, my eyes scanned China Beach which was a hang out for kids on those few hot days in spring, and I could see the bare outline of Dead Man's rock, where I fished, and scanning back to the bridge my vision focused on the distance between the lighthouse sitting upon huge rocks in the Gate channel and China Beach. I saw, in my mind's eye, my sister, the two of us swimming out to the lighthouse on a hot and glassy day. We waved up to the lighthouse keeper and swam back to the beach, a mile to shore. We never even thought about the Great White sharks that frequented that channel until in the early fifties when a young man swimming off China Beach was attacked and bled to death during rescue.

Instead of staying with the heavy traffic on 19th Avenue, we drove along the Bay's north point. The Presidio had kept the view pretty much as it had been years ago. I didn't care for the military, but knew that in their huge accumulation of lands they preserved them mostly in their original state. The Presidio remains a deeply forested acreage.

San Francisco is a great example for other urban regions. There are numerous parks, golf courses, Lake Merced, which is the same as it was in the early part of century, and the Spring Valley Lakes. Because of the isolation and protection these places have flourished as they did before man intervened. How many cities in the world, with a population near a million, have mountain lions roaming the outskirts, deer, rattlesnakes, raccoons, and an occasional black bear? Joan's parents have raccoons in their backyard at night; they drink water from a small pond and swim too.

Returning to Lunado Way after shopping, Joan and her mother prepared dinner while Paul and I watched a basketball game on television. I heard them speaking about their next-door neighbor, Jack, whom they had invited for dinner.

Dinner nearly ready, the table set by Paul and me, the doorbell rang. Joan answered it and I heard, oohs, and ahs, Joan asking Jack for a hug, and Jack asking her if she was still his sweetie?

Jack came into the television room and Joan introduced me as a colleague. Jack was quite elderly, but maintained childlike blue eyes which twinkled and focused right through you. I knew that he was

199

appraising me because he and Joan had been very close ever since she was a child, and he was protecting her as a real grandfather would.

Joanie, he called her. "We go back a long way, Joanie and me. She used to hand me daisies and flower bouquets through the fence, and helped me garden, too."

Jack was ninety-seven years old, but when asked he would say that he was three years away from a hundred. I liked Jack immediately. He was fluent in San Francisco history as he had been a settler long before the bridge, long before the 1906 earthquake, and as a teenager had attended the 1915 World's Fair in the Marina district, the only part of that remaining, the Palace of Fine Arts off Lombard Street.

After dinner, Jack and I settled into the living room, and Paul insisted on doing the dishes by himself. Joan and her mother had a private conversation.

I've always been interested in the old days in San Francisco. I've read every bit of history, and attempted to visit places that have now become zealously guarded museums.

Jack and I talked late into that evening, sipping Courvoisier. Jack sat back. He couldn't see very well, but he was articulately positive. Jack spoke of the early years in his life with fondness. He was proud of his affiliation with the Columbia Park Boys Club, and told of the first time that he went across to Marin County on the ferryboat, had to walk with the boys and counselors to Mill Valley where the overnight hike began. The Dip Sea trail started at the bottom of a huge Redwood tree covered mountain range, which terminated at Stinson Beach. You climbed and dropped into valleys filled with first and second growth Redwoods. The majority of Redwoods on ridges had been clear-cut in the 1800s. It took much longer to cut a Redwood tree down with handsaws, axes, and wedges. The men who cut those early forests were powerfully built. The destruction by the first timber men did not show as today when in a few minutes a Redwood tree can be felled, hundreds of acres in the time it took to fell one tree, hand prepare it to be pulled out by the horses and oxen.

Jack told me of how cold it was to sleep out on the Coast of Marin County with only a blanket for warmth. "I was a kid and endured. It was fun. They fed us beans, cooked potatoes, and rice. That was it until we climbed back onto the ferryboat and bought hamburgers crossing the bay back to San Francisco. Fred, I must be boring you, but I love California."

"Not at all. I appreciate those memories. I have some photos of the Gate entrance before the bridge. When I am in Hawaii, I just sit and look at them."

"Well Fred, I go back a long way. When I turned fourteen, the Columbia Park Boys Club decided that during the summer we would walk from San Francisco to Crescent City, a distance of three hundred and sixty-five miles, not counting side trips exploring. In those days there were hardly any cars on the road, mostly horses, and horse and buggies. Auto fumes were nearly non-existent. There was a lot of horse manure on the road, but that didn't harm your health."

"How long did it take?"

"Six to seven weeks. I'm not sure now, but it was most of the summer vacation. We averaged eighteen to twenty miles a day. It took a while to gain callouses on our feet instead of painful blisters."

"Where did you clean up, get water, supplies if there were so few towns?"

"The beauty of it, Fred, was that you could bend down and drink from all the streams, even the ones near San Francisco. We swam in streams, rivers, and lakes. Cleanliness was no problem."

"Did you carry back packs?"

"Only for personal needs; we had a horse drawn large wagon which carried food, extra clothing, and bedding needs. One of the older guys tended the horse and carriage. We were young and usually finished walking early in the afternoon, leaving time for setting up camp, cleaning up, swimming, and exploring. It was a slowed down time, Fred, a time when a kid had time to think, to focus. The towns we walked through were small settlements, some more prosperous than others, depending on whether the timber had been cut. Fishing villages filled the needs for food locally. Bartering was popular, trading fruits and vegetables for fish. There was no refrigeration, but ice sufficed. Twenty-five pounds would last about three days, and some towns had ice machines. They sold us shave ice, usually offering a myriad of flavors. That was a treat."

I partially filled Jack's snifter with brandy. "I can't imagine a world without automobiles everywhere."

"California was still in semi-wilderness. Communication was not instantaneous as it is now. The few automobiles up until around 1915 were two cylinder glorified horse carriages. You started them with a crank on the side. When the newer and improved models came in you had a choice of cranking, up front near the radiator, or pushing the car down hill and starting it in compression by putting it in gear and releasing the clutch. If that didn't work you cranked some more."

"Before you came to San Francisco, where did you live?"

"My father owned a hotel with a restaurant up in Coulterville. Do you know where that is?"

"Yes," I nodded. "I used to fish up there. I loved the area."

Jack leaned forward. "You know, Fred? We had the best of it." He sipped on his brandy.

I felt that Jack shared something with me that he guarded zealously, only feeding out this priceless information to those he felt truly appreciated. I loved California, old and new. There were far too many people moving into the state who did not share Jack's and my attachment to California.

They had come here to get a better job, make big money, develop the open land, build dams, and make a profit on mining and the remaining trees. They missed the point in that the development had already taken place. It was time to focus on what was left, take care of it, turn people's minds around to the incredible amount of money that could be made in recreation instead of plunder. I believe, with education, it could be turned around and the capitalistic system would not have to collapse.

The brandy separated the synapses in my brain and I saw Jack as a young kid living in tired skin. He knew what was valuable. He had experienced it and the benefits. It's sad that so many are content to sell our heritage down the drain for thirty pieces of silver. The worst thing is that education does not focus on teaching a value system that makes this finite world livable forever. Where is the joy in most money making endeavors? Jack was a jeweler on Union Square and spent a lot of time in down town San Francisco selling jewelry before retiring. He had a love in his life, and a family. His wife, Elsie, had died years ago, but Jack lived off the abundance he had been given in those early years.

Another oh so brief brandy, and Jack leaned toward me. "Fred, the next summer we walked to San Diego and visited all of the missions on Highway 101. Those adobe villas were great, cool in the hot sun, and warm at night when we slept on the floors. The Priests, although demanding and unbending, had an appreciation for their environment. Most of the trip to San Diego was hot, and we got sunburned. There were no sun protection products. We did not average as many miles, but it was clean. The streams ran freely with little demand from agriculture. Try to imagine Los Angeles with a navigable river running through it, oranges filling the otherwise desert land. Life was easier here in southern California. Things moved more slowly and the population was almost non-existent."

"In those early days when you lived up in Coulterville, did you ever get over to Yosemite Park?"

"You won't believe it Fred, but we either walked there, camping for a couple of weeks or we rode in a horse and wagon. I can vividly see Half Dome and El Capitan towering above the valley floor. Granite giants gazing down, revealing secrets to boys hungry for new wilderness adventures."

I tried to imagine what it must have been like to travel so slowed down, no smog covering the Sierra's, few people using Yosemite Valley, and the untouched canyons and streams filled with native rainbow trout.

The Napa River north of San Francisco today is a running cesspool, the depository for many chemical poisons, the sewer for agricultural and industrial waste, some of it legal, most not. I swam in it up until the Second World War. I don't even like the smell of it and would never consider eating fish caught in it.

Jack talks about a bunch of the guys taking the ferryboat over to Sausalito, disembarking, and riding horses to the Napa River. "Thirsty on our ride from Sausalito, we drank and swam in the river, then fished for trout, filling sacks with rainbows. Back home we kept a reasonable amount and gave the rest to neighbors."

I was very tired as Jack told me about how he did business by a handshake, never had any use for a lawyer, and that he had loaned the first owner of Harrah's Club in Reno $2,000. Forgetting the debt, some years later Harrah came into his store and handed him $5,000. The debt paid in full with interest.

I visited Jack in his new home once. He lives with his daughter in Atlanta, Georgia. Jack always shares something about California that touches my heart. Our communications take place over the phone. Jack tells me that he misses San Francisco, the Yosemite Valley, the ocean breeze, and we spend long moments swapping tales. Like the difference in Joan's and my age makes little difference after so many years together, Jack and I, when we talk, are transformed into two kids sharing a common love for California.

Joan and I talk about moving back to the Golden State. We look at property, make plans, read books, fantasize, but the thirty-five million people continue as a deterrent, the smog is overwhelming, but Californians are forward moving people. There are more anti-smog laws in California than any other state even though the smog continues to build. They get rid of one toxin only to have it replaced with two more.

Dining in San Francisco you do not have to worry about someone lighting a cigarette or cigar next to your table. Although polluted, perhaps beyond repair, there are more health conscious people in California than most other states. Californians are faddists from the word go, but they keep moving forward in a trend or fad to something more positive.

There are a group of elderly men and women who swim at the Aquatic Park in San Francisco, adjacent to the Municipal pier on the bay. These hardy souls, some in their eighties, swim every day around the pier and back, which is a mile, in water that gets as cold as forty-four degrees and rarely above fifty-eight degrees Fahrenheit. Most do not wear wet suits, only a protective cap upon their head.

Joan and I had one day left to play in San Francisco and opted to sit in the backyard. The west wind was picking up which meant that we would have fog by the afternoon. It was warm and sunny.

We sat in comfortable lounging chairs, and I faced away from the sun.

"Joan, I am going up to Lake Almanor after you leave and visit my parents who are camping. Are you coming back to California?"

"I'm planning on it, but I have to settle what's going on between Michael and me."

"I thought that it was settled after our trip together, how we get along, the things that we share. I've been through two marriages and never had the experiences that we have had in the past weeks."

"Well, that's part of it, two marriages, children, and you are so much older than me. I feel the same way as you, but there's too much baggage."

I felt the burning in my esophagus and throat that I remember from having an ulcer years ago. My world crashed. I felt cut in two. I didn't know if I could stand the separation. I felt so in tune with Joan and now she dropped this bombshell.

The rest of the day we sat together, but mostly in limbo. We didn't even kiss in the privacy of the yard. She seemed less affected than me. I didn't hear the music she was playing in her bedroom. It was like I was shell-shocked and wandered in a daze, suppressing the hurt the best I could. That evening her parents took us out to dinner at a neighborhood cafe. I ordered plain pasta and overlooked my favorite King salmon.

Joan's mother caught the vibrations between us and made some idle conversation. Joan laughed and frolicked with her dad who didn't think anything was amiss. I was glad when we left. Sitting in the back seat, I felt Joan put her hand on my leg and hold me close. I didn't get it. Joan packed in her room and I sat watching television.

Morning seemed to arrive more quickly than all the others. Joan kissed, hugged her parents. "I hope to be back in a week. I love you, bye."

I thanked them profusely and turned to leave. Bobbie said, "Have fun with your parents. I hope to see you again." Joan cried most of the way to the San Francisco Airport. Tipping a porter to load her bags, we walked to the waiting area for Hawaii bound passengers.

"If you come back would you take another trip with me? The summer has barely begun."

"I don't know. You're too pushy. It depends on what happens between Michael and me."

The departure call filled the room. To me it meant the end of the world I had found. I don't know what it meant to Joan. I thought I had it all figured. I felt like I was walking on my ears when she moved toward the departure gate, waved, turned to depart, swung around, and walked up to me. "It was real for me; I've never felt the feelings that I have with you."

Joan Marie hugged me, kissed my lips strongly and left, disappearing around the curve into the entry gate of the plane.

I was devastated, paid the parking fee, and stopped on the side of the freeway to watch her plane take off, and turn westward, tears rolling down my cheeks.

Driving to Lake Almanor I had to look at the map a couple of times, and arrived very late in the afternoon. My parents greeted me, glad to be with me again, but two minutes later the slings and arrows flew back and forth between them, like I imagined the Maginot line to be.

In two days it would be my parents anniversary, but today we were going to the beach on Lake Almanor. Their camp was on the east side next to the lake and, as early as it was in summer, very few campsites were occupied. After lunch, we strolled to the beach, set a blanket on the sand, and lay down.

The sarcasm, bickering continued, and I excused myself to a swim. The lake was about a mile across, and I couldn't see where it ended to the north. It was a large manmade lake. We were camped about a half-mile from the dam. I decided to swim there and back. I needed to clear my head of my parents constant tearing away at each other and Joan's sudden departure. Diving beneath the surface, the water was cold, but invigorating. I surfaced and swam, evenly spaced freestyle to the dam, climbed out and sat. This part of California maintained sunny weather most of the time from late spring until fall. Today was hot and the lake surface smooth, mirroring reflections of stately pines and fluffy cotton ball clouds. The evergreen forest surrounding the lake and the sky a deep clear blue, I understood why my parents camped here often. I appreciated that they had passed on to me their love of nature, but I did not understand their constant gnawing at each other's throats. My father told me how much he loved my mother, that there had never been another woman, but my mother was non-committal. She lost herself in her kids, sacrificing all individuality to that purpose. Billie, as we called her, by her actions, telegraphed to us that she did not like Doc. He had always been overly demonstrative in front of us. We all thought that our family was typical and that love was what they defined. As I rested on the other side of the lake, I thought of how my relationship, to date, with Joanie had been filled with demonstrations of love, but we were both private. The feelings I had developed in such a short time for Joan were not what I saw my parents manifest.

Standing up, a bit stiff from sitting, I dove into the water and swam a very slow freestyle back to where I could see my parents. Being on the outside, I viewed them with dismay.

I collected wood, built a fire, and Doc barbecued hamburgers. "Food tastes better off a charcoal grill in the outdoors. I showed you from a very young age that the outdoors was the place to be."

My mother interjected, "Well, you missed emphasizing that things happened because I cut wood, built the fire, and cleaned up, put the tent up, packed everything."

Darkness moved upon us and the fire lit up our little camp. There was not a breath of wind, and stars filled the universe above us.

Awaking early, I looked out from my sleeping bag, and saw my mother standing over the Coleman stove cooking breakfast, drinking her coffee. I asked what they wanted to do on their anniversary?

My father said, "We're all right. Don't bother to plan anything. I would like to have some trout for dinner."

Assembling my fly rod, choosing a fly, and light leader, I drove away, promising fish for dinner. I found a small stream where there were less fishermen, and moved up stream. Hours later, I had hooked and released one six inch rainbow. I walked to a larger stream and it was crowded with bait fishermen. Changing flies a number of times, I came up skunked.

It was early afternoon and it appeared that I was failing in my attempts to provide a trout anniversary dinner. Driving somewhat dejected, I came upon this sign that said it was a trout farm. Fishermen were welcome to try their luck. Parking, I chose the concrete pools that had the largest fish, and cast a dry fly near the middle. These trout were not choosy and I struck into what turned out to be an eighteen-incher, and caught another about fifteen inches. This was perfect. I asked the fee, a dollar an inch, and surrendered a traveler's check, receiving very little change.

Stopping at the camp store, I purchased a bottle of merlot, and picked out some flowers for my mother, signing a card to both of them.

Parking at their camp, I cautiously approached from behind my mother who was setting up the Coleman stove, and said, "Surprise, happy anniversary," and handed her the card and flowers. "I've got to clean these fish I caught," pulled them from the bag and my father said, "We knew that we could count on you to get fish."

Cleaning the fish by a faucet, I felt good. They would never know that I had caught these in a trout farm, and I think they enjoyed them as much as if they had been caught down behind our house in Boulder Creek. The truce only lasted until I heard them in their van, my father making an attempt at romance, and my mother turning away, my father angry, my mother silent. I had been so naive. My brother had told me that their marriage was not what Doc tried to make it appear. At that time I did not realize that it was not my fault for what happened between them.

I had done what I could to make the anniversary perfect. Before falling asleep I thought of a time when I confronted my mother, asking her why she was never outwardly loving to my father. She was angry and replied, "You don't know what goes on in the bedroom." I fell asleep happy to count stars and listen for night sounds.

Driving away from my parents camp, I looked in the rear view mirror, and saw them standing together. A tear fell upon my lap.

I always met them somewhere in a camping ground. My father liked camping, maybe because my mother did the majority of the chores. She did them at home, too. There had been Yellowstone National Park, Bozeman, Montana, and many other memories where I had said goodbye, wondering if we would meet again the next year, if both of them would be alive? I arrived in San Francisco, called Joan's home, and asked when she would be coming back? "She's here now. I'll get her."

Joan had a special way of answering a phone. "Uh, uh, hello," she said.

"I'm in San Francisco. Can I come and see you? I've really missed you."

"Was your parent's anniversary a success?"

"Yeah, it was a blast."

"Fred, I don't want to see you right now. Michael came back with me. He's staying with his parents. I'll see you back in school. Are you going back to the islands soon? I've got to go."

"No I'm not going back to the islands. I don't know where I am going. I think I'll go down to Boulder Creek and visit my brother."

Joan hung up. I called my brother. His girlfriend answered. "Fred, why don't you come down and stay with us? Peter would love it. Is Joan with you?"

I burst into tears and sobbed. "She dropped me, just like that. I'm devastated. Are you sure you want to see me now?"

She told me yes and to hurry down. I went to the first liquor store and purchased a six-pack of beer. Driving the Skyline Boulevard highway, I opened beer after beer, stopping at Woodside about half way to Boulder Creek, finished the beer, and went into the country store, purchasing another six pack, and continued to drive. I nearly went off the road on an unbanked curve. I put the beers in the back seat, arrived at Peter's an hour later, and climbed the steep stairs to his deck. Knocking on the door, Gayle met me and I fell into her arms. She assisted me to the couch and I lay there drunk, but more in a state of shock. Peter came home and we talked into the wee hours.

When I awakened early, I looked out and the Redwoods, the ferns growing beneath, and the bluest sky in California greeted me. It was too beautiful a morning to worry about Joan. I made a pact with myself: I would go on a purely ascetic diet, work out as I never had. I would start now. Putting on my running shoes and bathing suit, I ran from Peter's house to Ben Lomond, and back, a distance of about eight miles.

Stopping at the Junction on the way back, which was about a mile from Peter's, I decided to swim. The dam was in place and no one else was on the sandy beach. Reminiscing about Carol, my job at the high school, dives from the thirty-foot high ledge, I waded into the stream.

The sun warmed me, but I had to immerse my body in order to swim. Waiting a time, I looked up at the trees hanging over the river, peered deeply into the crystal clear water, and dove.

The ice cream headache disappeared as soon as I stroked toward the dam. As icy as the water was, the swimming seemed to warm me some, and I got into a rhythm, stroke, breathe, focus on physical things. Swimming under the bridge just short of the dam, suddenly the water dropped degrees until I swam back into the sun. I touched the dam and turned.

I was pumped and the swim back to the Junction was a joy. I sprinted the last hundred yards, stood up in shallow water, and walked the beach to my running shoes, donned them, and headed to Peter's.

The sun beat down on the porch and I was dry and warm in no time, Gayle bringing me a hot cup of chocolate. This was the way it went, day after day. I got bronzed tan, did a hundred and fifty push-ups before running, and looked forward eagerly to the daily endorphin high. It lasted a short time, but made the work out worth it, even though I pushed through both physical and Joan pain.

In three weeks I felt like an Olympic athlete. My body was tuned to its peak, my head cleared of Joan or as I thought. I had lost ten pounds, gained solid muscle, felt better than when I was in high school. I called Joan a few times in the first week, but I think her mother was protecting her from me.

It seemed all right now and one day when I finished a work out, and was eating out on the deck, Gayle handed me the phone. "A lady wants to talk to you, a lady I think you'd like to hear from."

I grabbed the phone and said, "Yes."

"Uh, uh, hello. I can borrow my father's car and visit you in about two hours, that is if you are interested."

Speech issued forth in muddled tones. "Yes, come. I'll meet you at the Junction. It's easy to find. Ask at the fire station and bring a bathing suit."

Walking to the swimming hole, suddenly the world had a rainbow in every nook and cranny. Spider webs vibrated in sunshine. The morning dew dried, disappeared into the atmosphere, but I saw through my eyes the kaleidoscopic colors that my fogged lenses portrayed. Life slowed and everything at the Junction moved in stopgap slow motion. I waited. Eternities seemed to pass. I sat by the river watching the baby trout swim back and forth, surface for some minute insect.

Hearing a car come to a stop up in the parking lot, I looked to see dust settling. There was a V-8 Chrysler, and Joan had just closed the door. Like an apparition she came toward me, dressed in a flowing wrap around, powder, blue dress, fluttering above her knees. "Uh, Uh, hello you. Got a hug for me?"

Reluctant to rekindle the flame that had seared my heart and soul, I stood up and smiled. She put her arms around my neck, kissed me, and I let the pain depart my body. All was well down at the Junction that sunny day. Life moved again in regular cadence.

People moved into our space, kids kicking up dust, the sun directly overhead. "Do you know any private place where we can be alone?"

I said that there was a Redwood canyon that was rarely visited except during winter when steelhead fishermen walked the steep descent into the gorge. It was located on Highway 9 about four miles from Santa Cruz.

One of the reasons why I came back as often as possible to the Santa Cruz Mountains was its immediate affect on me. No matter what pressures I endured away, the first entrance into the tunnel of Redwoods that surrounded the narrow highway, the mottled trunks each reaching to its own sky, the shadows that wrapped the highway in softness, the occasional deer standing by the roadside, all of the forest immediately touched me like an extra strength valium. I felt muscles, nerves in my body, my eyes shift into another mode. It was a change that happened each time, and it was now, the sweetness and fragrances, the silence, the almost complete lack of outside man made interferences.

We stopped at the sign that said the Rincon Trail. It ascended into the canyon where the river lay. Our fingers entwined, we walked down the slippery trail. It wound through heavy gardens of ferns, very little sun penetrating. The coolness was a natural air conditioning force. Near the river the land opened into scattered trees, and warmth dominated a clear sky.

Settling into a sandy spot amongst the huge boulders, we sat down. Joan stripped to nakedness, and I followed suit. We hugged and lay on our towels, the sun massaging sensually. We kissed; I touched her all over, and she pushed me away. "Why not?" I asked, not thinking with my brain.

"I need time. I haven't been with you for a while. I'm pretty much finished with Michael. Can we change the subject? How about a swim?"

Diving into the icy depths, my body wanted to sprint. The length of the pool stretched to about fifty yards, and upon reaching shallow water, I turned seeing Joan's synchronized swimming stroke moving toward me. I swam, head down, enjoying and transforming desire into explosive physical energy. Joan grabbed my leg as I started to pass her, held and kissed me, but it was different in the freezing water. The mood had passed.

We lay in the sun until the Redwoods shadowed out the beach. Walking up the trail, the air cooled, and we quickened our pace. "That is a special place. We'll go there again," said Joan.

We saw the Chrysler looming through trees, like some derelict that didn't fit the environment, but it was pleasant to drive with the heat turned to high. No shrouds of sun remained. I talked about the Santa Cruz Mountains and the special attachment I felt, that I could come back any time. Joan said that she felt much the same.

Joan drove and I started to unfold a story about Santa Cruz. It had been a good day and I had wanted to share this story about a seal in Santa Cruz with Joan a number of times, but always had held back because I didn't want her to get the impression that I was maybe some kind of nut. I felt that I had nothing to lose now.

I used to hitchhike down to Santa Cruz when I was attending San Francisco State University. There was so little traffic that sometimes I'd get stuck somewhere in the apricot filled orchards of Cupertino. This time I finally got a ride after dark and the man left me near Cowell's Beach. I walked, my sleeping bag wrapped around my neck, and found a suitable spot in the sand, fell asleep, and awakened to the resounding sound of the shorebreak. It was a glassy May day clothed in fog. I saw a four-foot wave breaking off the point. I sprinted to not miss any more of these perfect waves. Just a beginner," I told Joan, *"I usually stayed away from Steamer Lane, but today was small and Steamer looked negotiable. I*

212

paddled out to the Lane, and saw a huge wave break outside me, reform into a windowpane wave, framed in kelp. I caught the edge of soup and dropped. Climbing to the shoulder, I swung back into the wall and slid into Cowell's point, and kicked out. Shouting out the beauty of Steamer's waves, the cliffs echoed my voice, and then stood mute.

Paddling back to the line up, I saw a seal frolicking near the outside peak catch a wave. I watched him in awe as foam sprayed from his chest. He dipped his head into the wave and disappeared.

I was scared sitting out there alone. Slowly my tail block sank. I froze, stole a glance backward. There he was, a half grown seal, his paws looking like a cat's perched on my board. He barked at me, "Ark, ark, ark."

I sprinted to the low tide beach against the cliffs, hoping to escape this beast. I kneel paddled so that less of my body was in the water, and looked below to the seal swimming under my board, staring me in the eyes, and smiling. Flipping a shower of water into my face, he disappeared as suddenly as he had appeared. That was enough for me. I caught a wave, proned it so as not to wipe out, and climbed out of the water at the Cowell's shorebreak. Later that night I built a fire, and settled into my sleeping bag. I carried my board to the cliffs that hung above Steamer Lane. I slept soundly.

The next morning I carried my board out to Steamer Lane, waxed it, timed the set, dropped the board upon the wave passing, and paddled as fast as I could to avoid getting caught inside and smashed against the cliffs. The swell that capped over my head dissipated its strength after it passed me, and I arrived to sit in the line up awaiting a wave. I watched the kelp rise behind me, and a mid-sized seal rode past me, and swam to catch another wave.

Oh, to have that judgment, to know exactly where to sit for a wave. I envied the seal. I wished that I was a seal. Hearing an "Ark, ark, ark," I looked behind to the seal that had ridden those waves. He placed both of his paws on my board and barked into my face. At first he terrified me, but when I looked into his eyes they appeared to be friendly.

The seal swam to the outside peak, looking back toward me. He seemed to be mocking me. Riding wave after wave, he skimmed by, occasionally stopping to put his paws upon my board. Up close his breath smelled like he had eaten a pound of rotten fish.

The seal stationed himself out where he had caught so many waves, and barked incessantly. He passed up wave after wave and continued barking at me."

I thought it impossible that the seal wanted to put me in the perfect position to catch a wave, maybe just coincidence, but why shouldn't I at least chance it? No one was around to criticize, make fun of me. I paddled to the place where he was finning. He stopped barking, moved another twenty-five feet out, and barked again. Sprinting to where he was positioned I thought the wave would break on my head, but paddled anyway. And sure enough, a wave came. Standing up, I maneuvered across the best Steamer Lane wave I had ever caught, made two turns, and kicked out where I usually sat. Paddling back out, the seal sat in the same line up. We rode wave after wave. As long as I followed the seal I was in the perfect place. What a day! Catching one more wave, I made it into Cowell's beach and took off for the highway.

At school the next day, I wondered what had happened? Was the experience real or was I fantasizing alone at Steamer lane?

I told my brother, Gene, that I had been really close to a seal, and that by following where he took off, I caught more waves than I ever had. My brother said, "So what, there's always a bunch of seals at Steamer."

Dave walked up behind me and caustically spoke to me. "I heard that you surfed with a seal buddy. Fred, I know that finals are approaching, but come on, let's be real."

The next time I rode Steamer Lane, the surf was junk, and I was ready to paddle to shore when I heard a bark. There he was, finning fifty feet outside me. Paddling for the spot, he dove under my board. I saw a wave approaching and thought, I'm so far out; I'll never catch it.

The wave steepened and I leaned into it with only one stroke. I made it to the bottom, but spun out in the strong northwest wind blowing. Surfacing, I was clutched in the midst of kelp.

I panicked, thinking of drowning and no one knowing I was out there, and then thought of the swim to the cliffs with no one to retrieve my board before it got smashed.

Extricating myself from the kelp, I swam toward the cove, hoping that the inside rip would not catch me and push to Cowell's.

I saw the board sitting out in the channel, far from the surf line. I sprinted the last five yards and climbed on my board, noticing a slight ding mark on the rail. However, it appeared to resemble a bite mark instead of a ding.

Paddling to the line up, I thought, no it couldn't be. Dave was right. Finals were catching up to me. Surfing into Cowell's I put my board against the beach cliffs and left.

The next morning at school, I ran into Dave and Gene at the snack bar. "Suppose you met your seal buddy yesterday?" They both squelched snickers.

I leaned closer to Dave and Gene. "I think he retrieved my board for me."

"You sure it wasn't a mermaid," Dave sassily spluttered?

After class driving home I wondered, but knew that dings did not look like the teeth marks in my board. The seal had saved my board.

My next trip to Santa Cruz I paddled out to small, choppy surf. It was too close to the summer and Steamer lay dormant except for where a weak south swell touched the point. I surfed cautiously, fearing that I would lose my board into the blowhole, which was too dangerous to swim into at high tide.

The sun set and I waited, waited until darkness descended, and paddled toward Cowell's point. Out of the night a wave formed which I could barely see. I caught it, pearled, and lost the board in darkness.

Two waves broke on my head. The sets stopped, and I swam toward where I figured the board might be. I saw the board, dimly reflecting starlight, sitting in the abated foam. "What luck, thank you," I shouted. I heard an "Ark, ark, ark," somewhere out in the blackness. In my state, I was fairly sure that the barking had said. "You are welcome."

It was cold that night and I welcomed dawn, walked over to the pier bathhouse, and ate breakfast amongst the fishermen. One of them spoke loudly. "If I see another seal around my nets, I'll shoot it. They stealing my fish and tearing holes in the nets."

Standing up to pay my bill, I passed the fisherman and said, "Did it ever occur to you that the seals were here long before you, and that you might be stealing their fish? "

Opening the door to the sea, a cold blast of air massaged my face. I walked back along the pier, seeing two fishermen working feverishly at pulling up the hoist from down in the hold of their boat.

Turning away, I heard one of the fisherman say, "That god damma seal won't steal no more fish or tear my nets apart no more."

Freezing on the spot, I turned abruptly. One of the fishermen had put a grappling hook through a seal. They lifted it on the hoist into the back of a pickup truck. "Hurry, hurry, before the game warden see us." A bullet hole pierced the seal's head. The driver shifted and drove away rapidly.

Cold air, fog, wind, chop, I didn't care. I wanted to know. Was that my seal friend? I paddled the distance to Steamer Lane faster than ever. Sitting on my board, I looked down into the depths, tracing the shimmering kelp to darkness.

There he was, suspended deep beneath my board. He looked up through the kelp and was smiling. Elated, he hadn't been caught in the net and shot. I thought, well, not this time.

He nuzzled his nose against my leg, surfaced, barked at me, "Ark, ark, ark," and sped away to the Cormorant bird rock, which we all used as a line up for the middle peak.

Five minutes later I saw him surface, holding a big Ling Cod in his teeth. Swimming toward me, he gently nudged my hand, which hung in the water, and put the fish between my legs. God, I thought, they'll never believe this. I yelled at the seal, "Whoopee, ark, ark, ark."

Cleaning the fish in the shorebreak at Cowell's I threw the entrails to the circling and screaming seagulls, walked up the beach, gathered firewood, and cooked the fish over the coals.

After dinner, I settled in front of the fire, and fell fast asleep. Long before dawn, I was awakened by a pounding shorebreak.

It was a glorious morning, almost warm, with no fog or wind.

I tried a few Cowell's waves, each time returning to the line up to look out to Steamer Lane. It was big. Waves broke out farther than I had seen. I heard a bark out at the Lane. Paddling closer, I heard more barks. At first it sounded like the seal barking, "Ark, ark, ark," but I realized that it was not barking that I heard now. "Come sur wi me," slurred but definitely intelligible.

I called to him, "I'm coming, wait for me!" The seal sat on the outside fringe of kelp, and just before I reached him, he took off on a huge single peak, feathered his fin, and cut out right in front of me. He looked me in the eye and barked, "Ark, ark, ark," but I heard, "I want to be friend. What you name? My name Colisko Boski."

I answered as if one of my professors at San Francisco State had asked me to stand and recite. Tongue tied, attempting to maintain one of the many realities I moved back and forth from, "My name, uh, uh, name uh, Fred Van Dyke."

Colisko Boski told me that he wanted to teach me how to surf better, to improve my judgment for he said that judgment was the crowning point of surfing.

By late afternoon, we were conversing just as if I were sitting out there with Dave and Gene. Colisko told me that he had escaped from the aquarium in San Francisco. He spoke of when he was a seal pup following his mother from his birthplace, Alaska, and how he got caught in a net. The next thing he remembered was life in the San Francisco Aquarium. Colisko said that they treated him well, but he did not like the confinement.

I warned him of the dangers outside the aquarium, the fishermen, and what I had heard while eating breakfast. Colisko Boski assured me that no dumb fisherman would catch him in a net. He had learned that lesson while, after capture as a seal pup, he swam the boring short laps in the pool where he lived.

The fog moved back into Steamer; the day slipped away. I left my new friend, feeling deep pangs of loneliness, much like when you left me, Joan, to go back to Hawaii.

I lay in front of the fire that night feeling good about the seal, yet knowing that if I told the story I would be ridiculed. I saw myself talking to my master teacher, answering his questions in class about my lesson plans. "Uh, professor, I didn't make any lesson plans. You see, I met this seal who spoke to me in English and taught me to surf better. "

If I told the story my teaching credential would be history. Dave and Gene would mock and jeer at me.

Saturday morning Gene, Dave, and I sat in the Pier Bathhouse and ate breakfast. I told them how big Steamer had been.

Dave asked me, "Wasn't it scary surfing big Steamer alone?"

"I didn't surf alone. I'll tell you the story." As we paddled out to Steamer Lane I told them the story of Colisko Boski, including the fish that Colisko had given me. Gene and Dave dropped back, and I heard them mumbling over the roar of Steamer.

Dave in his sardonic manner paddled up to me and said, "Well I guess all you have to do is cut out of school during the week and hire a seal."

Gene interrupted, "There's a seal out there. Is that your buddy seal? Why don't you ask him if it is going to get bigger today?"

There he was, swimming toward the seal rock. I yelled, "Colisko Boski, Colisko Boski, come meet my friends."

He remained well beyond the sets of waves. "I can't. I've got to swim to Alaska for my first mating season." Colisko Boski climbed upon the seaward side of the seal rock and barked at a young female seal. They both dove into the sea and headed northwest.

"So, what's the big deal?" Dave yelled. "So, a seal barks at another seal on seal rock."

Gene laughed uproariously. We all laughed, I for a completely different reason. All that they heard was, " Ark, ark, ark." That was probably all that they would ever hear from seals, poor fools.

Joan laughed, "Well, I believe the story. It is a wonderful relationship that you had with Colisko."

We arrived at Peter's house, and Joan let me out. She turned off the motor and walked up the stairway into the sky. Peter met us and asked if we wanted a beer. "Why not?" I replied.

Joan said that she had to get back to the city and took a rain check. I walked her to the car. "You know, I like being with you. It is easy and I find you very attractive. You've been working out? Why don't you come up to the city and we'll take it from there? I'm pretty sure that Michael is out of the picture soon. I asked him to move. I just don't want to jump from one relationship right away to another I've got to go. My father will have the Highway Patrol searching for me. Give me a hug and a kiss."

She kissed me like she meant it, and I walked up the stairs to Peter's. Gayle was ecstatic and told me that she had known that Joan would not stay away too long. It was all right with me.

After dinner I sat on the deck, drinking a beer. Looking over to the other side of the valley; the second growth Redwood trees shone in moonlight. The air cooled as I remembered it. I took Airgorn for a walk. Gayle's dog loved running the valley with me, but tonight we walked leisurely, devouring all the shadowy sights, enjoying the scents. "Airgorn, do you like to walk?"

He barked so loud that Peter yelled, "Quiet that dog."

Walking the long line of stairs, I heard the phone ring, and Gayle came out the door, "Someone on the phone for you."

She handed it to me and the familiar, "Uh, uh, hello," carried into my ears like Hershey kisses sliding down my throat.

Joan told me that her dad and mother, with tongue in cheek, thought that we were still just good friends." Why don't you come up tomorrow?" We talked for an hour, at least, and Peter said that he was glad the bill was not on him.

The next morning I thanked Gayle and Peter profusely, telling them that their home had saved me from totally losing it. I drove to San Francisco a renewed person, noticed the fog moving off the coast, a little rain shower that created a double rainbow, and slowed for a number of deer crossing the road. I saw one handsome and healthy coyote. It was a good trip. Most of what I had left was still there, the Redwood forest, second growth, which stretched to the horizon, the Spring Valley Lakes. The highway near San Francisco was a freeway, and the traffic got heavier and faster, but I was falling in love with California, again, like it was my first sight.

Chapter 24

Will You Promise Me?

Back in Hawaii, I first of all experienced the heavy humidity closing in on me. My beach house on the North Shore lay impeccably trimmed in ocean, surf, and sky. When you walk through the wooden gate, you are met by greenery: plumeria, ginger, papaya, banana trees, watered by the trade wind showers that built in the evening and dawn hours. The temperature, as soon as you passed over the summit at Schofield and left Honolulu behind, dropped at least five degrees Fahrenheit. It was a different world, somewhat like the contrast between San Francisco and Boulder Creek.

Scanning my land for the first time in weeks, I was pleased with this oasis surrounded by palm trees and walked to the surf check platform shadowed and cool beneath the trees to watch the ocean. Surf at this time of the year was most often non-existent. I decided to make a dive, assembled the cobweb-covered fins, facemask, snorkel, spear, stringer to hang fish, and walked across the beach to the sea.

It was a beautiful day, and the water as clear as looking into a mirror. I wanted fish for dinner and scanned the reef below. Certain parts of a reef harbor particular fish, and others are barren. I knew all the holes and moved to one up toward Rocky Point, aptly named for the deep crevices, tunnels, and protrusions that meant fish lived there.

Hyperventilating, I dove the twenty feet to the lava reef, held tightly to a piece of coral, looked deeply into the hole, a sandy bottom, and sun streamed through from cracks in the lava. I hung as motionless as possible, held my breath and saw an aweoweo, a red snapper-like fish, holding on the edge of the hole.

The fish turned sideways, and I let fly the spear, which punctured the reef fish just above its gills. It quivered, but was speared solidly. Pulling the spear from the hole, I grabbed the fish and surfaced, killed it, and hung it on the stringer. I was thinking of how I could entice Joan to come out and have dinner with me, maybe stay the night. I needed more fish and I knew how she loved lobster.

The second aweoweo was an easy shot. Once these fish sight you, they have an uncanny curiosity to come closer. That is the moment. If you wait, the fish darts into a cave. I didn't wait, and the fish was on my stringer as I swam the reef in search of the feelers that lobsters stuck out from their protective place in the reef.

No feelers showing so I dove one hole after another and found them. They sat fairly far back in this narrow crevice, each set of feelers pointing at me. I was being monitored.

A trick I use, and it works, is to prod your spear from one angle, distract the radar antennae, and then slowly reach from the opposite angle. Two of them fell for the ploy and I had them strung quickly. The others scattered when I went down again.

Thanking the reef God, I swam to shore, cleaned the fish, walked up to my house, and boiled water, dropped the lobsters in and waited. They turned a solid red and I turned the flame off. The fish were refrigerated and the lobsters left to cool.

The next step was to entice Joan. I dialed her number, and the familiar, "Uh, uh, hello," filled my mind with solace. I asked her how it felt to be back? Was she ready to go to the first teacher's meetings soon?

"I hit the jackpot today and I am inviting you for dinner, All right?" "What do you mean, jackpot?"

"I got lobster and reef fish today, and I want you to share them with me."

"That's an invitation I can't turn down. What time should I come? Should I bring something?"

"Just yourself. I'll take care of the rest. Come right now and we can swim before dinner." Setting the table and gathering flowers

221

from my garden, I spread them throughout the house. Marinating the fish in wine, lemon juice, soy sauce, and pressed garlic spread freely, I moved to preparing a salad, refrigerated it all, and changed to my bathing suit.

I filled the wait by digging up weeds on the ocean side of the house and got lost in the task, until I heard from behind, "Uh, uh, hello."

Joanie moved toward me and removed her shirt, revealing a trim body bikini clad. She moved toward the beach. I followed with two towels, placed them near the sea, and lay down. Wispy clouds passed, cooling the sun only slightly as they moved offshore. We both drifted in and out of napping.

I felt hot and moved to swim, followed by Joan. We dove in and swam a hundred yards out, stopped and looked back to the vines, shrubbery, Norfolk pine trees interspersed, and kissed. On the North Shore the ocean is a few degrees cooler than Waikiki. We didn't hold the kiss for long and swam to shore. We showered together in my unique outdoor set up which consisted of an open space on top and below for the trade winds to circulate, while the wood screened our bodies from knees to neck.

Joan dressed in warmer clothes, and I met her out on the surf check platform, handing her a glass of cabernet.

The sun slowly lowered in the west, and we looked for the green flash that supposedly springs from behind the horizon as the sun sets. Joan told me to close my eyes and when she said open, do it immediately. I was skeptical after having never seen the flash, but followed her orders.

"Open now. It's a few seconds away. Hold on; the sun is setting." The sun dropped below the horizon, and the flash occurred so quickly that I almost missed it, but definitely experienced the perpendicular, narrow, tear shaped green figure.

"I saw it! I saw it! It really does happen." I toasted and kissed her. The best part of the day was right now, the wind barely moving the coconut palms, the last of light and strings of red, blue, green, spreading into the sky, and Joan Marie sitting next to me.

Mosquitoes finished the moment and drove us indoors. Heating up the lobsters and butter, I sauteed the fish in garlic. The dinner ready, I toasted that we were together again. Joan said, "I'll drink to that." She really made the best of the moment, savoring each tender bit of lobster. I passed her a filet of aweoweo. She tasted it and said that it was gourmet. I told her that the aweoweo fed on crustaceans, especially lobster.

Joan did stay and we spent the rest of the evening talking, climbing into bed early, and sleeping until dawn. We took a walk on the beach, and time passed into noon, and my fairy princess drove away in her Maverick. She called me later that night, crying into the phone. "Michael and I fought from the time I arrived home, and he knew where I had been. I asked him to pack his belongings and move out. It was a terrible scene."

I knew that they were not on the closest terms, and that their relationship was heading without an anchor onto the rocks. He had his chance and now it was mine, and I was not going to lose her again.

"School starts in a few days. Come stay with me until the meetings. It's the best thing to do, and the safest. Give Michael a chance to exit first."

It was a wonderful few days, and the night before school, we left my place and drove to Honolulu, parking her car, and unloading my clothes for school. All that was Michael was gone. We made the bed together, a waterbed, which took me some time getting used to the ocean like undulations; being a surfer I accommodated. The bottom line was that I was with Joanie.

We established a comfortable routine, spending the school week at Joan's house, and my beach house on most weekends. When I first kissed Joan, I knew that surfing would take a back seat, that I had found the woman for my life. I realized big wave riding had been my way of getting love and great amounts of recognition, but I didn't need that anymore.

After I met and spent time with Joan, I realized how empty my life had been with the newspaper, television, magazine glory that I had basked in for so long as a living legend. There were about fifty of us in the entire surfing world. Now when I drove up to my favorite surf spot and saw my friends riding wave after wave, I was not interested. I had done it. I didn't have to do it anymore. Every time that I had gone out in twenty-five foot waves, my life had been on the line.

Before, when I listened to the huge waves breaking out in front of my beach house, I rarely slept, but lay there sweating, grinding my teeth, in deep fear that the dawn would come and I'd have to bite the bullet. But now I enjoyed riding small waves, and probably will for the rest of my life. I'm free and acquiring my big wave now, is to gain love forever from Joan Marie.

The thing about our relationship, as it grew, was that we had fun in whatever we did. Joan was very conservative in ways, but loved the free life. When I surfed, big waves, I had only thought of one thing. Nothing came into compete, not former wives, children or job. My career was seeking big waves. I lied, cheated to be out when the surf was huge. In retrospect I do not know how I survived. Friends of mine were not as fortunate as me. But now I found life in everything again.

Joan and I flew to San Francisco for Christmas with Joan's parents, her sister, Carol, and her boyfriend, Michael. It was the first year that I had given up Christmas vacation, which usually produced the biggest waves of the year. We had been together for a little more than five months. We had skirted marriage, agreeing that it could ruin our relationship, and left the idea in the back seat.

In San Francisco, a crisp and sunny day, we walked the beach, me sneaking side glances at Joan, grasping her hand, and I felt a change in my psyche take control. It was a revelation in its least form.

I thought. This is the woman I searched for, saw disguised in my LSD trip, fell in love with the first time I saw her walking across the pool on top of the water, the woman who freed me from the bonds of trying to keep up with the gang out surfing, who showed me love as I had never experienced, had given me a chance to be a man instead of a macho boy.

Driving down Lunado Way, I dropped Joan at her house, and said that I was going out to buy beer. She said not to stay away too long. I still carried some of the rituals of surfing. Driving back to the beach, I parked, looked out into the sea where I had first swum out beyond the breakers with Cliff. However, a plan formed in my mind.

224

Why not? I thought. I'll be a damned fool if I don't. I'm going to buy her a ring.

Driving into a West Portal jeweler, I looked at engagement rings.

I was humming like a bumblebee when I rang the door at Lunado, the ring burning a hole in my shirt. Joan's mother answered. "Well don't you look like the cat that just swallowed the canary." I hugged her. I knew that they both thought that I was too old for their daughter, but they had visited us in Hawaii, and that seemed to be a plus.

The next morning dawned, sunshine and cold, but a beautiful brisk San Francisco, a little frost on the grass. It looked like it would warm up by afternoon so I asked Joan to take a ride down the coast. I wanted to show her a secret beach that was isolated.

Quickly finishing breakfast, I waited while Joan showered, dressed, and stepped into the living room, awaiting approval.

"Yes, you're beautiful. Let's get going."

As we drove the coastline beyond Pedro Point, a squall moved in and drenched the area, rain dropping so heavily that it was difficult to see the road. We stopped at Pomponio Beach, but had to keep the windshield working. Otherwise, you couldn't see the beach I wanted to walk with Joan, sit down behind a dune, and make my proposal. The rain did not stop and it got colder, enough so that I flipped on the heater switch. The windows fogged and we were definitely alone. I waited, but the rain continued, me getting more of a knot in my stomach.

I had wanted this magical moment to be perfect, my fantasies, a romantic setting washed away into a storm drain. I felt bitter that on this day of all days that nature had failed me. I even thought of forgetting the whole thing, wait for a nice day, but Joan broke the silence. "Is this your secret beach? What's going on with you? How come the silence?"

I looked to the ocean. "Let's walk. To hell with the storm."

"We'll get soaked. It's half freezing already."

Wrapping her in the woolen blanket that lay across the back seat, I persuaded her to step into the rain. We held close to each other and the rain pelted our faces. We walked and walked, and I couldn't get the words in my head to sound right, to flow.

I thought, Joan, you are the most special person in my universe, blurting out finally to her, "I love you."

She stopped and turned to me. "So, you had to take me forty miles down the coast in a blinding storm to tell me that?"

I smiled and laughed like an awkward teenager. "Joan, I love you." Reaching deep into my pocket, I pulled out the little square box that held the ring, grabbed Joan's hands between mine and said, "Will you marry me?"

Joan looked up at me. "I didn't think you'd ever ask. Yes. Hold me."

Placing the ring on her finger, I sighed deep inside. However, Joan was shivering almost uncontrollably. We rushed to the car. I turned the heat up full and drove toward San Francisco, and said in passing. "You know, we don't have to get married right away, maybe wait a while, and see where it takes us." If my foot could have fit, I would have stuffed it in my mouth.

"Just like a man," said Joan. "You just proposed and now you're trying to back out."

"Nah, just kidding." I knew that I was scared, thinking about the things that made it appear impossible that a marriage could be the right thing to do, my children from my earlier marriages always in the background wanting their share of me, whether her parents would put up resistance because of the age difference.

I peered through the windshield, the wipers creating a semi-hypnotic state in me, and thought of the joy we experienced when together, how we spent nearly twenty four hours a day together and had little friction. I had to admit to myself that giving up my freedom was a huge step as I had been burned in the past. I didn't think I'd ever get married again, but it seemed so right.

Joan screamed, "You're running off the road!"

Swerving, I gained control. "Yeah, sorry, I was just thinking."

Arriving in San Francisco, Joan called her parents and told them to meet us at the Cafe across the street from their office. We got into the restaurant just before her parents came. I told Joan to hide the ring.

Seated, we made idle comments, talked about what was on the menu, listened to the waitress describe the specials. Neither one of

226

us cared much about the specials, but played the game. It was only two in the afternoon, but I ordered a bottle of champagne and said, "It's after five somewhere in the world."

When the four of us finished lunch, I poured the last of the champagne, and raised my arm to make a toast. "I want to share with you that Joan, in a driving sleet storm, wet and freezing, accepted my proposal of marriage."

I wasn't sure how the news was received, but Paul did shake my hand, and Bobbie, "Well, I'm not surprised after the way you acted yesterday, Fred."

I know that when we went home to their house, I still had to sleep on the couch, not too consoling for me. We did hold off on the wedding until the following Christmas. Joan thought that we should practice a little more before taking such a grandiose step. I agreed. The time passed and in mid fall, Joan spent a great deal of time planning with her mother and Carol, her sister. Our phone bill was an astronomical disaster, but all moved toward a smooth conclusion.

I knew that Joan's father felt that I was too old for her, but he seemed outwardly accepting, and that was enough for me. Her mother may have seemed relieved. I went with Joan when she picked out the wedding dress, a lovely, stylish dress, simple in its creation, but an eye catcher, as I felt Joan Marie was.

Christmas Vacation came, and we flew the red-eye to San Francisco, Paul picking us up at the airport near dawn. It was cold, but felt good to me. We drove home and I told Paul that I needed to buy a new suit for the wedding. He took me to visit his tailor and I was measured, ended up buying two suits, one for summer and winter visits. The wedding was to be in San Rafael, performed by a friend, a former chaplain from Punahou School where we taught. The reception was to be in San Francisco at Paul's club, The World Trade Club, in the Ferry Building on the bay.

Wedding day, December twenty-sixth arrived, and I ran to the Ocean Beach, took a dip in the winter water, and ran back around Lake Merced, a perfect day, warm for winter, and not a breath of wind. Much of my joy seemed controlled by glassy days, whether fishing, surfing, diving or an upcoming wedding.

227

The place was in utter turmoil when I arrived and opened the door, Joan and Carol, Bobbie putting the finishing touches on dress up. Sam Wilson, my best man, and his wife had flown up from Santa Monica, and he was attempting to assuage my manifest anxiety. All came together near departure time, and friends from Montana arrived. The house was filling to capacity. Michael, Carol's boyfriend, opened two bottles of champagne, and everyone toasted in guarded sips, not glass fulls.

The church was in a wonderfully quiet, wooded neighborhood, and when our two cars arrived, I saw many people milling in the sunny, but brisk day. There were about fifty people, and I shook all of their hands, knowing some, meeting others for the first time. I saw my parents standing off to the side, and hastened to them. "I'm so happy that you came. Let's go into the church." I seated my parents on one side and helped Bobbie and Paul to the other pew. People filed in; my eyes blurred. It's really happening, I thought.

In a daze I followed Sam to the alter, looked back to the sea of faces, and saw Joan Marie, my queen to be, enter, Paul leading her to me. The critical moment arrived; the Chaplain asked, "Who gives this woman away?"

Paul appearing somewhat overcome, and Joan standing in beauty, said, "I do." He walked to his wife, sat down, and tears streamed down his cheeks. I didn't know if this was a positive or negative expression.

I assumed the best and smiled into the crowd. Joan and I read an acknowledgment of love and gratitude to both of our parents. More tears. I faced Joan, saw Oregon, northern California, the rainy beach, and said, "Yes, I do." Joan expressed likewise. The chaplain pronounced us man and wife, said that I could kiss the bride. I did, and we walked out to the street, quickly surrounded by relatives and friends from both sides.

Half the party followed my parents and about half Sam, his wife, Dodie, Joan, and me. The club, downtown at the edge of the bay, was about a twenty-minute drive. On Bush Street, I turned toward the beach and most of the wedding party followed the others to the club.

It was sunset time, and I didn't want to miss that green flash on the day of my wedding, or neglect to check the surf. The glassiness dominated, the surf perfectly formed, and we hugged while our Montana friends and Dodie took pictures. The flashes came from all directions, and then it was dark, and time to make our appearance at the reception. Traffic was heavy, and we arrived about a half an hour later than the early arrivals. No one had taken a drink, and Bobbie appeared a bit miffed.

Jerry, a professor from Montana State University, had hand carried a crated magnum of French champagne that we had won last summer in a Montana triathlon. The waiters held the bottle like it was a sheep waiting to be sheered and the cork slid out. They poured champagne and Sam, the best man, proposed a toast.

We drank to that toast and the waiter approached me and asked if Joan and I would care for a refill? Before he could pour, I heard this familiar voice behind me pronounce loudly, "Waiter, my son has had enough." Laughter nearly brought the house down. Here I was a grown man and my mother was squelching my alcohol consumption. Someone whispered to me that mothers don't change.

The food exquisite, Joan and I felt very loved and proposed a toast to Paul and Bobbie, my parents, Sam and Dodie, and finally, to love.

Carol and Michael had reserved a room for us in the Queen Anne, a wonderful old refurbished Victorian mansion, high above the city on Bush Street. The next morning we lay in bed relaxed, in love, and hungry. Sam called and said that he had made reservations for brunch at the Palace Hotel.

It was an exotic meal, Sam, his wife and son, my new mother and father-in-law, and Carol and Michael feasted and spoke of getting together this summer when we traveled to California.

Joan had an aunt, Carmen, whose husband always took her to Yosemite in the fall. No one understood why they went when winter was around the corner. I asked Joan where she would like to go on our honeymoon, and she replied, "Yosemite."

I got to sleep with Joan in her old bedroom. We left the next day, Joan's mother insisting that we call them the moment we arrived and telling us to drive carefully on the icy roads.

We drove the distance in about four hours. The higher we got into the mountains, the thicker the snow. It was a majestic drive and suddenly we rounded a corner, and the Yosemite Valley unfolded beneath us.

Swirling mist rose through the trees, snow clinging to their needles, appearing like a Christmas tree. Huge slabs of granite lay in our path down the curving road. I put the car into the lowest gear and descended very slowly. Dropping into the forest the air cooled considerably, and I had to turn the heat up.

Stopping at the Ahwahnee Lodge, we added a woolen sweater and walked up to the desk. "Sorry sir, but we are booked a year in advance."

On the way out, Joan saw the restaurant, a majestic place with ceilings that reached for sky. We made a reservation for dinner, and searched around the park for lodging. It was mid-week so there were openings at a group of log cabins. We chose the most isolated.

The cabin was small, but warm and quaintly cheerful. We lay around for a while, decided on a walk, and added clothes. Yosemite in the winter, during the week, is a delight. Deer, squirrels, chipmunks, and blue jays were everywhere, and we petted a few deer.

A slight powdery snow fell, and we returned to our cabin, shed our clothes, and fell into one another's arms. Our cabin felt overly warm after walking the valley floor.

Yosemite was another aspect of California's diversity, from mountains, desert to sea, each with its own specific climate, but Yosemite touched me nearly as strongly as the Redwoods. There was a definite starkness in Yosemite whereas the Redwoods blanketed, softened to the outside world. John Muir wrote passionately of his affair with Yosemite. It broke his heart and some of the spirit he displayed when engineers created a dam in the valley just north of Yosemite to trap water for San Francisco. The water was necessary, but the dam could have been built farther down the system. Now dams are built at sea level trapping the water that eventually ends in the sea. Hetch Hetchy Dam is a continuing travesty on nature. The lake behind the dam during drought conditions exposes flora, which are destroyed by outside invading bacteria, creating fetidness in a once ecologically balanced self-propagating system.

Designed to blend in with the surrounding forest and austere cliff backdrop, stood the hotel's granite facade. The Ahwahnee Hotel was delightful, a huge fireplace standing far higher than me, intricately placed huge river rocks, kept it toasty. Priceless Native American baskets, paintings, and photographs adorned the interior.

Seated, we craned our necks upward, admiring the chandeliers, the designs hand-painted on the log support beams, and the superb architecture. We ordered deboned rainbow trout, bathed in a delicious sauce, a salad of crisp spinach leaves, and finely sliced tomatoes seasoned with a balsamic, garlic, vinaigrette dressing. Bread was baked daily, and dessert, strawberries and cream.

Walking to our cabin it was so dark, the sky filled with billions of stars, that we followed the road by the break in the trees. Checking at the manager's office about places to visit, he said that Badger Pass ski lodge would be exciting if it didn't snow tonight.

Our cabin was cozy, not like the log rooms up at Shingletown with a fireplace, but we settled for the beauty that lay all around us. Morning came crispy, with a clear sky and no wind. There wasn't much snow on the ground in the valley, but as we ascended deeper piles lay by the roadside. The turn off for Badger Ski area loomed, and I made a right turn, climbed up a freshly plowed road, and soon watched skiers descending the white mountain. We stopped in the parking lot, and walked to the edge where you needed snowshoes or skis.

Neither one of us had watched skiing up close, and it looked exciting to see these people zooming down the mountain, to turn out in front of the ski lift and do it again.

We both hit on an idea when we saw a young kid, not over four years of age, ski down and make turns. "Are you game?" asked Joan.

"We're really not dressed for skiing and I don't want to try the lift. Sure, we'll hike up the mountain as we improve, and maybe by the end of the day try the lift."

Renting skis, boots, and poles, we ascended the bunny run, clamped our skis in place, and leaned forward. Little kids of varying ages skied by us, and we fell about ten times on the way down the one hundred foot long beginner's slope. We were excited and tried the rope tow, lessening our loss of energy. Two hours later, we ascended the rope tow with ease, and soon were making wide turns to the bottom.

It was time to go higher and steeper, but it was getting late to use the lift. We decided on the safest, but most difficult, to take off skis, and climb the mountain to the steepness we could negotiate.

Looking down from three-hundred yards up, I was not sure that I had made the right decision, but leaned forward on an angle, and swoosh, the skis moved lightning like, leaving me flat on my back. The slope was much steeper than the bunny run, and the next challenge was to stand up. Sitting up, I watched Joan move a hundred yards down, making many turns, and fall.

I made some turns catching up to Joan. Stopping, I bent to help her. We both ended up face forward in the snow, sat up, and decided that we would ski the remaining down hill, and call it quits. We made it without a fall, felt like accomplished skiers, stepped out of the bindings, bent and picked up our skis, trying to appear as well seasoned.

There was a little refreshment bar near the car, and we ordered brandy. It hit our bloodstreams like an anesthesiologist's needle filled with morphine. We sat on the deck, the sun already behind trees, and hugged. Joan said that she had more fun today than ever. We were hooked on skiing, and couldn't wait until the next attempt.

Driving back to San Francisco eased in difficulty as soon as we were below the snow level. Entering the Interstate 80 freeway, I held at seventy miles an hour, drove across the Bay Bridge, and coasted into Lunado Way. We were tired, sore, hungry, but so stoked on our new adventure. Joan ran the stairs, rang the doorbell, and embraced her father. "We had so much fun skiing today."

I climbed slowly, trying to bring all the clothes in one trip. I didn't want to do the stairs again. After dinner we had no romantic illusions, and fell into deep sleep, awaking the next morning with stiff muscles, but otherwise feeling wonderful.

"Joan there's a place I want to show you. I mentioned it a couple of times, Sutro Forest." The forest, what was not turned into housing developments, still stood as originally when my friends and I explored. I had told Joan about the cliff that the big kids had trapped me on, and how I had jumped, slid to the bottom only getting some heavy scratches.

Part of the hill had been gouged out to make room for the high-rise condominiums, but there was still the cliff, and I pointed out where I had jumped and slid. One did not drink the water from the stream further up 7th Avenue, and the mountain lions and deer were gone, but raccoons still flourished, and who knew what animals hid in the remaining forest?

Visiting the forest was a 360-degree recall for me, and I was happy that I had shared some of it with my wife, Joan Marie.

Chapter 25

Magic Sparkles
Ever more

The atomic bomb brought the Japanese to surrender on August 15th 1945. There had never been such a fell swoop destruction in the history of man, two cities wiped out, the survivors faced with inevitable cancers that would manifest later, possibly, in generations to follow. Our leaders had assumed that such a victory had no encumbrances attached. It looked good for a short time. The bomb had stopped World War II, saving thousands of lives down the line. Had Harry Truman, then President of the United States, done the right thing?

Groups of scientists traced the wind currents, suspecting that a possible fallout over the northern hemisphere could occur. Atomic scientists scoffed at the hypothesis. The fallout had long gone into the atmosphere and dissipated they argued.

The caribou in Alaska ate lichens, which were a staple in their diet; the lichens had become radioactive, and the caribou followed suit as they grazed. Eskimos hunt caribou as a staple in their diets. Cancer began to show up in these people, far above what could normally be expected. The radioactive fallout had traveled those miles across the ocean and infected the entire food chain in Alaska. The suffering that the Japanese and peoples downwind of the Atomic explosion may have more than equaled the stopping the war short.

A so-called wonder spray was developed that destroyed all forms of insect life, mosquitoes, fleas, lice, vegetable parasites. DDT! It was lauded as the miracle of the century. RKO Movie News photographed children in Europe, bending their heads forward as machines filled with DDT drove down the streets spraying for lice.

Crop dusters sprayed fields, which blew into surrounding neighborhoods. Soon it was found in the tissues of all plants and animals, including man. In the 50's and 60's Hawaii used more insecticides than any other state in the U.S.A. Crop dusters in Hawaii sprayed fields to kill the multitudes of differing insects. The Filipino workers in the fields got direct spraying with resultant problems. Too little was known about the affects of spraying without any protection, like facemasks for example. Before the migration of conquerors, traders, missionaries, and colonizers came to Hawaii, including the Hawaiians themselves, there were no mosquitoes, no pigs, no parasites, no introduced species of flora and fauna. Hawaii was truly a paradise then.

Bureaucratic agencies associated with the war effort mostly folded when the war ended, except for the Army Corp. of Engineers. They immediately transferred efforts from war to saving our country from the neglect of the war years. Their selling point wherever they went was received with open arms by trusting Americans. They showed slides, scientific evidence to back up their created needs, built dams on as many rivers as they deemed dangerous to progress, cleared swampland to make it productive.

The Army Corp. of Engineers facilitated the movement of many rivers to the sea by cementing them into culverts, passageways with not a curve to slow down the water moving to the ocean.

The Los Angeles River, once a meandering navigable body of water, had a spawning run of salmon and steelhead before the creation of culverts. The upper portions of the river had a substantial population of rainbow trout. Except during heavy storm rains, which are not usual in Los Angeles, the culvert is dry, and punks race up and down its length shooting at each other. Whatever water might have been allowed to flow seaward is pumped out by the agriculture industry, which has become, in most cases, an organized conglomerate that slowly, but surely engulfs the small subsistence farmer. DDT has, except illegally, been replaced by a number of other cancer producing agents. The cancer rate soars, for many reasons, but the bottom line is that California remains one of the healthiest states to reside in.

Land developers bulldozed forests, streams, and entire mountains to create homes, business offices, and roadways to these newly named tracts. After denuding and leveling of all plots, the developer on completion of the house or office, landscaped the area with the same flora destroyed. Where one hundred year old trees grew, now are seedlings, and lawns to replace indigenous wildflowers. Spraying of wildflower seeking poisons are used flagrantly with little fear of the potential destruction to other plant and animal species. Somehow the FDA passes on these chemicals and then years later a major discovery shows the deleterious affects.

The golf course lawns, trimmed hedges make a great appearance, but the thousands of pounds of insecticides used to maintain these decorative flora eventually drains into our drinking water sources, and the ocean. The Public Health Department issues statements, often, about the affects of eating fish from lakes, streams, and the ocean. Pregnant women are warned not to eat fish from certain sources and from some waters eating the fish is a calculated health hazard. The striped bass I so loved to supply my family with during the war is considered toxic enough that it is unsafe to eat more than once a month, and even then you take a chance.

The Farallon Islands, nearly thirty miles west of San Francisco, are a small group of inert volcanoes, a portion of the Pacific Belt of Fire. The islands are one of the main sources of fishing off San Francisco. Fish in abundance, cod, snappers, smelt, perch, salmon, striped bass, halibut, and others inhabit the reef.

After the Second World War, the waste from atomic energy piled up, stored in fifty-gallon oil drums. The Atomic industry, under pressure from environmental groups and private citizens, had to get rid of this potentially lethal threat to large populations. They submerged these barrels off the Farallon Islands, dumped a poisonous substance, the most cancer-producing agent, into the ocean. The atomic waste has a half-life of many generations. Less than fifty years after dumping, some of the drums filled with these poisons have eroded and leaked.

A huge public outcry forced the industry to do something again. They made futile attempts to collect the remaining barrels for in the sea everything grows and gets covered up. Metal disintegrates, but atomic waste is much slower. Testing showed that the fish, the seals, crabs, most of the sea life were contaminated, especially clams, oysters, abalone, who are the scavengers of the reef. There has been little believable evidence that this dilemma will not work its way up the food chain and affect man.

The Coast Guard, in its zeal to protect our coastlines during the war, depth charged much of the sea population, and post war the fishing industry, able to get unlimited gasoline, fished out the sardines in a brief period of time. This affected the entire ecological web dependent upon sardines for food. Other lesser bait fishes had to suffice as food.

The sardine, considered extinct by scientists since 1947, has begun to show in small numbers. Hypotheses continue. The sardines migrated from areas not fished out, or considered extinct some must have survived, and many other theories abound. The positive, undeniable fact, is that if given a chance, nature can heal itself and replenish its abundance.

Some things are irretrievable tragedies, like the golf course up at the source of Boulder Creek, the bulldozing of near impenetrable brush and forest, the side pond filled with carp which drains into Boulder Creek, and leaves it dry in places that were salmon and steelhead spawning beds. The sell-out by the butcher who loved steelhead fishing of some of that land at the golf course for college educations for his children, I can't fathom.

Through it all, I still get the same feeling of relaxation and wonder when I drive into that first cover of redwoods on Highway 9. Walking in the Big Basin State Park is a continuing dreamland fantasy for me. I took Joan and my in-laws to visit the park. We hiked the path of giant Redwoods, and Paul, after looking at the trees, said, "Fred, you get a sore neck looking up at these trees."

The last time I had gone down into the Dinky Creek gorge out of Fresno was 1948. It had been a long time. I talked Joan into packing a large lunch. Fresno was about a five-hour drive. We drove over the

Pacheco Pass into the San Joaquin Valley and I noticed that a freeway system was expanded, bypassing most of the towns I remembered hitchhiking through. I remembered Fresno as holding a population of about 25,000 people. The Fresno off ramps unfolded, one after another, the population now exceeding 350,000 people. My last visit I had driven into the town on Highway 99, a three laner, the middle lane a passing area for both sides of the road. It was dangerous.

I didn't see the Fresno State College campus from the freeway and passed to the road heading eastward. Fresno expanded in all directions, housing tract upon tract.

We drove into open space, rolling hills, and approached where the Trimmer bar had been located. I stopped at a small filling station and asked the attendant, "How far to the Trimmer bar?"

Bursting into laughter, he said, "It's about a mile down the road around a corner, but you ain't gonna get no beer there. It's somewhere buried under that huge dam that was built."

Driving up and around the dam, I continued to Dinky Creek and then Oak Flat where I had camped. Where I had feared to drive, lay a paved road and a camp filled with Winnebagos. People sat in their camps, drinking beer. Some teenagers played the car stereo loud enough for the entire camp to hear, but no one seemed bothered.

Hiking the brief distance to the overlook, I peered into the same huge granite slopes, tree filled gorge, and a posted sign that reassured me for a time. "Dinky Creek 2 miles — Watch for rattlesnakes." The new trail seemed to be well maintained, unlike the "struggle-through-brush-throw-rocks- ahead-to-warn-snakes" trail that we had blazed.

Voices resounded up the granite cliffs. I saw a serpentine of people walking up the many switchbacks, an occasional peg of iron stuck into the granite as a hand support. They reached the top, one carrying a creel. My curiosity wetted, I asked if I could look at his catch. "Sure," he proudly handed me the creel.

I looked. There were three dried out trout, the biggest not over nine inches.

"Fishing's been lousy all summer since they ain't put no helicopter drop of hatchery trout in the gorge. Even if they did, they'd all get caught in a couple of days."

I talked to him of the pre-fifties and the twenty inch trout landed when the limit was twenty-five. I told him that we slid down on our bottoms across granite slabs, and protectively wrapped our trout in damp ferns before attempting the near perpendicular ascent in blazing sun.

I told him that there was a stretch below the gorge where we never even tried, the fishing being so good at the bottom of the descent, why bother? We left when he lit a cigar, stopping along the road to the King's river where a deep hole lay. It was a magnificent place, framed granite thousands of feet high rose into the blue sky. Pine trees swayed in a gentle, but warm breeze. It was too tempting and we stripped into bathing suits and swam, the water cold, but not icy. We lay in a small sand spit and soaked up the sun. I wasn't going to drink the creek water, but Dinky creek had retained a good part of its ruggedness. Shadows stretched across the creek, leaving only a sparse sun spot to lie in. It was time to leave, but I felt glad that I had found this deep hole.

The day before we left for Hawaii, Joan and I walked the beach in San Francisco from Sloat Boulevard to the Cliff House and back. The beach was overrun with people, a beach which had signs prominent every so often that laid down rules on unbendable metal, a beach covered with oil waste from ships emptying their bilges at sea, a beach littered with aluminum cans, plastic fast food wrappers, empty cigarette packages and soggy butts.

I talked to fishermen who told me that few striped bass are caught, that the smelt are all but gone, and an occasional redtail perch might be landed if you were persistent and lucky.

The old wire Redwood fence netting to hold sand, prevent erosion, the native grasses were being replanted. The newly growing grasses were protected by a sign in their midst which read, "Dune Restoration." We learned quickly that you don't walk on those grasses because of the piercing thorns that also carry a painful poison.

Back at the car, we looked into the deep hole, like a bomb had exploded, where the Fleishacker pool had been for so many years. I remember the letters to Council people, visits to high-ranking city officials to enlist aid to keep the pool, but all efforts had failed. The pool had been the birthplace of the Far Western Swimming and

Diving Championships where great athletes like Duke Kahanamoku, Johnny Weissmuller, Jon Hall, Buster Crabbe, and others had competed. There had been talk of filling the pool area, one thousand feet long and fifty yards wide, the largest pool in the world, to make it a parking lot.

Returning by Lake Merced, we stopped at Petrini's, the local supermarket a few blocks from Joan's parents home. We grabbed a shopping cart and bought some wine, vegetables, salad ingredients, and stopped at the fish market. Petrini's seafood display made up for the higher than other market prices. The fish was fresh, and the presentation flawless, tempted you to buy with abandon.

I considered the toxicity levels that could not be seen in the fish. Joan said, "How do you like these abalone prices?"

The price tag read forty-nine dollars a pound. I asked the fish man? "Are you serious, abalone forty-nine dollars a pound? Get real."

"Hey man, they're on special this week, last week fifty-three dollars a pound." He pointed to some small smelt. "Used to throw them away. Sold the cod for ten cents a pound in the fifties. They ain't hardly none left."

The fish man and I talked of the old days, the bass runs, the abalone stuck to nearly every rock, the unappreciated abundance. I bought some hatchery raised steelhead, pink meated, took them home, and they were good. No one knew the difference except for the fish man and me. I can tell the difference between pond reared salmon and wild fish. Much of the catch you buy in the supermarket comes from ponds. They are reared to sell, catfish, striped bass, salmon, steelhead, trout and others.

I do have to say that I find it a convenience to have certain fishes any time of the year, but I won't forget the taste of wild fish. It's like the difference between Courvoisier and less expensive brandy.

Boonville, Boulder Creek, Santa Cruz, Southern California, Marin County, the Russian River, Dinky Creek, San Francisco, Fleishacker Pool, Sutro Forest, the untimely demise of Carol, wounded me deeply. Wounds heal if taken care of properly. I grow in acceptance and inner strength each visit to California. The state grows in population, but it now has many more protectorates than when the early timber barons and gold rush obsessives tore into everything in the environment to make fortunes, caring nothing about the devastation they left.

With each visit I see that California has begun to heal in places. I thought it was on a path into hell, irretrievable, but in many places California is shedding its scars, helpfully being covered with new tissue. Environmental laws go a long way, but many Californians are more cognizant of what they could further lose and are devoted to preventing this atrocity. Education of its youth toward more friendly involvement with their environment will help to heal more scars.

All told, California flows in Abundance, not like in the old days, but in a more meaningful and planned manner. There will probably never be the freedom of movement once so prevalent, but with that loss other positive factors compensate, health, safety, abundance of food, and more citizen involvement in what will be the California of the coming years. Attitudes, not in mass, are changing, and these new feelings will not be squelched.

I thought of what Lindy, my fly fishing buddy, had said when we climbed out of the gorge, sweating, dying for a beer, creels filled with fat, native, wild trout "This place will be here long after we're all gone."

So will California and the abundance I experienced, I hope!

About the Author

Fred Van Dyke, a native San Franciscan, is described by friends and commentators as a Maverick, one who marches to a different drumbeat. Ocean lovers know of Fred as a living legend, the young Californian who pioneered Hawaii's frontier coastline of huge, thirty-foot waves. Many know him as a teacher for thirty years at Punahou School in Honolulu. Most know Fred as a passionate man—about health & physical fitness, an avid outdoorsman : fly fisherman, hiker, jogger, swimmer, surfer, skier, an activist to protect Nature's precious beauty & resources. Fred lives with his wife, Joan Marie, in the mountains of Montana and on the beach in Hawaii. California will always live deeply in Fred's heart and soul.

BOOKS BY ANOAI PRESS

Stories from Hawaii

Mango Lady and Other Stories From Hawaii
Ted Gugelyk

Squid Eye
Ian MacMillan

Exiles from Time
Ian MacMillan

Short-Timers in Paradise
John Wythe White

Poetry from Hawaii

Dancing the Waves and Other Poems
Steven Curry

Waxing the Lunar Mountain Apple
Steven Curry

Children's Books

Two Surf Stories for Children
Fred Van Dyke

Mama is Hāpai
Written by Chaika Piilani Hale
Illustrated by Dennis Asato

A Dolphin Day in Hawaii
Dennis Asato

Hawaiian Oral History

The Separating Sickness
Ted Gugelyk
Milton Bloombaum
(Published for the Ma'i Ho'oka'awale Foundation)

Anoai Surfing Classics

Surfing Huge Waves With Ease
Fred Van Dyke

Once Upon Abundance
Fred Van Dyke

ANOAI PRESS publishes literature of all types-novels, short stories, oral history, poetry and children's books. We are particularly interested in Hawaiian-Pacific and East-West themes. Topics of interest to senior surfers are also a specialty.